EVERYTHING YOU NEED TO KNOW TO MAKE A PROFIT IN ANTIQUES & COLLECTIBLES

• Authentic English furniture up to 1840 • American Colonial, Shaker, and Federal furniture • Victorian furniture • Fine silver, glass, and china • Pre-1900 original oil paintings • Art Nouveau • Art Deco • Mission Oak • Quilts and rugs • Folk Art • Cast-iron toys and banks • Depression glass • American Indian crafts • Stained glass windows • Cameras • Clocks and watches • Beer cans • Bottles • Marbles • Baseball cards • Children's toys • Fountain pens • Books and magazines • Commemoratives • Limited edition plates and prints • Comic books • Fifties furniture • Advertising art And more

DON'T MISS THIS INDISPENSABLE GUIDE TO A MAJOR MONEY-MAKING OPPORTUNITY!

By Bruce E. Johnson
Published by Ballantine Books:

HOW TO MAKE $20,000 A YEAR IN ANTIQUES &
    COLLECTIBLES WITHOUT LEAVING YOUR JOB
THE WEEKEND REFINISHER
THE WOOD FINISHER
50 SIMPLE WAYS TO SAVE YOUR HOUSE

HOW TO MAKE UP TO $20,000 A YEAR IN ANTIQUES & COLLECTIBLES WITHOUT LEAVING YOUR JOB

Bruce E. Johnson

Illustrations by Randy Kraciun

BALLANTINE BOOKS • NEW YORK

Copyright © 1986 by Bruce E. Johnson

All rights reserved under International and Pan-American Copyright Conventions. Published in the United States by Ballantine Books, a division of Random House, Inc., New York, and simultaneously in Canada by Random House of Canada Limited, Toronto.

http://www.randomhouse.com

Library of Congress Catalog Card Number: 85-43341

ISBN 0-345-34624-6

This edition published by arrangement with Rawson Associates, a division of Scribner.

Manufactured in the United States of America

First Ballantine Books Edition: October 1987

20 19 18 17 16 15 14 13 12 11

For my grandmother,
Violet Hickok,
who somehow knew those early lessons
in family heirlooms would not be lost
amid a boy's jumble of
batting averages, bicycles,
and bubble gum

Contents

Acknowledgments

No writer can ever claim to have written a book by himself, for without the information, materials, experiences, and encouragement that can only come from his friends he would sit in a vacuum, surrounded only by his limited exposure to life. I have been fortunate to have had many people more knowledgeable than myself pierce that vacuum and while I can only list them here, I hope each of them knows how truly grateful I am and will continue to be for their assistance.

First, let me thank three talented people who have invested their time, their energy and their reputations in me: my publisher, Eleanor Rawson; my editor, Grace Shaw; and my agent, Susan Urstadt. Without each of them, this book might have remained just another manuscript.

Second, I would like to thank a number of people who helped ensure that this book would be the most accurate of its kind. Each will know and, hopefully, will recognize their contribution to this book:

Bill Ackerman, Ackerman's Antiques, Iowa City, IA; Fred Bachmann, Iowa City Cabinet Shop, Iowa City, IA; Judy Ball, Antiques In The Olde White Church, Hills, IA; Becky Barnhart, *Press-Citizen*, Iowa City, IA; Bert Cuthbert, Heritage Clocks of Massachusetts, Sturbridge, MA; Mary Davin, Mary

Davin's Antiques, Iowa City, IA; Tom Dawson, Dawson's Antiques, Washington, IA; Enchanted Valley Doll Hospital, Modesto, CA; Ray Errett, Glass Repair and Restoration, Corning, NY; Jo Ferris, Trust Antiques, Iowa City, IA; Bonnie Fechner; Dean Finley, Nu-Mirror, Iowa City, IA; Mike Finley, Lafayette Furniture & Repair, Iowa City, IA; Phil Gabe, 20th Century, Ltd., Iowa City, IA; Neal Gerichten, Neal's Antiques, Bloomfield, NJ; Pat Gilpin, Gilpin Paint & Glass, Iowa City, IA; Janet Goetz, Cottage Antiques, Iowa City, IA; Rosine Green Associates, Inc., Brookline, MA; Glen Hanson, Glen Hanson Upholstery, Iowa City, IA; Sandy Hanson, Highway One Antique Company, Solon, IA; Inzer Pianos, Inc., Marietta, GA; Ross Jasper, The Glass Doctor, Davenport, IA; Dr. Lydia Jeffries, Moral Support, Iowa City, IA; Grace Jochimsen, The Glass Case, Iowa City, IA; Ed Johnson, Johnson Watch Repair, Greeley, CO; Grace Johnson, Unicorn Antiques, Lake City, FL; Karen Kennedy; Nancy Kennedy, Re: Antiques, Iowa City, IA; Shirl Kenney, Trunk Restorations, Cedar Rapids, IA; Randy Kraciun, R. James Graphic Studio, Iowa City, IA; W. B. Lewis; Jon Maney, Novel Antiques, Salt Lake City, UT; Wendel and Mary Marine, The Rocking Chair, Iowa City, IA; Steve Maxon, MaxCast, Iowa City, IA; Carlton McLendon, Carlton's Rare Woods & Veneers, Atlanta, GA; Conny (Pence) Lynch, Antique Doll Restoration, West Branch, IA; Joe and Pam Michaud, The Book Nook, Iowa City, IA; Elaine Milin, The Consortium, Chicago, IL; Helen Miller; The Musical Museum, Deansboro, NY; Norma Myers, Country Cousin Antiques, Iowa City, IA; New York Marble Works, Inc., New York, NY; Bob Niman; Ray Northway, Ray Northway Photography, Iowa City, IA; Muriel Owen, Quiltwright Quilting Frame, Cedar Rapids, IA; John and Lil Peterka, Peterka's Cane & Wicker, Swisher, IA; Peter Pflock, Metal Restoration Services, Newport, RI; Chuck Ping, Chuck Ping Restorations, Iowa City, IA; Mike Pitlick, Knock On Wood Antique Repair & Restoration, Iowa City, IA; Steve Salek, Steve Salek Restorations, Iowa City, IA; Thompsons Studio, Inc., Damariscotta, ME; Becky Uber, The Butterfly Shop, Ferndale, MI; Alan Weinstein, The Barn, Iowa City, IA; Maureen Collins Williams, Antiques of Marion, Marion, IA; Marilyn Woodin, The Woodin Wheel, Kalona, IA; Yesteryears Museum, Sandwich, MA.

Introduction

It may be too late to cash in on the real estate boom. The stock market may never see a rally like the one it saw a few years ago. But there is still a field left where, with just a little money and a lot of savvy, you can add thousands of dollars to your income each year without jeopardizing your current job.

Where?

In antiques.

Antiques Fever—It's an Epidemic!

Antiques fever has reached epidemic proportions. College students, young professionals, couples with combined incomes approaching six figures, investors, interior designers, housewives, grandparents: all are buying antiques—and not just Chippendale chairs and Sheraton couches. Today, baseball cards, paperweights, advertising art, Amish quilts, Persian rugs, folk art, postcards, pottery, and even old stock certificates are being bought, sold, and collected in every county in the nation. We're caught up in a collecting mania that shows no sign of ever subsiding—an unprecedented opportunity that is ripe and ready for anyone who has an interest in antiques and collectibles, a few extra hours each week, and a desire to increase his or her income.

You Don't Need a Shop to Be in the Antiques Business

There once was a time when people thought that to make money in the antiques business you needed a full-time shop, had to have spent years studying century-old glassware or furniture, and look as if you'd just stepped out of a Norman Rockwell painting. Today nothing is further from the truth. While a few dealers still fit this description, more and more people with an interest in antiques are discovering that they can make money without the overhead associated with a full-time shop, without spending years becoming an expert in dusty old furniture, and without looking as if they'd just stepped from the cover of an old *Saturday Evening Post* magazine.

The New Approach to Buying and Selling

The antiques business is ready—right now—and exploding with a new group of part-time dealers *with a fresh approach to buying and selling antiques and collectibles*. A new generation of collectors with more cash than time on their hands is waiting for someone to find them an unlimited number of antiques, ranging from Chippendale chairs to Art Deco ashtrays. They are more than willing to reward you generously for the time and effort you invest in finding a piece that they want to add to their home or collection. It matters not to them that you paid only $35 for a 1930s bronze Lorenzl nude figurine that you spotted in a parking lot flea market; its actual value in a shop or at one of the major auction houses is closer to $800—and they'll be thanking *you* as they write out the check.

Getting into the Antiques Business

How, then, do you get into the antiques business?

How about "How *not* to get into the antiques business"?

You don't begin with your life's savings in cash, a tank full of gas, an empty building on Main Street, and an appointment with a salesperson from the Yellow Pages.

Instead, sit down with a new notebook and take a few moments to think about just exactly what you would like to do in the field of antiques. Start by making a list of the areas that interest you the most. Your interest may be as general as oak furniture or as specific as presidential postcards—that is not what matters; what is important is that you begin to think about concentrating on two or three specific areas, time periods, or types of antiques.

But, you may be thinking, am I not going to miss out on all sorts of great deals if I look for just one or two kinds of antiques?

Perhaps, but not as often as you might think. Antiques, like the field of medicine, has grown too large and too complicated for one person to know enough about every area to be able to differentiate between what appears to be a fabulous deal and what in truth is little more than a fancy lemon. Just as the number of general practitioners has steadily declined over the past few years, so has the number of antiques dealers who handle a little bit of everything and know a lot about nothing.

Don't take that to mean, however, that just because you happen to have a special interest in antique cast-iron toys that you have to turn down your neighbor's offer to trade you his old oak roll-top desk for your worn out riding lawn mower. When I was young and foolish (as opposed to now when I generally am just foolish), my grandmother took me to a yard sale held by some friends who were moving to California. They had a son my age with an unbelievable collection of baseball cards dating from the late forties and early fifties; his parents had decided the collection was too heavy to move and too insignificant to sell, and I thought I had died and gone to

xiv   *Introduction*

While the majority of the furniture produced during the American Art Deco period (c. 1920–1930) has yet to attract much sustained interest, accessories of the period, such as this 10-inch nude holding a removable pottery ashtray, continue to command impressive prices. Fine examples can still be purchased very inexpensively in rural and small town shops where the demand for them is low. Consequently, urban dealers are anxious to buy them to satisfy the demand of their clientele.

heaven when they offered to *give* it to me—shoebox after shoebox after shoebox of cards.

But, as I said, I was young and foolish and infatuated at the time with Mickey Mantle and the Bronx Bombers. I insisted on taking just the New York Yankees cards. No doubt my grandmother thought I was daft, and, judging by the puzzled look on the boy's face, so did hë, but I was ecstatic. It wasn't until years later that I fully realized how foolish I had been; I had blinded myself to a great deal by in effect "overspecializing." I worked up the nerve to ask my grandmother if she could remember what had happened to the rest of the cards. "No one else wanted them," she said, "so they burned them."

Young—and foolish.

Choose an Area That Interests You

Naturally, you won't make any of the mistakes I made—at least none of the ones I'm going to confess to—so you'll be able to choose an area that interests you and at the same time be aware of what else is going on around you in a shop, at an auction, or in the midst of a monstrous flea market. Once you step into the world of antiques and collectibles, though, you will literally be exposed to, immersed in, and seduced by thousands and thousands of items. The only way to make sense out of it all, the only way you can bring order to a nonorderly world, is to enter it looking for something specific, something you can recognize, evaluate, and buy with confidence.

I

BUYING ANTIQUES

1

Getting Started

List the Kinds of Antiques That Interest You

The best way to begin in this business of antiques is to sit down with a new notebook and start making lists. List Number One is going to consist of any areas that interest you, regardless of how remote they may seem. If there is a jar of old clay marbles on your bureau that has always fascinated you, put it down; if you love walnut Victorian furniture, note that: if you've always wanted to collect first edition books, that goes on your list, too.

The purpose of this list is twofold: first, it will make you realize that today's antiques and collectibles aren't restricted to French Provincial furniture, Sandwich glass, Duncan Phyfe tables, and Chinese porcelain; second, it will put you in touch with what you enjoy. George Bernard Shaw is credited with saying, "Happy is the man who can make his living from his hobby," and that is our goal, or, at the very least "adding to our living."

List Number One doesn't have to be limited to areas in which you already have started to collect, either. Perhaps you don't own any old quilts, but if you have fond memories of your grandmother's quilting frame surrounded by a half dozen

While eighteenth- and nineteenth-century blanket chests still survive in a variety of styles and conditions, those that feature original milk paint finishes, dovetail joints, extremely wide plank sides, hand-forged hardware, and unique construction details (such as the half moon cutouts on this example) are highly sought after by dealers and collectors. Regardless of condition, authentic milk paint finishes and hardware should be preserved and not replaced.

of her friends on a sunny winter's afternoon, trading gossip and piecing together a coverlet for a sick neighbor, you may have the urge to learn more about quilts and eventually to start buying, collecting, and selling them.

Right now, though, it is not imperative that you narrow your field of interest to just one specific area. Let it grow to four or five areas, for experience may soon teach you that because of factors beyond your control, such as where you live, one of your choices may realistically be impractical. Early American antiques, for example, are harder to find in Seattle, Washington, than they are in Providence, Rhode Island. That does not entirely rule them out as one of your interests if you live in Seattle, however, for if no one else there expects to run across a legitimate hand-grained blanket chest or knows how to identify one, you can find some great "steals" where no one else even bothered to look. But in general, keeping your options open to several different possibilities will prevent you from prematurely specializing in an area that may not turn out to be your best choice.

The law of supply and demand is a major consideration we

need to examine closely. In the field of antiques, people don't collect what they can't find. You may be fascinated by matchbook covers from North Dakota, but if not enough of them are available to spur an interest in collectors outside of North Dakota, then your accumulation is destined to remain a novelty rather than a valuable collectible.

Fortunately for us, there seems to be a collector for nearly every type of antique and collectible, including, perhaps, matchbook covers from North Dakota. Still, the greater the supply, the more easily you can build your inventory; the greater the demand, the faster you can both sell your antiques and count your profits.

The Three General Antiques Categories

Hundreds of items already have established themselves as being blue chip antiques investments; these we will label *Establishment Antiques,* a category that includes such standard-bearers as Chippendale chairs and Derby porcelain. Others have just recently attracted national attention—especially from a new and younger generation of collectors—and will remain in the category of *Collectibles* until interest in them stabilizes and is reflected in steadily escalating prices. Coca-Cola memorabilia and Maxfield Parrish prints are but two of dozens of collectibles that are currently hot. And then there are those that are just about to burst onto the antiques scene. *Tomorrow's Antiques* some dealers like to call them. If you can predict what those will be, chances are that you can snap them up at bargain prices and then simply wait for the rest of the country to suddenly sit up and take notice.

A recent example of this most profitable—yet somewhat risky—betting on the future occurred when the farm implement giant International Harvester folded late in 1984. The day after the closing announcement was made a friend of mine drove to several International Harvester dealerships and bought nearly $900 worth of the I.H. toy tractors, plows, and wagons that the company had for sale on its counters. Without even

The Coca-Cola company has been a forerunner in advertising ever since it started in 1886. This figure-eight Baird clock appeared in the 1890s. The cases of such clocks were often made from pressed paper and painted dark with light-colored lettering. Even though collectors may not consider Coca-Cola to be "The Ideal Brain Tonic" today, they will still pay almost $4,000 for a near mint-condition clock such as this.

disturbing the original boxes he packed them all away in his attic, figuring that within a year he could sell just half of his inventory and recoup all of his $900 investment. The rest would be pure profit. Judging from the number of antique toy collectors who are already anxious to add pieces of International Harvester to their collections, his profit will be more than just a modest one.

To give you an idea of some of your possible areas of interest in all three categories, consider the following (keeping in mind that these lists are neither complete nor exclusive):

ESTABLISHMENT ANTIQUES

Authentic English furniture up to 1840
American Colonial, Shaker, and Federal furniture
Select quality Victorian furniture
Fine silver, glass, and china
Pre-1900 original oil paintings

COLLECTIBLES

Art Nouveau   Cast-iron toys and banks
Art Deco   Depression glass
Mission Oak   American Indian crafts
Quilts and rugs   Stained glass windows
Folk art   Cameras

Needless to say, the best of the Collectibles are already making their way into the major auction houses and thus are destined someday to make the jump to Establishment Antiques; these are the stuff success stories are made of, for unlike an original Picasso painting, a signed Gustav Stickley bookcase can still be uncovered in the back of an antiques shop or in the basement of a house and bought for but a fraction of its current value. The smart collector will hopefully find something on his or her List Number One that falls under the category of Collectibles, for here is where profits are made by those who are sharp enough to spot what others, including (or especially!) the more traditional auctioneers and dealers, are too blind to see.

TOMORROW'S ANTIQUES

Our third category is to the antiques collector what penny stocks are to the Wall Street investor: cheap long shots. Most of the items now classified as Collectibles were at one time considered cheap long shots, but while a few of Tomorrow's Antiques may someday move up a category, most are destined in our lifetime to remain novelties that require little investment and offer only long shot profit potential. This category includes such items as:

Beer cans
Marbles
Baseball cards
Children's toys
Bottles
Fountain pens
Books and magazines

Commemoratives
Limited edition plates,
  prints, and the like
Comic books
Fifties furniture
Advertising art

Inventory the Antiques You Already Own

Once you have completed List Number One (realizing, of course, that it is subject to constant change, revision, and sharpening of focus as you get further and further into the antiques field and begin to discover what your interests are, what is available in your area, and what is in demand by dealers and collectors), start a second list in your notebook. This one is an inventory of the antiques you already own. Some, such as family pieces or those with sentimental significance, should never be sold, but those that you have grown tired of, that don't fit your decorating scheme any longer, or that you never got around to repairing or refinishing should be identified, appraised, and considered as potential selling or trading material for the antiques you are going to be seeking.

Your inventory list will be undergoing constant change, so get into the habit of both updating it regularly and including every piece of important information regarding each item. Your description should be detailed. Right now you may only have one "Oak Rocking Chair," but will that be true six, twelve, or eighteen months from now when you have a buyer interested in an oak rocker of yours, but you can't recall whether that's the one you paid $10 for at a yard sale or $70 at an auction? Change "Oak Rocking Chair" to "Pressed Back Oak Rocker, Hand Caned Seat, Eight Spindle Back, No Arms, Height 47 in., Original Finish." Along with a description, assign a number to each piece and include where and when you obtained it, the purchase price, any repairs or restoration costs and any historical significance unique to it. All of this information will be invaluable when you determine your selling price and thus how much profit you made on each particular item.

Start Reading Everything in the Field

At this point you have List Number One, a preliminary list of perhaps four or five areas that interest you, and List Number two, an inventory of your antiques and collectibles. Your next step is to *start reading*. If you don't already subscribe to your local daily newspaper, call the circulation department today and get delivery started immediately. And keep your receipt, even if it is just the stub from the paper carrier. The antiques business is exactly like any other business, and since you are going to have to pay income tax on the profits you show, you had better take the legitimate business deductions the IRS has determined you are entitled to (more on that later—for the time being follow this one basic bookkeeping rule: save and label everything).

Savvy stock investors learn to read newspapers from back to front, not because they don't know any better, but simply because the information that is most important to them—the daily stock quotations—is printed in the back of the *Wall Street Journal*. Even though we may be reading the *Daily Babble* or the *Evening Disappointment* rather than the *Journal*, anyone interested in antiques should be practicing the same technique. Up until now, reading the classified section may only have signified that the paper was ready for the bottom of the birdcage, but tucked inside that fine print the astute reader can find antiques and collectibles that thousands of other subscribers don't even know exist.

Start making it a habit to read the "Antiques for Sale," "Household Goods," "Miscellaneous for Sale," "Garage Sales," and "Upcoming Auction" classifieds before you begin worrying about the headlines on the front page. You'll also find it advantageous either to look through the classified section as soon as you get home from work or, if possible, within minutes of press time, just to get the jump on other dealers and collectors. You should also make it a point to pick up a copy of any weeklies and advertisers on the day that they are published; their ads are generally unclassified, so you have to read the entire paper to make sure you don't miss anything of special interest to you.

At this point you are not so much concerned with making calls or buying or selling antiques as you are with getting both a reading habit established and a feel for what is being bought and sold through classified ads. If you do spot any "Wanted to Buy" ads with references to items that are or might be on your list of areas of interest, copy the name, phone number, and information into your notebook. Later, even if weeks or months later, you will have someone to call when you have something to sell. Do the same for any ads that offer services you might someday have a need for; if American glassware is one of your interests, for instance, it will pay you to know whom to call when you are in need of a glass restoration specialist.

Another reading habit you are going to want to establish will involve bookstores and libraries. Reading has become popular again, as shown by the number of bookstores in all the shopping malls across the country. While your spouse is trying on shoes or debating which Baskin-Robbins flavor will tempt you off your diet, slip into a nearby bookstore to check out the selections in the Antiques aisle. You could invest a small fortune in all the antiques books available, but you will need only one or two to begin with.

You'll Need to Buy Only a Few Books

First, pick out a book that covers one or more of your areas of interest in detail. Depending on your field of interest there may only be one or two to choose from or there may be a half dozen. Antiques books don't generally get extensively reviewed, so you are going to have to rely on your own judgment to determine which is the best for you.

Naturally, sharp, clear photographs and/or illustrations are a plus, as is a detailed index. Check out the author's credentials on the back flyleaf as well. Blurbs from antiques publications are pretty much meaningless, since just about any publishing house can find someone somewhere to say something nice about the book, even if just for a free examination copy.

A Good Price Guide Is a Must

Your second selection should be a good price guide. Here more than anywhere else the publication date is very important, for an out-of-date price guide is about as useful as an old prom dress. Any price guides more than three years old run the risk of being both outdated and misleading. When given the choice, select the newer of two price guides.

The growing trend is for any publisher or antiques writer who has published or written everything he or she has to say about antiques to come out with their own price guide. Read the introduction carefully to see where the suggested prices came from, for many times there will be a great deal of difference between a price guide based on major East Coast auction houses and one that represents an informal survey of antiques dealers across the country. If you live on the East Coast and plan to frequent the major auction houses, then select a price guide reflecting their prices. If you are more apt to be traveling around the country, shop for a price guide based on a cross-section of regional dealers.

At best, a price guide can only give you a general idea of what some antiques are selling for in some sections of the country, for they have several inherent weaknesses. First, most of them are out of date before they ever reach the bookstore; second, they generally do not take into consideration geographical influences on prices. California, for instance, has more demand for than supply of Victorian oak furniture when compared with Maine; thus the prices for oak furniture on the West Coast are generally higher than those in the East. Finally, the single most important factor affecting the value of any antique is its condition and I still have not found a price guide with an acceptable grading system that can enable readers to make an accurate comparison between their less-than-perfect antiques and those antiques pictured in the book. So, buy a good price guide, but just use it as you get started to get a feel for what the antiques that interest you are selling for. Don't ever depend on a price guide alone to decide whether or not to make a purchase. Later, after you have gained some experience, you will be able to establish your own mental price guide.

Your Public Library Can Help You Educate Yourself on Antiques

Your public library may have an extensive collection of books on antiques. You will find, however, that you are going to want to own the best ones in your field so that you can take them with you wherever you go. Use the library to help determine which books you are going to buy and which you can rely on the library to have when you need them. Don't hesitate to recommend that your library order a particular book that you feel would improve its collection; many of the books with extensive color plates may be too costly for you, but may be affordable within the library's acquisitions budget. And while photographs may not reproduce well, you can always photocopy short sections of text that pertain to your particular areas and file them away in your notebook.

Perhaps the most valuable service your library can perform for you, however, won't even be in the book section. Specialized publications are doing better today than even the once popular general interest magazines such as *Life* and *Look,* and the antiques field is not without its share of both glossy magazines and weekly and monthly tabloids. While once again your budget may not permit you to subscribe to half a dozen antiques publications, the library's may. And here again you can browse through their selections and decide which ones you want to subscribe to (another business deduction) and which you can stop in to read once every few weeks and, if necessary, photocopy important articles from them.

Inside some of these antiques periodicals you are going to come across ads for book clubs specializing in or at least offering books on antiques. Many of these books never show up in libraries or bookstores, so pay close attention to them. You may wish to become a member, but if not, at least study their ads closely for any books you would like either your bookstore or library to order.

Start Visiting Shops and Auctions

While you are in the process of making and revising your lists, evaluating your inventory, reading your new books, and studying antiques publications, start making it a habit to drop in on antiques shops and swing by auctions in your spare time just to get a feel for what is going on. Some people complain of feeling uncomfortable in antiques shops or intimidated at auctions, but that generally is just a matter of getting accustomed to new surroundings. If you remind yourself that an antiques shop is just another retail store and that both antiques dealers and auctioneers are dependent on people like yourself to make their living, then you will soon begin to feel more comfortable and confident in either place.

You are not yet out to do any serious bargaining or buying, but only to see how what you have been reading about stacks up against what is really going on in your area. Don't be afraid to take your price guide with you and certainly tuck your notebook under your arm. Compare some of the shop prices to those in your price guide and you'll see what was meant by using it only to get a general idea of an antique's value.

Establish Rapport with Dealers and Collectors

One of the best things you can do in both antiques shops and at auctions is to talk with the people around you. Antiques dealers are a storehouse of information. Some of it is accurate, some you may need to check out before you take it as gospel, but almost all of it is based on the one element you may be short of—experience.

When you do find a dealer in a shop or a collector at an auction who knows what he or she is talking about, stick to them like mud on a stick. Ask questions, pick their brains, especially if their field of expertise includes an area you are anxious to work in.

- How are things selling? How much of a problem is keeping up an inventory?
- What sorts of items are hot? What's not?
- How far do they have to travel to buy?
- Do they do shows or flea markets? Which ones?
- Which magazines or newspapers do they find helpful?

Most people you will encounter in the antiques business enjoy talking about their interests, though a few burnt out wizards may get suspicious and give you little more than a few grunts and shrugs if you come on too strong or appear overzealous. Keep in mind, especially when establishing a rapport with dealers and auctioneers, that these people may soon be your regular customers. Become more than just a twice a year visitor. Study their merchandise and tactfully offer some of your new information to show them that you are serious about antiques. If you are looking for something, let them know about it, if for no other reason than to acquaint them with your name and interests. Appear as an intelligent, informed collector, buy something you want from them, and chances are they'll remember you the next time you stop in or they come across a piece that's of special interest to you.

And that's about all it takes to get started in the antiques business. No big bank roll, no splashy ads in the phone book. Just a few areas of special interest, some background information, a feel for what is happening in your locale, and good rapport with your dealers and auctioneers. Keep your notebook close at hand and when it fills up, start another, because once you're hooked, you're destined to stay in the antiques business for the rest of your life.

Be Businesslike—Keep Accurate Records

Before becoming too deeply engrossed in the antiques business, you have to realize that antiques are only half of the antiques business. Along with the fun and profit comes the responsibility of records and taxes. As much as you may dislike doing them, keeping clear, accurate records has its own rewards. First, they will go a long way toward keeping the Internal Revenue Service off your back. Second, they will insure that you do not lose any of your legitimate business deductions, thus saving you hundreds of dollars a year. And, third, they will enable you to tell at a glance exactly how well your new business venture is doing—and why or why not.

You'll Need a Few Business Supplies

Start by giving yourself and your new business a desk. Later, if you have the space, you may wish to expand to fill an entire room or you may decide to incorporate your desk into your antiques restoration area in the garage or basement. By doing so you may qualify for a substantial business-in-the-home deduction on your federal tax return. For right now, however, a desk that is designated solely for your antiques business use will suffice. At first it may seem large and empty, but resist the temptation to share space with either your household accounts or the paperwork from your nine-to-five job. In an amazingly short span of time your desk is going to fill up with books, magazine articles, business cards, pamphlets, newspapers, auction bills, price guides, and, naturally, notebooks. If you don't already have a desk that you can clean out and claim, start looking for one. It can be your second business deduction—right after the cost of this book.

Next you will need to stop in at an office supply store and pick up a simple, basic bookkeeping ledge and a box of manila envelopes. In your ledger you will enter each of your daily expenditures and, eventually, your sources of income. If it makes you feel more comfortable, pick up a simple bookkeeping manual that will familiarize you with some of the more widely used financial terms such as "debits," "credits," and "accounts receivable." And take some advice from a non-CPA antiques dealer who has found the secret to keeping good books—keep everything simple and don't put off recording your transactions. When you come home from a morning of yard sales or an afternoon at an auction, sit down immediately, pull out your ledger, and enter your expenses: $20.00 for an oak office chair, $3.00 for a box of old books, $7.50 for an Art Deco vase, $2.00 for coffee and doughnuts, and twenty-two miles on your car.

You're Eligible for Legitimate Tax Deductions

On the first of each month label three large manila envelopes: *Cash Receipts, Check Receipts,* and *Invoices.* Every time you buy something for your business, whether it be a $2 can of stain or a $200 table, enter the transaction in your ledger, write on the back of the receipt what it was for, and drop it in the appropriate envelope. Every time you make a sale, enter it in the ledger and slip the duplicate invoice in the Invoice envelope. At the end of each month (and do make sure you have the month and year marked on the outside of each envelope, too) you will have all of your cash and check receipts at hand and all of your sales invoices collected. This

way you won't lose any legitimate tax deductions and you
will know exactly where your back deposits come from.

Choosing a Name for Your Business

If you haven't already done so, now is the time to consider
a name for your business. A review of the shops and dealers
listed in the Yellow Pages of your phone book will help you
eliminate any potential names that could be confused with that
of an existing business. The Yellow Pages or a directory of
area antiques shops will also help you formulate a name. Some
of the examples may strike you as too coy (e.g., Yee Olde
Junque Shoppe), too bland (L&M Antiques), or too overused
(Attic Antiques). Some will be directional, as in Main Street
Antiques or Highway One Antiques Company. Others will
identify the owner—Mary Davin's Antiques, Harman's Bazaar, Dawson's Antiques—or both the owner and the address,
as in Ackerman's Newton Road Antiques.

Naturally, the more a name can do to identify you, your
business, and your location, the better, but brevity must be a
serious consideration. Long and overused names are easily
forgotten or confused; your first responsibility is to indicate,
either covertly or obviously, what your business is. After that
the field is wide open. If you want to stress your location,
consider a directional name—but remember: if later you decide to move your business either to another street or to another town, do you keep what could become a confusing name
or do you change it and risk sacrificing your hard-earned reputation? Can Main Street Antiques really expect to be found
on Jefferson Avenue?

The trend today appears to be moving steadily away from
the cutesy names of the sixties and seventies to those that
stress reputation and personal service: Charles Ellis, Antiques; or Antiques by the Bullards are but two examples.
Using your personal name in your business name implies
pride, trust, and dependability. Customers will know that if
they have a question, they don't just call Basement Antiques,

they call Elizabeth Ashton, Antiques. Others rely on alliteration (Country Collectibles, The Wooden Wheel, Collectible Corner) for easy recall; still others inject a little humor (Antiques and Temptations, Don's Den of Antiquity) for the same reason.

No matter which style you lean toward, give name selection for your business long and thoughtful consideration. Once people come to know you by it, you won't want to change it. As one businessman, tongue (or foot?) planted firmly in cheek, declared, "I'd sooner change wives than change the name of my business."

State and Local Permits, Forms, and Fees

In most cities and states the only license that you and your new business need apply for is a state sales tax permit (but do check with both your city and state authorities for any requirements unique to your situation or area). The procedure is quite simple, the fee generally inexpensive, and the effect twofold: first, you become a tax collector for the state, and, second, you become exempt from paying sales tax on certain items. As holder of a state sales tax permit you agree to collect and remit to the state whatever percentage of sales tax the state is currently affixing to each transaction. The only persons exempt from a sales tax surcharge are other dealers with a state sales tax permit who are buying something from you that they intent to resell. The idea is that only the last person in line, i.e., the consumer, is to pay sales tax; therefore, anything that you as a middleperson and not as a consumer buy in order to sell for a profit is also exempt from the sales tax. The forms and a detailed explanation of how the system works are available from your area representative of the state revenue department.

Use a Separate Checking Account for Your Business

One of the worst mistakes you can make in setting up a new business (besides not sending the state the sales tax you have collected) is failing to separate your business finances from your personal finances. As soon as you have a name for your business, go to your bank and start a new checking account, even if it means lending yourself a hundred dollars from your personal account just to open it. Then, whenever possible, pay for everything with a check. Not only will it make your bookkeeping duties easier, it also will keep you from paying for business expenditures with your personal cash, thus saving your hundreds of dollars each year in lost tax deductions. A separate checking account will also enable you to take your business pulse at any given moment without having to make adjustments for nonbusiness deposits and withdrawals.

A Business Card Is Vital

Even though many new businesses start out with thousands of dollars of printing expenses—personalized stationery, envelopes, fancy invoices, receipts, three-color flyers, time cards, T-shirts, bumper stickers, and baseball caps—the only printed material you will need to get started in the antiques business is a business card. This little two-inch by three-inch piece of thin cardboard has been known to serve as a notebook, a bookmark, a sales receipt, a press pass, even a contract. Carried with you at all times, your business cards make introductions at shops, shows, auctions, and parties easy and permanent. A few years ago while vacationing twelve hundred miles from home I walked into an antiques shop where something surprisingly familiar caught my attention—my own business card tacked on the bulletin board. The owners had picked it up at a show I had done, carried it all the way back home, and posted it in their shop. It probably didn't bring me much

Country pottery has become one of the more recent "hot" antique items. Collectors will pay premiums for decorated crocks or jugs in excellent condition, especially for those with the name of the pottery impressed in them. Deep cobalt decorations of lions, deer, or ships are considered scarce and can command prices in excess of $2,000. This 14-inch example was made at the Lyons pottery in upstate New York about the time of the Civil War. Both the undamaged handles and the deep cobalt flower decoration will keep the value of this piece well over $100.

business that far from home, but it taught me that if someone twelve hundred miles away had saved it, a lot of people closer to home probably had, too.

And while you know not every business card you hand out will be saved, you can increase your chances of winning attention by remembering this undocumented but certainly proven rule of business cards: attractive, creative, interesting cards outlive plain, dull, boring ones by at least three to one. A unique logo, a different lettering style, or an unusual arrangement of the two on anything but white stock will guarantee your card a longer lifespan. Spend some time studying the examples displayed in print shops, but don't just look at other antiques business cards. Borrow one idea from a music company, another from a real estate agent. Take the lettering used on a restaurant card and combine it with the layout a department store executive paid a graphic artist several hundred dollars to design. Take one of the few opportunities available today to express yourself, your business, and your personality for everyone you meet to see, save, and remember.

2

Where to Find Antiques

Fortunately for us, antiques are everywhere.

It doesn't matter if you live in midtown Manhattan; Lawrence, Kansas; Albuquerque, New Mexico; or San Francisco, California. Antiques recognize no geographic, economic, or social boundaries; we stand as good a chance of finding a Victorian clawfoot round oak table, a #7 Shaker rocker, or a signed Tiffany lamp along Cherokee Street in St. Louis as we do in Charleston's famous King Street.

Antiques Are Everywhere—Just Look Around You

And now the Establishment Antiques, the Chippendales, Hepplewhites, and Hitchcocks, have had to move over to make room for their Yuppie-ish neighbors, the Art Deco lamps, oak iceboxes, Maxfield Parrish prints, Coca-Cola trays, copper weathervanes, Shirley Temple glasses, and Hoosier kitchen cabinets. And what many people are madly searching for today, only a few years ago someone else was hauling to the dump. People are still throwing out treasures with their trash,

A #7 Shaker rocker from the Mt. Lebanon, New York, colony. This was the largest of six sizes offered by the Mt. Lebanon craftsmen. It featured a woven tape seat, mushroom cap posts, and a unique top rung for attaching a cushion. Chairs and rockers with the Shaker number or decal on the rear of the back top slat were intended to be sold rather than used in Shaker homes. When two identical pieces are sold, the one with the Shaker decal or number will command a slightly higher price.

but thrift stores, yard sales, auctions, and flea markets have now replaced the old town dump.

One of the most exciting aspects of antiques hunting is the diversity of sources for us to comb. If you want to buy carpet for your bedroom you have to go to a carpet store, but if you want an original Amana braided rug you can hit the yard and garage sale circuit Saturday morning, attend a farm auction Thursday afternoon, browse through antiques shops, shows, and galleries on your lunch hours, stop at a secondhand furniture store on your way home from work and set up private appointments in the evening.

Family and Friends Can Be a Rich Source

As for sources of antiques, we have several to consider. One wellspring of furniture, glassware, and other antiques ready to come onto the market is within your own circle of family and friends. Don't interpret this as encouragement for you to rush over to your neighbor's house, talk her out of her prized heirlooms, and sell them for a quick and tidy profit. Family pieces are meant to remain within the family and those persons who literally pry someone's fingers off his grandfather's old Morris chair or a set of her mother's Haviland are destined to spend eternity stripping paint from the inside of Hoosier cabinets.

Pieces, though, that the family has decided have no sentimental value or need to be disposed of are just what you are looking for. Odd chairs, extra dressers, old china, bedroom sets, books, and prints take up space, can deteriorate if not stored and cared for properly, and don't sell themselves. Almost always their owners are glad to find someone who can help them sell these items well and profitably. The best approach is a direct one, so simply inform your family and your circle of friends that you are interested in seeing and possibly buying any antiques and old furnishings they would like to dispose of. You will be surprised at how many will contact you, thankful that they now have someone they know and can trust to give them a fair price for their antiques.

Get Buying Experience at Yard and Garage Sales

One of the fastest and easiest ways to gain experience in buying antiques is at yard and garage sales, even though in some areas this part of the business is quite seasonal. An activity that barely existed twenty years ago is currently challenging professional baseball for the title of National Pastime. And the sale that used to be a Saturday morning event now stretches from Tuesday through Sunday—with a couple of Monday afternoon sales thrown in just to keep you on your toes as you are driving home from work. America has discovered that yard and garage sales are an easy means of disposing of unwanted furniture, clothing, glassware, hamsters, books, and an accumulation of other belongings sure to boggle the mind.

Yard sales fall into several different categories, including the single household I'm-Telling-You-If-You-Don't-Get-Rid-of-That-Junk-I'm-Going-to-Burn-It sale, the neighborhood get-together sale, the service organization charity bazaar, the pseudo antiques dealer monthly sale, and the ultimate sale of sales—the moving sale.

The wide range of types of sales and their proven success insures that, weather permitting, they can be found nearly every day of the week every week of the year. Most sales still actually take place in the front yard, garage, porch, or driveway, but some of the larger and more organized sales are held in school gymnasiums and church basements. And while Friday afternoons and Saturday mornings are still the favorites, you will see that some of the best deals await those yard sale addicts who don't wait.

Read the Local Ads to Locate Sales

It seems, too, that every community or neighborhood has one publication that almost everyone uses to advertise their yard or garage sale. Be it the local weekly, the classified section of the daily paper or one of the throwaways simply called "advertisers," find it, get it early, and study it. Thousands of antiques and near-antiques change hands each year through sales advertised in these papers and most of the time for less than half of their retail value. Each yard sale addict will have his or her own story about the Heisey serving platter picked up for 50¢, the four drawer oak file cabinet for $60, or the 1952 Mickey Mantle stuck in a pile of worthless Topps trading cards.

Antiques Shops—One of the Best Sources

Many amateur antiquers find it hard to believe, but among the best and most reliable sources of antiques for either the casual collector or the profit hunter are the local antiques shops. Rather than avoiding them with the misconception that you can't afford anything that a dealer has bought, repaired, cleaned, and marked up, attack them with the controlled aggressiveness needed to quietly spot a bargain, analyze its strengths and weaknesses, and negotiate a lower price.

Spotting Good Deals in Shops

Antiques dealers are a strange breed. I don't say this derisively, for I've been one for several years and intend to stay one for many years to come. Although each dealer has a special field in which he or she is most interested and most knowledgeable, we all have one common vice—we can't pass up a good deal. And sometimes we don't even know how good a deal it is when we either buy *or* sell it.

Not long ago a dark, dirty, but signed Gustav Stickley music cabinet was pulled across the stage at a well-attended Midwest auction. Over a dozen dealers were in attendence, but the music cabinet barely attracted any attention, and the auctioneer could only coax a bid of $50 out of his audience. The dealer who did buy it promptly sold it to another dealer the next morning for $200; she, in turn, marked the music cabinet at $500, having, by this time, realized it was a signed Stickley. Two area dealers looked it over that same day, but passed on it. A third, a rather new and inexperienced dealer, had read about the resurgence of interest in the furniture of Gustav Stickley and knew that it had to be worth more than the new owner was asking. He offered $450, she accepted, and he left with the music cabinet in the back of his rusty van. The next day he simply cleaned it, took some color photographs, and began doing some ad-

This example of an oak Arts and Crafts Morris chair was inspired by the English writer and designer William Morris (1834–1896), who advocated a return to traditional woods, hand craftsmanship, and the natural beauty of the wood. Like most Morris chairs, this Gustav Stickley designed model (c. 1902) featured an adjustable back and loose cushions. The curved arms, arched tops and sides, and pegged joints are all indicative of the quality of design and construction found in the best Mission Oak furniture.

ditional research. Three months later the call came from Christie's in New York: they had sold his $450 music cabinet for $15,000.

All three dealers had each made a quick and tidy profit from each sale of the cabinet, but it was the one who recognized the piece, followed his instincts, researched his find, and found the best market for it who clearly achieved the greatest profit.

Most antiques shops end up being an eclectic collection of everything from cuckoo clocks to cookie cutters, candlesticks to Chippendale, and china cupboards to cut glass. And that's just the C's. For some strange reason, every dealer is presumed to know everything there is to know—date, origin, craftsman, wood, finish, glaze, history, current *and* future value—about every clock, painting, statue, piece of furniture, glassware, pottery, and paper doll ever created since Michelangelo was hired to do some painting for the pope. And let's

To enable customers to distinguish his furniture from that of his competitors, Mission Oak furniture designer and manufacturer Gustav Stickley had his craftsmen apply either decals or paper labels with his shopmark—a joiner's compass and the Flemish words "Als ik kan" (as best I can)—to the furniture they produced. Fierce competition, cheap imitations, overexpansion, and a change in public taste led to his bankruptcy in 1915 and signaled the end of the Mission Oak era (1898-1915).

face it—if any antiques dealer were that smart, she wouldn't have to be selling antiques. So if you think that little old lady or young bearded man sitting behind the counter with his or her nose stuck in a back issue of the *Antique Trader Weekly* knows the real value of everything in the shop, then you're missing out on some great bargains.

A young college chap who used to work in our shop had the uncanny ability to spot these great "steals," as we called them, right in the middle of some of the largest shops in town. He claimed it was more out of necessity than luck, since at the time he was living on stale peanut butter sandwiches and what little I was paying him.

His once-in-a-lifetime steal (I think it was his third that semester) was a small, unsigned original painting stuck irreverently in the corner of a very busy and very successful antiques shop. Although he had no formal training in art or art history, he sensed the painting was worth more than the $35 being asked for it. Naturally I lent him the last $10 he needed to buy it, never thinking I should have bought a one-third interest in it instead. He took the painting home, went to the art library and did some research, discovered it was the work of a recognized and collected nineteenth-century artist, took photographs of it and mailed them to five major art dealers in New York City. Three weeks later, after a minor bidding battle between two of the dealers, he collected $4,500 for his efforts.

You Can Still Find Treasures at Antiques Shows and Flea Markets

More and more dealers are avoiding the overhead associated with a full-time shop by selling their merchandise at antiques shows and flea markets. These brave and hardy souls haul their treasured antiques from exhibition halls to gymnasiums to shopping malls just so they can sit for three days while people manhandle their merchandise, belittle their prices, and smother them with stories about what grandma had (and as one dealer is fond of saying, "the only person interested in what grandma had was grandpa"). Then, just when they are on the brink of exhaustion, these exhibitors have to pack up what's left and haul it back home.

While it is difficult to find many hidden treasures at a show, the smart buyer can still come away with several good deals and, once in a while, a steal. Dealers generally bring only their best merchandise, know its value, and realize that their sales have to cover all of their expenses—plus leave them with enough money to replenish their inventory *and* pay for next week's groceries. Some exhibitors approach shows with the philosophy that they are going to keep their prices down and go for volume; others may bring fewer pieces, generally larger ones, and hope to make as much on a few sales as the volume dealers do on several. Even though it may be tougher to find a good deal at an antiques show than in a shop, you can increase your odds by coordinating your arrival time with the appropriate bargaining techniques—all of which we will explore later.

Auctions Can Be Fun—and Highly Profitable

Near the top of the list of hackneyed lines antiques dealers tire of hearing at shows as well as in their shops is "I bet you go to a lot of auctions, don't you?" In truth, few dealers today have the time, energy, or money to depend on auctions for the majority of their inventory. So, rather than avoiding auctions on the premise that they are dealer dominated, seek them out, for you are going to have an advantage over both the dealers and the crowd of curious friends, relatives, and neighbors who show up for this traditional postmortem.

Auctions, whether estate, farm, household, antiques, or consignment, are an excellent source of antiques and a means of taking the pulse of what's happening, not in the shops or at the shows, but in the *real* marketplace. When dealers talk about market price, what they are really talking about is auction price. If round oak tables are hot, you'll know it by the spirited bidding at an auction. If they start to fall out of favor, the first place you'll sense it will be at the auctions when the auctioneer has trouble coaxing bids out of the crowd.

In spite of the investment of time you must make, using special tactics and techniques at auctions is great fun—and highly profitable. They help make up for the fact that, unlike exploring shops and shows, you can't just breeze through in a few minutes and decide what you'll buy and what you'll leave. Murphy forgot at least one law when he was compiling his infamous list: no matter what item you decide you want at an auction, you can be sure it will be among that last up for bids. And there's one other point Murphy should have considered: just as soon as you slip away for a sandwich or a cup of coffee, the auctioneer will immediately reverse direction and throw your item up for bids.

Assembling Your Antiques Inspection Kit

Now you have a preview of the major sources of antiques: private individuals, yard and garage sales, antiques shops, antiques shows, flea markets, and auctions. But before you grab your checkbook and car keys, take a few minutes to assemble what will prove to be your most valuable companion on all of your antiques outings: your Antiques Inspection Kit.

The Kit itself can be an old gym bag, knapsack, or even a discarded briefcase. In it you are going to collect an assortment of items that will help you make smart decisions when face to face with any of the thousands of antiques you are going to encounter in the next few months. Keep it in the trunk of your car or behind the seat in your van or pickup. And make sure everyone in the family knows the Rule: everything in the kit stays in the Kit. No borrowing permitted or the day will come when you are on your hands and knees peering inside an eighteenth-century sideboard at the remains of an original label and you reach for your flashlight only to discover that it is still up in the attic under the burnt out light bulb.

The first item, then, to go in your Kit is a flashlight with a fresh set of batteries. A small, inexpensive model will enable you to peer into the dark corners of barns and basements, identify dirty labels, and flag down help when your old van finally calls it quits on the way back from an all-day auction.

Along with it goes an assortment of basic tools for dismantling large pieces of furniture: screwdrivers, pliers, a crescent wrench, and one of those large pocket knives with all the exotic accessories. You'll soon find that only when you are alone do you buy a bargain that is too large to move by yourself. Now you can reach for your Kit, whip out your screwdrivers, and in a few minutes time, remove the top from a desk, the mirror from the back of a dresser or the fragile sugar canister from the inside of a Hoosier kitchen cabinet.

A small magnet will enable you to distinguish between a brass-plated lamp, a brass-painted lamp, and a legitimate solid brass lamp—distinctions that could mean a difference of more than $100 in retail value. A magnifying glass will take the guesswork out of identifying worn pottery, porcelain, or china trademarks; distinguishing printed signatures from real ones; and recognizing recent repairs. A tape measure is essential for distinguishing three-quarter from full-sized beds, comparing measurements of a piece of furniture in a catalogue illustration with one you are considering buying and seeing if it is then going to fit in your car trunk.

You will also want to toss in a notebook and pen for names, addresses, and auction observations. Trying to remember five hours later when the auctioneer finally puts them up for bids which chair had the split seat and which did not need any restoration and how much you decided you would pay for either of them can be difficult—if not expensive. Take notes you can refer to later and you'll never have to worry about paying too much for the wrong piece when the time comes to bid.

It is also a good idea to include in your Kit a general (or specific, if appropriate) price guide to help you determine how much one of your finds is worth when you are too far from your home reference library to go back and check. It's going to take a real beating down in the bottom of your Kit, so make it a paperback that can easily be replaced when the pages start falling out, or keep it in a plastic bag as it rides in the Kit.

Finally, tuck a twenty-dollar bill in a plain white envelope and drop it in the bottom of your Kit. The day will eventually come when you spend your last five dollars on a ten gallon Red Wing crock only to discover that neither your kids nor your car are going to make it home without being fed. The Kit's emergency cash fund will give you just enough cushion to get you home without losing that last great deal.

The Next Step

Now you are set. You know where to go and what to take with you. What comes next is learning the tricks of the trade that will enable you to spot the great steals and turn them into usable cash. And in today's antiques business the time

Even though he died of tuberculosis in 1904 at the age of thirty-five while he and his pottery firm were both still young, Artus Van Briggle's designs and company continued to flourish under the direction of his wife. Van Briggle pottery is clearly incised with his trademark. The one pictured here was used beginning in 1920. It is Van Briggle work prior to that year, before the words "Colo. Spigs." (for Colorado Springs) were included in their trademark, that inspires the most interest in collectors.

is right: sources are plentiful, quality is high, and buyers are ready.

So if you're excited, energetic, and ambitious, now is the time. The buyers, the sellers, and the antiques are all out there, waiting just for you.

3

Buying Privately

So where are we now?

You have an idea of the antiques areas where you want to concentrate, you have an inventory of all your personal antiques, you have a desk and some books on antiques, perhaps a price guide or two, and some antiques publications, a bookkeeping ledger, some manila envelopes, business cards on order, and a new checking account that even shows the same balance as the bank does.

Amazing.

And you thought it would be hard starting your own business.

So let's find some antiques.

Buying from People You Know

As we said earlier, your circle of family and friends is one of the first sources of antiques you could consider, but buying from people you know is like playing with a double-edged sword. They are close, convenient, and trusting, *but* if you take unfair advantage of them or misrepresent your intentions, you may inflict permanent damage on an irreplaceable relationship. Make sure that everyone you deal with knows that you are now in the business of buying and selling antiques. If your aunt lets you have a butternut dresser for $25 because she thinks you are going to fix it up and use it in your son's room, but later learns that you turned around and sold it for $225 the next week, don't bother looking for a Christmas card from her this year.

Build a Reputation for Fair and Honest Deals

If anything, don't expect to reap great profits from your family and friends. You may even have to insist that your aunt take three or four times as much as she is asking for her dresser if she is unaware that this type of dresser has seen a drastic increase in value in the past twenty years. You are better off building a reputation as being fair and trustworthy and by doing so establishing a regular clientele than making a tremendous profit from one deal and never getting to see another antique from the individuals involved or any of their friends again. No town or neighborhood is so big that you can make it your business to take advantage of any of your customers. Be honest about your intentions, be fair in your offers, build a reputation that you can be proud of, and you won't have any problems being successful in the antiques business.

One of the traditional rules of the antiques business is that the seller must first name his or her asking price, but be prepared to bend it when dealing with your family and friends. Once you put out the word that you are going to be buying and selling antiques, they are going to be coming to you presuming—and we hope not incorrectly—that they can trust you to tell them how much their antiques are worth.

With family and friends, however, you are often going to have to explain to them the difference between the wholesale and the retail value of their antiques. Since you are, in effect, the middleman of the transaction, you cannot expect or be expected to pay full retail value and then transport, clean, repair, possibly refinish, advertise, negotiate a sale, and possibly transport it again without showing a loss. Be candid with the seller when you explain what happens with the piece after you buy it and how much time and money you must invest in it before you can sell it. In almost every case they will understand that the work just begins after the first sale is made and will be willing to accept a wholesale price for it rather than assume—as you will be doing—all the responsibilities of the retailer.

Estimating Your Costs and Your Profits

You must first approximate what you can eventually and easily sell the piece for. Naturally you want to get all you can for the butternut dresser, but you cannot keep your money tied up too long in one piece or you will have to pass up several other profit-making opportunities until your cash is again available. Most dealers would prefer to buy five less expensive antiques for a total of $1,000 and turn them all over in a matter of days than invest the same amount of money in one major piece that will take several weeks if not months to find the right buyer for. The sooner you get your money—and your profit—out of a piece, the sooner you can invest it in another.

Based on your reading and your trips to local antiques shops and auction houses, approximate the amount you can expect to sell the dresser for. Before you can start figuring your profit, though, subtract any costs you will need to incur between the two sales. Let's assume that the dresser is in excellent shape and won't require refinishing, but you still have to consider transportation costs, including paying your neighbor's son $5 to help you load and unload it, cleaning and refurbishing materials such as mineral spirits and lemon oil, and any advertising you plan to do to sell it.

After giving it some thought, you decide that the local retail value of the butternut dresser is $225 and your preparation costs will be approximately $30. Your gross profit now stands at $195, as long as you pay less than that you will show a net

Toward the end of the Victorian era several things were happening to furniture, as evidenced in this dresser. First, applied trim and spoon carvings were disappearing; second, elm and ash were being substituted for oak, and third, panel sides were replacing heavier, more expensive solid sides. The result was a lighter, less durable— and less valuable— piece of furniture.

profit. If you were a real cad and took the dresser from your aunt for only $25, then you are going to show a net profit of $170 for your time. If you were more considerate of both her interests and your reputation and paid her $90 for it, then you still would make $105 after expenses. Divide that by the amount of time you spent on the project and you will know exactly how much you have made per hour.

The Two Key Elements to Successful Antiques Investment

The two key elements to a successful investment are the selling price and preparation costs. It may seem awkward at first, but in the antiques business you have to figure backwards: selling price, preparation costs, and then purchase price. Only after you compute the first two can you accurately determine how much you can afford to pay for a piece and still justify your investment of both time and money. If, for instance, the dresser required refinishing or a drawer needed to be repaired, the preparation cost would have more than doubled, but your selling price would not necessarily have increased. The only way you could have insured your profit would be by paying less for the dresser in the first place.

Use Psychology on the Seller

That brings us to the problem of the seller who is convinced that her antique is worth far more than it actually is. If your aunt has seen a dresser similar to hers priced at an antiques show for $350, she'll scream when you offer $90 for hers. Once the walls stop shaking you may be able to explain to her that although the show dealer's asking price was $350, his actual selling price most likely would be less than that. In addition, his price has to include costs that she might be unwilling to undertake: booth rental at the show, leasing a trailer to transport the dresser, restoration costs, insurance, meals and lodging while on the road, and a babysitter to watch the kids at home.

If she still hasn't stopped screaming, then save your breath and your money. Whatever you do, don't be intimidated into paying too much for it and don't get into a fight with her. Apologize for not being able to pay her any more than $90 for the dresser, thank her for the opportunity to look at it, and ask her to keep you in mind if she ever decides to sell anything else. If you close the conversation on a pleasant note and leave the door open for future transactions, chances are that she will be calling you back in a few days, having, as she will say, "reconsidered" your offer. Loosely translated, that means she called in another dealer and he offered her only $75 for it.

Buying from Classified Ads

Naturally, you can't make even a part-time living from the small number of antiques your family and friends are ready to dispose of, so that's why you will want to get into the habit of reading the classified ads each day. People have been buying and selling cars, homes, property, livestock, furniture, and antiques through classified ads for years, yet it is amazing how many antiques dealers never bother to take advantage of this ready source. Two annoying problems associated with antiquing are solved in classified sales: first, someone else paid for the advertising and, second, you don't have to worry about whether or not they are serious about selling.

Realize, however, that you can't sit down with the paper at nine o'clock at night, leisurely flip it open to the classifieds, and expect to have a dozen great deals drop in your lap. Editors have regular press times and these are generally several hours before most people even begin to think about reading their newspaper. If you spot an ad for a $50 antique quilt six hours after press time, don't even bother calling. If you are serious about buying antiques through the classified ad section of your newspaper, you are going to have to make a few adjustments in your schedule to insure that you are, indeed, one of the early birds checking out those worms.

Read the Classifieds Early to Get a Jump on Your Competitors

Morning papers are generally delivered before most people even hear their alarm go off, so simply getting up a little earlier and reading the classifieds before you go to work can

Curved glass china cupboards have experienced a revival. Not only are they sought after by people who appreciate quality Victorian oak furniture, but collectors of glassware and other fragile antiques use them as display cabinets. Several companies advertising in major antiques publications now offer replacement curved glass at reasonable prices. This particular example features paw feet, a top splashboard, and adjustable shelves—all of which combine to make it highly desirable.

give you a jump on everyone else. Afternoon dailies are printed as early as one o'clock, so a slight adjustment in your lunch hour may be all that is necessary for you to be able to pick up an early copy, make a few phone calls, and even drive over to see a collection of Hummel figurines while everyone else in the office is picking at their spinach salad or sipping the first of their three martinis.

One of the rather bizarre aspects of buying through the classifieds is discovering the ways in which people think. A friend and part-time dealer stopped by the shop one day to gloat over his most recent find—a late Victorian oak curved glass china cupboard in nearly perfect condition, bought for only $50 through an ad in the local paper the previous night.

At first I was skeptical, since I had read—or so I thought—that same paper and had seen no such ad, but he showed it to me—listed under the category "Firewood." It seems the owner was a woodcutter and to avoid the cost of a second ad had listed the china cupboard in with his regular firewood ad. I watched that $50 china cupboard sell at a consignment auction less than a month later, and when the bidding finally stopped a young couple was taking it home, but only after they had paid $675 for it.

Responding to Ads by Phone

Buying through the classified ad section of either your daily paper or one of the free weeklies begins with the telephone conversation you have with the owner. Like the ad itself, not everything you hear can be taken literally. Don't assume, for instance, that the owner can distinguish cherry from mahogany, much less differentiate between false grained and real oak. Unless you enjoy driving around town or wandering miles out into the country only to discover that what you had been told was a piece of early China brass was clearly stamped "India" on the bottom, you are going to want to develop a line of questioning that would leave an experienced attorney envious. Your time and gas are too valuable to waste on items that are of no interest to you or people who have an inflated idea of the value of their antiques.

Ask Questions and Take Notes on the Answers

First, don't begin calling without your notebook or a pad of paper and a pen in front of you. If you have to concentrate on remembering all the answers, chances are you will forget a few vital questions. In fact, some dealers keep a printed questionnaire next to the phone. Take that idea a step farther and slip a piece of carbon paper under the top sheet; you'll have one copy to take with you and a duplicate for your files. At the top you'll want space for the time and date of the call and the owner's first and last names, street address, and, if different from yours, city, state, and ZIP. Also leave a space for directions and for distinguishing characteristics of their house or apartment building. It is much easier to find a two-story green house with white shutters and a detached garage than it is to locate 1215 S. Locust at dusk.

Naturally you already have their phone number, but leave a space for a work number as well. It is also convenient to leave room to tape the ad to the form or at least write down the important information, including the name and date of the paper it appeared in. As time consuming as that may seem, clipping out the ad and attaching it to the form is a safety device that can keep you from either losing it or doing as I once did and writing down the wrong house number.

The Right Questions to Ask the Advertiser

The more specific questions will vary according to the type of antique you are buying, but most will be designed to draw out more information than the ad had room for. Leave the majority of your information sheet empty for the notes you will take as you ask questions. If you are buying furniture, for instance, you will want to know the type of wood it is made of, the type of finish on it, the condition of both the wood and the finish, what repairs it needs, whether or not the hardware is missing or original, whether or not any parts, such as leaves or drawers, have been lost, approximately how old it is, what its dimensions are, and, of course, how much it will cost.

Trying to Establish a Ballpark Price

This last little question is the one that may lead to a sudden case of stammering on the part of the seller. Most people are afraid of selling their antiques too cheaply, so would prefer that you make them an offer rather than have to commit themselves to a figure. If you are tactful, however, and firm without being demanding, you can coax a figure out of them over the phone that will at least give you an idea whether or not the two of you are even playing in the same ballpark. Rather than barking at them "How much do ya want for it?", ease into it with a line like "Well, about how much were you hoping to get for it?" or "What do you think would be a fair price for it?"

Chances are you are going to get a reply similar to "I don't know. How much would you give me for it?" or "I was hoping you'd tell me" or, worse yet, "I'll trust you to tell me what it's worth." What they are doing is asking you to play two conflicting roles: those of appraiser and buyer.

If you like, you can get angry, tell them if they want it appraised to go pay an appraiser and to quit wasting your time; you may feel better, but you'll lose that sale and any future ones as well from them. Bite your tongue and be polite. "Well, it's difficult for me to know how much it's worth since I haven't seen it yet. Maybe if you can remember how much you gave for it that will at least give us a place to start."

They probably didn't give anything or at least not very much for it and you guessed that, but it will serve as a reminder to them that they don't have much invested so anything they get for it will in all likelihood be almost all profit. Another good line with a psychological slant is "Well, when it comes right down to it, all that really matters is what it is worth to you." Naturally it isn't the most important thing in their life or they wouldn't be trying to sell it. Some time before they placed the ad they decided that either they needed the money, the space, or something else more than the piece you are trying to buy—so you may need to give them the opportunity to remember that.

Finally, you may just have to remind the person on the other end of the line that you can't be expected to take the time to drive over to see it without at least some idea what his or her expectations are. As evasive as they may seem, somewhere in their mind they have a figure floating around; it may be too high, it may be enticingly low, but you need to get at least a glimpse of it before you go galloping off toward the sunset. If that doesn't work—and, remember, you are still being polite—then you are going to have to follow your instincts. If you sense that the prospective seller isn't all that serious about selling or may be expecting far more than it will be worth even ten years from now, then you can leave your name and phone number and ask that the person call when he or she either has had it appraised or decided how much they are going to ask for it. Or you can go ahead and set up an appointment to see it. Before you've gotten very far into the antiques business you will have done both and there will have been times you shouldn't have bothered going and times you'll wish you had. That is just the nature of the antiques business—and of people.

In addition to your notes, leave room on your form for the date and time of the appointment. If you are interested in buying the piece, however, don't make the appointment for next week or even the next day. Obviously, the person you are talking to is at home now, so see if you can't go over now. Their phone is going to keep ringing all evening, but the first one to come up with the cash, regardless of whether she was the first or the fifteenth caller, is going to be the one leaving with the antique.

The Early Bird Clinches the Deal

And once in a while that means you have to go to a few extra lengths to be the first one there. Several years ago I spotted an ad in the paper for a player piano—low in price—but with the notation beside the phone number "After Six." Realizing that by six o'clock half the people in town would have read the ad and several would be standing by their phones with the number memorized, I took a different approach. A call to the public library put me in touch with a young lady at the information desk who had a current city directory in front of her; she looked up the phone number from the ad and gave me the address that matched it, so at five thirty, instead of standing next to my phone, I was sitting parked in front of the house. At five minutes before six when the owner of the player piano pulled in, I got out of my truck and met him halfway across the yard. He never even made it to the house, but took me right to the garage where the piano was waiting. And just about the time I started writing out the check, the phone started ringing.

Placing Your Own Classified Ad

Before we examine what happens when you do arrive, let's consider the other principal means of establishing contacts with individuals who have antiques for sale. Once you become serious about getting into the buying and selling of antiques, you are going to want to consider placing your own classified ad. The reason for this is very simple: far more people want to place a classified ad than actually ever do. So what do they do instead? They read them—religiously. The little old lady with the collection of Sandwich glass that is now doing nothing but collecting dust wants to sell it, but doesn't know how much it is worth or who might be interested in buying it. Each night, however, she scans the antiques section of the classified ad page, hoping to find an ad by someone else that mentions a price for Sandwich glass.

If this is where potential sellers are looking, then this is also where you as a potential buyer should be advertising. A simple, inexpensive ad describing the type of antique that interests you is all it takes to get started:

Oak and Walnut Furniture Wanted.
Top Prices Paid. F. Smith.
Tel. 333-3333

Top Prices Paid For Persian Rugs
Call F. Smith Evenings 333-3333.

Get your notebook out again and play with several different possible ads. Naturally, the more words you use the more it costs, so be precise, but don't leave out any crucial informa-

One sign of the decline of the elegant
Victorian period (1840–1910) was a
reduction in both the size and the grandeur
of its furniture. This early twentieth-century
hall tree, unlike its predecessors, is
lightweight, features only a few carvings, is
made of oak rather than walnut, does not
have a seat, and is nearly a foot shorter
than earlier models. What some collectors
would view as shortcomings, however,
have made hall trees such as this one
popular with today's apartment dwellers
and condominium owners.

tion. People scan classified ads with their minds programed to
search and find key words, so mention what it is you are
interested in early in your ad and possibly in bold print. If
you want plenty of phone calls, then make it general, as in
the first example above. If you are only interested in a few
accurate calls, let your ad screen them for you by being very
specific about exactly what you are interested in buying.

Not all buyers include their names in their ads, but giving
the reader a last name to ask for when they call is more personal and takes the first step toward building that all-important
trust between you and the seller. It isn't necessary or perhaps
even advisable to include your first name or your address, but
make sure that your phone number and, if applicable, the time
of day you would like them to call is included and is correct.

Advertise Locally at First

Once your ad is written your next step is to decide which publications you want it to appear in. Rates generally are printed in each issue, but you may want to call the circulation department to find out how many copies of each issue are printed and what the range of distribution is. With that information entered in your notebook you should be able to decide which publication—the local daily, weekly, or advertiser, a monthly magazine, an arts and entertainment guide, or even a theater program—offers you the best opportunity to reach as many people as possible for the least amount of money.

Don't worry right now about advertising in the national antiques newspapers and magazines. Unless you are planning to be extremely specialized, your local publications will generate enough calls to let you gain some experience in buying antiques close to home—and that is an important consideration when you realize that transportation costs can easily become one of the largest portions of your overhead. Later, especially if you choose to specialize in one particular type of item such as Shirley Temple memorabilia or Hummel figurines, you may want to expand your advertising to include some of the regional and national antiques publications.

You next must decide how many times you want your ad to appear. As we said earlier, papers charge by the word and the number of times the ad runs, so you can figure exactly what your costs will be in each publication. Don't, however, expect to be able to run an ad once and be flooded with calls; experience will bear out the theory that most people will need to see an ad more than once before they respond. The rationale is easy to understand: If your ad has run several times, then your business must be successful; and to be successful in the antiques business people have to be able to trust you, so more people call. And when they do, don't hesitate to ask in the course of your conversation where they saw your ad, for it will help you decide just where your advertising dollars were spent wisely.

Handbills Will Also Spread the Word

A historic and still very successful means of spreading the word about your new business interest is the handbill. Posted in grocery stores, public bulletin boards, auction houses, and anywhere else people are apt to read them, they can alert potential sellers to your service at a very low cost. Handbills, or flyers as they are also called, give you more space to work with than a classified ad, so take advantage of them. A standard 8½ by 11-inch sheet of paper will give you more than enough space to detail precisely what types and kinds of antiques you want to buy and even to include artwork from either copyright-free drawings called "clip art" (ask your printer to let you see his books) or reprints of old Sears and Roebuck catalogues. The drawings in these catalogues may be photocopied and then trimmed to fit in among the words on your handbill, business card, or stationery. In addition to adding another dimension to your handbill, they also let people know you are a professional and not just another opportunist looking for a victim.

Advertising, be it newspaper, sight and sound media, or handbills, brings with it the old good news/bad news dilemma. The good news is that your phone is going to start ringing. The bad news is you're not always going to be there to answer it. At this point you're not even going to consider giving up your present job and the hours you do have to yourself are not going to be spent staring at the phone. The antiques business, like any business, is led by those who don't sit and wait, but, instead, go out and make something happen.

Make Sure Your Phone Is Answered at All Times

While you are out making contacts, buying and selling pieces, and running errands you are going to need to make sure you aren't losing potential buyers and sellers. To do so you should look into a phone answering service. At first, either an in-home mechanical device or a personal answering service may seem unnecessarily extravagant for a new, part-time business, but you will soon find that it becomes your least expensive, most trusted, most valuable employee. Besides, it's tax deductable and it doesn't complain about the hours.

Answering services fall into two basic categories—a mechanical device that you purchase and hook onto your phone line or a human being who sits in an office other than yours and takes messages when your phone rings. Choosing one or the other will be a matter of comparing costs and convenience. Some people complain that they feel uncomfortable talking to a machine, thus many businesses hire a phone answering service. Such services work on a monthly basis wherein the rate is determined by the number of hours per day and the number of days per week you wish to have their service in operation. Most offer a variety of options, ranging from taking all of your calls to only answering after a certain number of rings. To pick up your messages you simply call the service.

Mechanical devices are simple to install and are activated with just the turn of a dial. You record a message which your callers will hear after a certain number of rings; they then are given the opportunity to leave a message for you. Since people are somewhat put off by recorded messages and talking into a tape recorder, a personal phone answering service will save a greater percentage of your calls, but does tend to cost more over a long period of time. One problem with the mechanical devices that people could correct, however, is the recorded message that the caller hears. If you get a phone recorder, spend some time thinking about—and rehearsing— what you want your caller to hear when the phone rings. A natural sounding, pleasing recording will go much further toward keeping the caller on the line than a stiff, formal "I'm sorry but I am not in the office at the moment. . . ."

Setting Up Appointments to See Antiques

Naturally, the sooner you can return any calls that came in while you were out, the sooner you can set up an appointment to see some more antiques. Moods and minds change easily, so catch your prospects while they still want to sell. Whether they call you or you call them, set up an appointment that is convenient for both of you and then be there on time. Not only is punctuality polite, but it's just plain smart as well. It shows them that you respect their time and their plans and gets the appointment off on the right foot.

Act Like a Professional and You'll Be Treated Like One

You don't need to show up dressed in a tuxedo (unless, of course, you're on your way to an opening night performance and your wife is keeping the car running while you check out "just one more" contact), but you shouldn't look as if you'd just finished changing the oil in your car either. You are a professional and you want to be treated like one, so you will have to prove that you are through how you look and act. Remember, every satisfied customer—be it buyer or seller— leads to two more. You are doing more than just looking at one particular antique; you are also laying the groundwork for future dealings with them and their family, friends, neighbors, and co-workers.

Putting the Seller at Ease

As you introduce yourself at the door, have one of your business cards ready to hand the seller and you won't have to worry about going through one of those awkward moments later if they suddenly forget your name. You are a stranger in their home, so help put them at ease with a few seconds of small talk while they start forming an opinion of you. The weather is the easiest to start with, since right now it is the only thing you know the two of you have in common and shouldn't spark any violent arguments. If it is appropriate, compliment them on their home or furnishings, but do not be insincere. If the plaster has just fallen or their Irish setter has gone into heat and ripped the couch to shreds, don't say something like, "Oh, I wish I could keep my apartment this clean" or "Having a dog must be so much fun"—or you may be leaving with one.

Let the Owner Carry the Conversation

Once you are led to the piece that is for sale, however, let the owner carry the conversation while you begin your inspection. You will learn to listen, make very neutral responses, and examine the antique all at the same time. Don't worry about holding a conversation on the level of Alistair Cooke; your main concern is to learn all you can about the antique from the owner while you check it over for damage that either detracts from the value of the piece or will have to be repaired. If it helps, take notes as you inspect it, especially if it is a large piece of furniture with several flaws (e.g., the bottom drawer needs to be reglued, there's a veneer chip missing from the top, the casters are not the originals, and the like).

Comment on the Item's Good Points

Just as being on time was both polite and smart, so is openly complimenting the owner on the good points of the antique. If the finish on her burled walnut chest of drawers is in excellent condition, say so. She knows it, so why appear to be either deceitful or stupid or both?

Starting a conversation by criticizing the piece will only risk offending the seller or putting her on the defensive. She has probably prepared herself by mentally listing all of the positive points about the chest of drawers, but if you state them for her or, at the very least, agree with them, then you've taken away her best bargaining weapon. What happens more often than you would think is that if you tell her what is right with the piece, she will show her appreciation by letting slip a few things that are not.

Nevertheless, you are going to have to point out some of the flaws in the piece, but hold off until you have heard her asking price stated again. Even though she may have told you over the phone, ask again. Rather than saying to her, "You wanted three hundred dollars, right?", inquire, "How much are you asking for it?" She may have had second thoughts since your conversation and may already have dropped the price. If just the opposite has happened you can politely remind her that it was $300 and not $350 that she quoted you earlier. By keeping your observations to yourself until you have heard her asking price again, you leave yourself some leverage.

Mention the Flaws Subtly

"You're absolutely correct, Mrs. Abernathy, it certainly is a beautiful piece and I think you're right, it is well over a hundred years old, but I'm afraid that the veneer on the bottom drawer is going to have to be replaced before it will ever be worth that much. And do you happen to have the pull that is missing off this other drawer?"

Mull over her answer in silence while you recheck your notes. Right now saying nothing is the smartest thing you can do. She has just realized that you know what you're doing and that the veneer problem and the missing hardware didn't escape you. Give her a chance to reconsider her asking price without any pressure from you. She is beginning to question her opinion of the chest of drawers and should also be realizing that if you don't buy it then she has to go through all of this again with someone else. If she refuses to budge, then you must decide whether your eventual selling price minus your restoration costs will leave you any profit if you pay her asking price of $300.

How to Make a Counteroffer

Chances are, though, she'll give you an opportunity to make a counteroffer. You have already decided that $250 is the very most you can pay for it and still show a profit, but don't be too eager to offer even that. As soon as you indicate to her that you want it, you've given away part of your bargaining strength. It doesn't matter if you've just come face to face with the one piece you've had your heart and your wallet set on all your life. Hesitate. Put her in a position where she is more concerned about losing you than vice versa.

"I just don't know, Mrs. Abernathy. It's going to take a lot of work. Burled walnut veneer is very hard to find and very expensive and I don't know where to even start looking for a pull like that. I probably shouldn't even buy it at all. [Pause. Deep breath.] What the heck—how about two hundred dollars?"

You know that she will probably have to turn down your offer since it is so much lower than what she had hoped to get for her chest of drawers, but you still have $50 to play with and you haven't put yourself in a position where you can't change your mind. If you announce, "Two hundred is my maximum," then what do you do if she refuses? This way you can't lose: if she accepts your offer, you just made an additional $50. If she refuses it, then you both have a natural compromise awaiting you—$250—which just happens to be your original limit. Antiques bargaining is no different from playing chess or checkers: the winners are the ones who train themselves to think two or three moves ahead.

The Best Deal Is Often a Compromise

And the nice thing about a compromise is that no one leaves feeling taken. Mrs. Abernathy didn't get her $300, but then she also knows you didn't get it for $200. She doesn't know that $250 has been your intended price all along, but then you don't know that it hasn't been hers either. And that's what keeps antiques deals interesting.

Before leaving—with or without the chest of drawers—make sure that no feelings have been hurt or toes stepped on. Thank her for the opportunity to see the piece and be sure to ask if there is anything else she might be thinking about selling; she has invested a good portion of her evening in this transaction and knows that you came prepared to buy something. If it is not her chest of drawers, then it might just as well be that unused set of walnut chairs down in the basement. And if there is nothing else she wants to sell right now, make sure she knows you would be interested in coming back another time and that you would appreciate it if she would let her friends know about you as well. If she seems responsive, leave some extra business cards with her. They don't do any good in your glove compartment.

Be on the Lookout for "That Old Thing Nobody Wants"

One of my best customers told me about the time she heard that an elderly gentleman down the street from her home had a swivel office chair he wanted to sell. She called him that evening, set up a time to see it, liked it immediately, and bought it for just what he asked—$35. In the course of the conversation he casually mentioned that he had used the chair and an old roll-top desk to start his first business. Alertly she just as casually asked about the desk.

"Oh, that old thing," he laughed. "I've still got it, but you wouldn't be interested in it. My brother sawed the legs off to get it out of the office when we moved the business, so it's no good anymore."

Needless to say, she carefully pursued the matter and since the old man liked her (she paid him what he wanted for the chair without haggling over a few dollars, remember?), he took her down to the basement to see the desk. The funny thing was, she said, all the while she was looking it over and

This 1897 Montgomery Ward roll-top desk featured a ''lap joint, dust and knife proof curtain [roll]'', two sliding arm rests, and solid oak construction. At $19.50 it certainly was an ''extra good value.'' The same features that made it popular then maintain its popularity today.

glancing through the drawers he kept trying to talk her out of wanting to buy it, since he was sure it was beyond saving. She persisted, however, until he insisted on taking only the same as what she paid for the chair—$35. A few hours and a few friends later the desk was on its way to a new home where it was much wanted—with the eight sawed-off legs safely tucked away in the bottom drawer.

4

Buying at Yard and Garage Sales

No one seems to know exactly when the first garage sale was held, but at least one unreliable source has traced it back to Detroit, Michigan. It was there on May 17, 1895, that Clara Ford, while her husband was out in the countryside raising dust and frightening horses, started throwing wrenches and fenders and pistons out onto the lawn where passersby were startled by a huge, hand-painted sign—''No reasonable offer refused.''

Since no one in town had a reliable map (or a car, for that matter), and since Mrs. Ford, ignoring the advice of her friend Ina from across the street, had neglected to take out even a small ad in the *Press,* it was reported that the sale was a failure—much to the relief of Henry, who, upon his return home, rescued his precious parts, his tools, the Ford Motor Company, and the United States of America—all in that order.

Yard and Garage Sales Are Big Business Today

Today both the Ford Motor Company and the yard and garage sale industry are a part of big business. Over a billion dollars changes hands each year at over a million yard and garage sales—and the numbers continue to grow daily. What used to be just a lighthearted way of making a few dollars from the junk that had accumulated in closets, basements, garages, and attics has become for some a substantial contribution toward their annual income. Nonprofit organizations, neighborhoods, friends, relatives, and even antiques dealers have realized that yard and garage sales are an ideal way of disposing of unwanted merchandise while generating several hundred dollars.

How to Find Diamonds in the Rough

And amongst all that unwanted merchandise are literal diamonds amid the rough—Tiffany lamps alongside Waring blenders, first editions of *Uncle Tom's Cabin* separating Nancy Drew and the Hardy Boys, Amish quilts buried under Sears electric blankets. And the smarter you are, the earlier you are, and the faster you are, the richer you become.

Locating Yard and Garage Sales

The first step toward becoming a successful yard sale buyer is to determine where and when the yard and garage sales in your area are being advertised. They are generally divided between the classified ad section of the daily paper and special yard sale sections in the weekly giveaways known as Shoppers, Advertisers, or Penny-Savers. You should be reading both—or all, if that is the case—since you don't want to risk missing out on any great sales that might be listed in only one publication. (People have a strange way of holding grudges against newspapers; let just one daydreaming ten-year-old carrier toss just one paper into their shrubs and some people will refuse to have anything to do with the entire newspaper organization for the next ninety-nine years.)

While it is not necessary to be standing next to the press as the first paper comes off the line, it is important that you learn which day each of the weekly papers is published. Reading the paper on the same day it is printed will enable you to catch any last minute sales taking place that day and to adjust your next day's schedule and itinerary so that you can catch either an early morning sale on your way to work or to check out a Depression glass collection being disposed of at a church rummage sale starting late that afternoon.

Don't Overlook Early and Midweek Sales

Early in the week the listings are going to be slim, but that doesn't mean you should ignore them. One of the best sales I ever attended was being held for one day only—on a Tuesday—because the family was suddenly being transferred out of the country and everything except the barest necessities had to be disposed of before the weekend. Needless to say, the bargains were unbelievable: desks, tables and chairs, bookcases and boxes and boxes of books, all for only a fraction of what they would cost new—or old.

One friend of mine supplements her babysitting income by selling to dealers the antiques and collectibles she buys at early and midweek sales when nearly everyone else, including the shop dealers, are tied down to their regular jobs. Then Saturday morning when everyone else is running from sale to sale, she sleeps in, makes the rounds selling to the shop dealers what she had bought the day before, or holds her own one-day yard sale. She claims she can find more bargains during the week with less hassle than she can on any given Saturday—but I still see her out on many a Saturday morning with her list in one hand, a map and a cup of coffee in the other, scurrying from sale to sale.

Attending Late Week and Weekend Sales

Monday, Tuesday, and Wednesday sales don't require much advance preparation since there are generally only a few being advertised, and those you can hit on the way home from work or the store. But when you open Wednesday's paper one day in May, watch out—the list of yard sales may knock you cold. In fact, it may seem so overwhelming that it takes the desire right out of you.

Don't despair. Follow the example of the old prospector who discovered Sutter's Mill. Rather than racing excitedly about, snatching up a few nuggets, and then racing back to Sacramento, he sat down, figured out the best place to begin and then started panning. By the time everyone else got done yelling and screaming and jumping up and down and running around, he had staked his claim and made his fortune. And so can you.

You are going to want to start on Wednesday night, not hitting the bricks, but reading the papers. First, separate the Thursday-Friday-Saturday sales from the Friday-Saturday Only sales from the Saturday Only sales. You can makes lists of addresses on separate sheets of paper or you can do as some serious yard salers do and actually cut out the ads and stack them together by category. Then you can start determining your priorities.

Plan Your Attendance Schedule—Bargains Don't Wait

First, if you are able to get away on Thursday, either during the day or after work, make a list of the sales you can attend starting that day. If however, you are restricted to Saturday morning, the sales that opened on either Thursday or Friday should become a lower priority than those that open for the first time on Saturday morning. Any bargains at Thursday's or Friday's sales will have been snapped up by Saturday, so don't waste prime time on them; you've got more important sales to attend that morning.

Whatever day or days you plan to do your yard saling, you are going to have to get organized. At no other time in your antiquing is being first going to be more important than in hitting the yard and garage sales. Bargains don't wait for anyone and you are going to be up against some stiff, experienced

Navaho blankets are among today's most popular and profitable collectibles. Dealers and collectors both prefer pre-1900 examples, but difficulty in dating and increasing demand make even early twentieth-century blankets and rugs desirable. Buyers are urged to consider wear, previous restoration, color, and design carefully before making a major purchase. Current interest has spawned several books and magazine articles dedicated solely to buying and selling Navaho rugs and blankets.

competition when you start playing the garage sale game seriously. Before you stow your Antiques Inspection Kit behind the front seat and back out of the garage you are going to have to know exactly where you are going and in what order, or you will end up spending valuable time backtracking, driving in circles or pulled over to the curb trying to find Yewell Street on your tattered map.

Get There Before the Competition

On Thursday after work, for instance, let's say there are two average sounding sales that, according to your map, are only a few blocks off your normal route home. Five miles in the opposite direction, however, is a large sale with several antiques listed. It, however, starts at noon. It may seem obvious to you that your chances of discovering a great deal would be better at the two smaller sales where you can be among the first to arrive, but apparently not everyone seems to think like that. Smart yard sale organizers know that the word "antiques" brings dealers and collectors out of the woodwork, whether or not they actually have any legitimate antiques. Don't be fooled, then, into driving several miles out of your way if you can't be among the first to arrive, because there may or may not be any antiques for sale (and if the owners know—or think—they have antiques, what is that going to do to the prices?). Being early, being able to catch two sales in close proximity to one another, and being at a sale where antiques aren't overemphasized will, in all likelihood, enable you to buy a valuable antique or collectible that no one else was even able to identify.

Remember: A sale in the hand is better than one out in the bushes.

On Saturday's list you can eliminate those sales that started on Thursday or Friday and that you either did not or were not able to attend. The problem you find, however, is that there are still more sales on Saturday alone than you could hit if you had two Saturdays and an extra Sunday thrown in just to do yard sales. Some are close to home, others are miles away; some list antiques that sound inviting, others are too vague to tell. Some start at eight o'clock, others not until ten—and three don't list any times at all.

Finding the Sales Nearest to You

Sound confusing—and maybe just a little discouraging? Certainly. But inherent in a successful yard sale buyer is the ability to pull order out of chaos. One way to do that is with what is often called "the shotgun approach." Spread a city map out on your table and begin cutting the ads out of the paper and placing them near their respective addresses. Grad-

ually you will see order emerging out of disorder. What you
are going to want to find are areas where you can cover several targets with one blast. Eliminate the ads for sales miles
away from you or the nearest other sale, for besides wasting
valuable time and fuel, they inevitably will be closer to home
for some other yard sale addict.

Pay closest attention to the areas nearest you that meet the
following criteria: (1) early starting times, (2) other sales
nearby, and (3) antiques advertised.

As we said before, this last criterion is not always the most
important. When people list "antiques" in their ads, they generally have already overestimated their value. This word in a
listing also tends to draw the largest crowd, and it doesn't
take a genius to figure out that even if the closest thing you
have to an antique is your grandmother's elephant-foot umbrella stand, just the mention of that one special word alone
is going to bring hordes of people to your sale.

How to Find Antiques That Have Not Been Advertised

What you want to do is to find the antiques that aren't
advertised. You want the antiques that no one else has figured
out actually are antiques—the matched pair of Art Deco lamps,
the stack of arts and crafts linens, the painted Windsor chair
or the oak box full of early woodworking tools. And you want
to find them before the late risers have their third cup of coffee
(you're drinking yours out of a Thermos at twenty-five miles
an hour), casually pick up the paper, and hit one or two sales
before they go out to the driving range or to K Mart that
afternoon. Believe me, there is no better feeling than to be
sitting over a Saturday afternoon lunch with your car crammed
full of great deals when you overhear someone in the next
booth talking about going to a yard sale—one that you have
already picked clean.

For that reason, finding a grouping of eight o'clock yard
sales not far from your home is the ideal place to start your

shotgun approach. Don't pay too much attention to the wording of the ads—about the only thing you can trust in them is the address. For all you know the owner may have been too cheap to spend an extra dollar on the words "set of six pressed back oak chairs" and instead merely listed "chairs." Or he may not have even known when he wrote the ad that his brother-in-law needed some quick cash for a down payment on a new boat, so is bringing his wife's walnut dresser over to sell out of his pickup.

Once you have combed all of the addresses in the first area, plan to move to the next closest grouping, but now, instead of heading for sales that started at eight o'clock, target the ones that advertised a nine o'clock opening, or, if it is getting late in the morning, a ten o'clock start. Chances are the eight o'clock sales have been picked over, but the later sales will still be fresh. You can continue this way throughout the day, but sales that start at noon or after are rare, so you can figure that by ten or eleven o'clock in the morning most of the bargains have been plucked.

Your Return Visit May Swing the Deal

Before calling it a day, however, there is one option open to you around noon. If you dropped in at an early morning sale that had an antique you were interested in, but the item was marked too high for you (and hopefully for anyone else) to buy, the owner might be willing to lower her price as it becomes clear that it is not going to sell as easily as she had hoped. It will be worth your while to swing back by the address, see if that is the case, take another look at the piece, and make her an offer—who knows, your best deal of the day may be your last.

Attending Sales When You Specialize

Not everyone employs the shotgun approach. Some swear by a more selective process whereby they put all of their emphasis in the wording of the ad. For instance, someone who only buys and sells glassware is going to arrange her list not according to close groupings, but by time and content. It won't matter if the first sale starts at eight and is nearly four miles away—just so long as the ad lists "glassware" for sale. She may then drive past six other sales to get to one on the other side of town that starts at nine and also offers what she is looking for.

Both approaches have their advantages and disadvantages and neither is entirely more preferable over the other. Many times the approach you choose may depend on the mood you are in, the type of merchandise you have found you can most easily resell in your area, or the number of sales going on. Regardless of which you feel most comfortable with on any given day, the key to a successful outing is going to be how well you organize your itinerary the night before.

Your City Map Is the Key to Yard and Garage Sales

One item in your Antiques Inspection Kit which you may want to tailor to your yard and garage sale excursions is your city map. Trying to fold, unfold, read, and understand a city map while driving twenty miles an hour down an alley used by the air force for practice bombing runs on Tuesdays can be tricky—and more than a little dangerous. One of the smartest solutions I have ever seen to this problem was designed by a regular yard saler in a town of approximately 80,000 people; he cut the city map into four segments (you could use more sections if your city is large or your eyes weak—and you could have them enlarged on a photocopier), highlighted the major street or avenue running through each with a brightly colored marker for easy reference, transferred the map's grid system to all four sides of each minimap, and then pasted each to a separate piece of cardboard. He then had each segment laminated not just to protect it from coffee spills, but to enable him to use a felt marker to trace his route the night before and mark each sale he was planning to attend. These he either kept beside him on the seat of his truck or attached with a clip to his dash to free his hands. As he moved from one section of town to another he would pull the appropriate minimap from his stack, find his starting point, and follow his pre-marked route from sale to sale. At the end of the day he simply wiped each map clean with a damp cloth to ready it for the next week's sale.

Take Packing Material for Fragile Items

If you anticipate buying glassware or other fragile items, slip a couple of sturdy boxes with lids and packing material inside your vehicle before you leave. Unlike antiques shops, yard sale merchants can't be expected to wrap your purchases for you. Here the rule is "You buy it, you carry it, you pack it." And if your newly purchased Candlewick goblet rolls off the back seat and lands on a soapstone footwarmer you bought two blocks ago, there's no one to blame but yourself.

Buying Excursions Alone or with Company

One of the last decisions you are going to have to make before you wrap up your Wednesday or Friday night prepa-rations is whether you prefer to travel alone when you are antiquing or like to have company. If this is simply a social enterprise for you and not a business outing, then by all means take the entire family, but don't expect to cover much ground. Getting everyone headed in the same direction at the same time can be difficult, if not impossible, especially when your twelve-year-old son discovers in someone's ga-rage a stack of old *Playboy* magazines just about the time

your youngest daughter tips a cage full of gerbils over on
the lawn.

On the other hand, having someone to help with the navigating and parking not only will ease the strain, but can enable
you to hit more yard sales in a single morning than you would
be able to visit alone. If you have a friend who also enjoys
getting up at seven o'clock on a Saturday morning just to dig
through someone else's junk, then you should be able to work
out a system that would enable the two of you to find some
great bargains while remaining good friends.

Here's one possibility: the passenger assumes responsibility
for guiding the driver to the proper address. Once there, the
driver pulls up directly in front of the house, the passenger
jumps out and heads for the bargains while the driver parks
the car and walks back. When they both are finished, they
reverse roles, with the driver then becoming navigator and
getting first crack at the next sale.

One problem with two yard sale addicts, though, is who
has first choice at an item? The best way to solve that is to
talk about it before it happens—and then to work different
sides of the same sale rather than to go down the tables or
through the garage together. That way there is no problem
enforcing the age old rule of antiquing: whoever spots it first

and indicates to the other that he/she has an interest in it has first option to buy. Only if that option is not exercised does the other partner have the right to buy it.

If you are in the mood to do some serious yard sale buying, want to travel light and fast, and don't want to worry about any conflicts with your partner, work out a deal with someone who can drive your car but has no interest in even getting out to browse. It may be a son or daughter, niece or nephew, husband or neighbor, but if you can convince them that you will make it worth their while to spend four hours Saturday morning chauffeuring you from sale to sale, you will have eliminated all the problems associated with navigating, parking, and partners.

That is not to say that you can't do some serious yard saling alone. I do most of mine alone simply because I find I travel faster that way and have learned a few tricks to keep from having to walk six blocks from where I parked to the sale. If you don't dawdle, you can usually—depending on how busy the street is—get away with five minutes of double parking. From a legal standpoint I certainly can't recommend it, but if you decide to leave your car parked illegally for a few minutes, be sure to put on your emergency flashers. And hurry.

Most yard salers are polite, so polite, in fact, that many times they will drive three blocks away rather than park in the owner's driveway or that of a neighbor. Once again, however, don't dawdle or you may get a ticket. And never, never leave enough space for someone else to pull in behind you. I once saw an experienced dealer make the mistake of pulling all the way into a long driveway where a sale was being held in the back yard. While she was back there someone else pulled in behind her, leaving her no exit. As I watched, the later arrival walked a few houses down the street to a neighboring yard sale. No sooner had he disappeared into the crowd than the dealer emerged from behind the house, ready to leave—but blocked in. She was furious, but had no one but herself to blame for her predicament.

(And don't do as one woman did and pull into a driveway too fast. She reportedly plowed through three tables of glassware and ran over a lawn mower before she finally got her car stopped.)

The smart solo buyer will first drive past the front of the house to see if there are any spaces available along the street or in the driveway. If not, don't automatically pull away or start circling the block. Instead, turn the corner and come in through the alley. Chances are you will be able to find a parking space back there that won't hinder any emergency vehicles or upset the seller's neighbor—so long as you don't park on his strawberry bed.

Making Your On-Site Inspection

Once you are out of the car don't waste any time. Take a quick lap around the entire layout, analyzing what is on and under the tables, what is set out in the yard, and what is still sitting in the garage. If the ad listed a specific item that interested you, but you don't immediately see the piece, ask about it. The owners may have left it in the house or it may already have been sold. Either way you don't want to waste valuable time wandering around looking for it. This isn't the time for needless window-shopping either. If you are interested in furniture, find it. While you stand there thinking you could use a few extra clay flowerpots, someone else is going to be carrying a stacking oak bookcase out of the garage.

And speaking of garages, don't pass up the opportunity to wander into the garage, even if it appears obvious from the doorway that there is nothing in there of interest to you. So what if you live in a third-floor condominium? Pretend you might want to buy that twelve horsepower John Deere tractor mower while you scan the walls and rafters for anything of real interest to you. I once spotted a superb set of oak library card catalogue files back in a corner of a garage. The woman holding the sale was surprised to see that I was interested in them since her late husband had only used them to store nuts and bolts. A few minutes and a few dollars later they were mine—as were nearly a hundred dollars worth of nuts, bolts, screws, washers, and nails that she had no need for. After a good cleaning all that the card catalogue needed was a new home—with an expert cook who needed a place to store her recipe cards.

Make Your Decision Quickly

When something does catch your eye, stop, inspect it and make a decision. If you want it, either carry it with you or take it directly to the cashier for her to hold until you are done looking. Set it back down on the table and you can be sure of only one thing—it will be gone when you return. There is a strange quirk in humans that sparks a desire for something only after we have seen someone else show an interest in it. And it works the same for antiques as it does for cars, clothes, houses, and spouses.

Bargaining and Buying at a Yard Sale

One of the best aspects of yard and garage sales is the bargaining that often takes place before cash changes hands. It rarely reaches the intensity witnessed in antiques shops or shows when a shrewd collector is pitted against a veteran dealer with a $3,000 Pennsylvania tilt-top table at stake, but it is the practice field on which future negotiators are trained. Unlike the shop and show dealers who know they will have more customers in next week, next month, or even next year, the yard sale host wants to get rid of everything with a price tag— and maybe a few other things as well. This gives you a distinct advantage over them, especially later in the day or just as soon as the first threatening cloud rumbles across the sky.

Never stay home just because the weather isn't perfect. While an unexpected storm may have cancelled some sales, those people who spent the entire night setting up tables, washing clothes, and pricing items are in too deep to cancel. The crowd will be small, thus the sellers will tend to be extremely flexible in their bargaining.

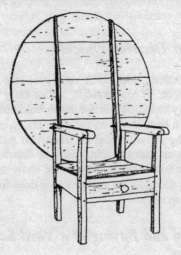

The chair table (c. 1660–1840) survives as a fine example of American country furniture. Though far more practical than its cousin, the tilt-top table, it never achieved the same popularity. This particular example featured pegged joints, curved finger grips, and a storage drawer beneath the seat. They were made in several different types of wood, including pine, maple, birch, and oak.

Understanding Prices—Theirs and Yours

If you've ever helped with or run your own yard sale, you will probably agree that the toughest part of the entire ordeal is pricing items. Emotional attachment—or detachment as the case often is—aside, people who are bank tellers, accountants, shop clerks, and plumbers have no idea of the actual market value of the antiques and collectibles they have accumulated over the years. As a result, some pieces will be greatly un-

derpriced, such as the old Heisey serving platter I bought for
50¢, and some will be overinflated, such as much of the
cheaply veneered bedroom furniture from the 1920s.

Before you get involved in any yard sale bargaining or buying, make sure that you have closely inspected the piece for
any flaws, cracks, chips, or potential problems that could
either detract from its resale value or add to your overhead.
Determine what you could resell it for or, if that is the case,
what it is worth to you as a personal possession. Once you
have a price in mind make that your top limit and resist any
temptation to exceed it.

The Fine Art of Negotiation

I don't make it a habit to haggle over a few cents—even
for the practice—especially if the item is priced far under its
market value to begin with. If I spot an antique I like, however, and know that it is priced too high or sense that the
owner is willing to negotiate a lower price, I'll start one of
my routines (and any dealer or collector who claims *not* to
have one or several routines needs to take a closer look at
herself sometime when she's bargaining). If I'm in a hurry or
don't really care whether I buy the piece or not, I'll just come
straight out and ask, "Can you do better on the price?" or
"Would you take less?" If not, and the price is still below
my limit, I might buy it; otherwise I'll walk away—and that
takes more practice than you first realize. Too many people
get too emotionally involved with a piece before any bargaining is done. Save your excitement for afterward and you'll
also be saving yourself some money.

When the Price Is Too High

If the piece warrants it and I am in the mood, I'll spend
more time bargaining, with the objective of thus spending less
money. As with all negotiating, the more time you can get
the seller to invest in you and the transaction, the more apt

he or she will be to drop the price in order to salvage something for the time invested. Asking questions about the piece
is the best approach: its history, how old it is, how long the
owner has had it, what it is made of.

After a while you are going to want to indicate that you are
seriously interested in the piece, but that the price is a little
high for you. That is also the time to point out any flaws in
the antique: scratches, chips, nicks, replaced hardware, missing casters. You are, in effect, acting much as an attorney
who is presenting his case to a jury would. You have your
price in mind and you are attempting to present the facts that
would support it and not that of the opposing side.

"You know, I really like this dresser, but I'm not so sure
those handles haven't been replaced. It's going to have to be
refinished, too. [Pause] Would you be willing to take something less than two hundred for it?"

Rather than make him your top offer, which in this case we'll
say is $175, leave the door open for him to commit himself. If
he answers with $150, close the deal or, if you're really in the
mood and feeling sharp, go for $125. You haven't got anything
to lose and only stand to increase your profit.

Start Your Offer Low

If he invites you to make an offer, start lower than your top
limit. One hundred and fifty dollars, for instance, gives you
room to compromise if he refuses your offer and gives you
the chance to make an extra $25 if he doesn't. If, however,
the two of you can't come to terms, prepare to leave—slowly.
Let him watch that $175 start to slip away. He may change
his mind, but if he doesn't, don't leave without first giving
him your name and phone number. By the end of the day he
may have undergone a change of heart and figure your $175
is better than nothing at all. At this point you tell him that
you found another dresser at the next sale priced at $150, but
if he is willing to sell his for that, you'll take it—you sly fox.

Getting Your Purchase Home

Once the bargaining is completed, only two things remain: paying for the piece and getting it home. Most of the time neither of these will pose any sort of a problem; cash is the preferred method of payment, although ironically the larger the amount, the more likely the seller is to accept a check—provided you have plenty of identification and an honest face. You then simply put your great buy in the car and you're off to the next sale.

What happens, though, if it is too big for you to fit in your car? One dealer tells the story of a dental cabinet he bought at a yard sale for $200, leaving the sellers a check and making arrangements to come back later after he had emptied his already brimming pickup. When he returned a few hours later, however, his dental cabinet was gone. The seller handed him back his check and informed him that someone else had come along and offered them $250 for the cabinet—and they accepted it.

Naturally, the dealer was incensed. He fumed and shouted and demanded back what he insisted was *his* dental cabinet, but to no avail. He even carried through with his threat to contact his attorney, but was advised not to attempt a breach of contract suit. He ended up short one dental cabinet, but long on experience.

Hopefully, most people would not do what was done to that dealer, but you do have several options open to you, should the same situation arise, that can prevent that from happening. If you have a partner, one of you could remain with the piece while the other goes for a larger vehicle. If you are alone, you could phone home for assistance—provided your teenagers don't have the lines tied up.

If none of these options is available, and it becomes apparent you will have to leave, take the following precautions: first, get a detailed receipt. It doesn't matter if it is written on a scrap of notebook paper or the back of a bank deposit slip. Just make sure the seller gives you an accurate description of the piece, notes the price and the date and signs it.

Second, explain to the owner—now the previous owner—that you will be returning as quickly as you can. Ask that the piece be moved out of the sale area (and help do so). Make sure the previous owner knows that you expect the piece to be there when you return.

Finally—and this is going to almost guarantee that it won't be sold out from under you—take part of it with you. If you just bought a large walnut dresser, take with you as many of the drawers as you possibly can cram into your car. Chances are no one is going to top your offer for a dresser without any drawers, a bed without one rail, or a lamp without a shade.

Nevertheless, don't delay your return. Even if your piece is still there when you do return, you would have a difficult time holding the previous owners responsible if the neighbor's dog mistook your umbrella stand for a fire hydrant or if someone's child pulled over your newly acquired Aladdin floor lamp, shattering the original glass globe. Get whatever it takes to get it home—a truck, a van, or a rental trailer—and get back there. Fast. If it is that good a deal, then it's worth skipping the rest of the morning's yard sales just to insure that you have indeed finalized the sale.

When You Get Your Purchase Home

And when you do get home, don't just collapse into the nearest chair and stay there for two days. Unpack your car slowly, piece by piece, entering each item and its description into your inventory notebook, along with the purchase price. If necessary, wipe each piece clean and set those that need to be repaired near your workbench. Pack glassware and pottery away carefully with your previous purchases and mark on the outside of each box exactly what it contains. That will save you from tearing open each box and pulling out half its contents and packing material when someone calls up wanting to buy a Rookwood vase you bought at a yard sale six months earlier. Your inventory is virtually worthless if you can't get to it quickly and easily when you have the chance to make a sale.

And if there's but one thing that the yard and garage sale circuit will give you in the course of only one summer, it is inventory. Start organized and stay organized and you'll find yourself halfway toward becoming a successful antiques dealer.

5

Buying at Antiques Shops

A couple of weeks on the yard and garage sale circuit is to the new antiques dealer what spring training is to the rookie shortstop: preparation for the pros. In our league the professionals don't wear numbers or swing bats, but they can throw you a few curves. We're going up against veteran antiques dealers, men and women who have spent years buying, selling, trading, and appraising antiques, people who are experts at bargaining—and refusing to bargain.

So why should we even bother going up against the pros?

Simple.

Some of the best deals in town are sitting right under their noses.

Don't Be Intimidated by Dealers

Many newcomers to the field of antiques are intimidated by antiques dealers, awed by their years of experience and their ability to apparently remain emotionally unmoved by the sight of a beautiful hand-stitched Amish quilt, an exquisite piece of Lalique glassware, or a lovely hand-tooled Roycroft book. What these rookies don't realize is that antiques dealers be-

Elbert Hubbard, founder of the Arts and Crafts colony he called Roycroft, adapted the orb-and-cross mark of a thirteenth-century bookbinder monk and insisted that it be prominently incised on all of the books, magazines, metalwork, and furniture produced in his East Aurora, New York, center. The internationally famous Hubbard died along with his wife when the *Lusitania* sank in 1915.

come just as excited, just as nervous, just as anxious as they, only the dealers have learned to mask their feelings from the scrutiny of an auctioneer, another dealer, or a customer.

More important to us, however, is that behind those masks of authority and experience is a realization that they can not even be sure of the true value of many of the antiques in their own shops.

After a long morning of dashing from house to house and garage to garage hoping to find just a few good antiques tucked in amid the clutter of broken bicycles, worn out wheelbarrows, lime leisure suits, and geriatric gerbils, a nice, clean, organized antiques shop can soothe the weary soul. I must confess to having slept late a few fine Saturday mornings when the paper was brimming with yard sales, too tired from the night before to rise to the emotional peak necessary to compete for the day's bounty, but anxious by noon to hit several antiques shops.

I also discovered, after a few months of always being a few minutes too late or a house or two behind him, one particular dealer who depended almost entirely on yard and garage sales for his inventory. By midsummer I was convinced that the man started at four in the morning, had an underground network of informants that identified key sales, used a CB radio to map his coordinates, and was taking funny little pills that enabled him to leap from his truck, hurdle kids, cars, and bikes, balance four chairs, a stack of books, two vases, and a Red Wing crock while he made change, and still catch his slowly moving truck before it reached the next intersection.

Unable to discover his "radio frequency," I changed my

plan of attack. Rather than compete with him, I pulled out of
the morning yard sale circuit one Saturday and chose instead
to wait for him at his shop that afternoon. About two o'clock,
he roared into the driveway, trunks, chairs, tables, wardrobes,
pottery, and glassware all bouncing precariously under a
hundred feet of clothesline rope, his cab littered with coffee
cups, newspapers, notes, maps, half-eaten doughnuts, and
$300 worth of defenseless Rockwood pottery. While he dashed
off to the phone to seal yet another deal, I calmly picked
through his loot, waited for him to fly back out of the house,
paid him his modest markup, and saved myself a good deal
of gas, a great deal of effort, and an unmeasurable amount of
frustration.

Dealers Provide a Service

Like my yard sale competitor, all dealers provide us with a
service—namely, finding, buying, cleaning, and sometimes
restoring antiques. They display them in a variety of ways,
ranging from glass-enclosed display cases in new shopping
malls to hundred-and-fifty-year-old barns with chairs literally
hanging from the rafters. A good portion of their markup is
justified, for if they cannot meet their overhead expenses and
stay in business, then many of us are going to have to take
more time off from our regular jobs to scour the country lanes
and city streets for antiques.

Use the Antiques Shop as a Classroom

Most dealers carry what is referred to as a general line of
antiques. This means that in most shops you can expect to
find anything from a country pine cupboard to an Art Deco
lamp. Each antiques shop is also a classroom and each dealer
a qualified instructor in some aspect of antiques. Even if you
can't find anything you are interested in or feel you can afford,
if you leave a shop without learning something, you have only
yourself to blame. Pull out your Kit notebook and jot down

prices, bits of information you might pick up in your conversations, the names of unusual pieces that you might later want to research, titles of books or periodicals, and other such valuable information.

Not long ago I journeyed up near the Minnesota border to pick up some signed Gustav Stickley chairs I had bought over the phone from a shop dealer. Her specialty, it turned out, was Red Wing stoneware, a field I knew less than nothing about. While I asked her a few basic questions and looked over her inventory, I sensed that I would never become a Red Wing enthusiast, but my interest was piqued when she mentioned that the rarest and most valuable Red Wing stoneware could be identified by a raised diamond stamped on the bottom. That, I knew, was something I could easily remember and watch for. Less than a month later at a small show three hundred miles away I casually picked up what at first glance appeared to be just another piece of Red Wing and discovered on the bottom the rare raised diamond.

Getting the Word Out about Your Specialty

It pays to strike up a conversation with the dealer and to introduce yourself. If you are searching for a specific item that the dealer apparently does not have, ask if he or she ever comes across one, do they know of any other dealer who might, and would they give you a call if one ever does come in. Successful dealers generally have more inventory than they are able to display at one time; and the aggressive ones are always searching for specific pieces to sell to a particular collector or another dealer. Letting them identify you with your specialty not only gives them a reason to remember you, but it, in effect, provides you with a nonsalaried employee who is out actively searching for antiques on your behalf.

A Gustav Stickley spindle-back side chair with leather seat, c. 1910. Stickley's signature, in the form of a postage stamp size black decal, would often appear on either the inside or the outside of the rear stretcher. The combination of narrow spindles on the back and underneath the seat make this a highly desirable example of his work.

Do Your Homework about Your Specialty

While all dealers have one or two areas in which they specialize, none of them are able to know all there is to know about each of the antiques lining their walls and hanging from their ceilings. And while an experienced dealer can teach you more in an hour than you could learn in a day in the library, when you are out in search of a specific item that is your specialty, you can save yourself a good deal of money if you have done your homework first. You can give yourself a decided edge over more dealers if you take the time to research the antiques you are after.

Chances are greatly improved that when you enter a shop loaded with information on the styles, makers, markings, conditions, and prices of the particular antique you are looking for, you are going to know more than the dealer behind the oak roll-top desk. With just a few minutes of discreet inspec-

Estimated by experts to have been the world's largest art pottery in 1915, the Weller Pottery Company produced hundreds of different models between the time of its founding in 1882 and its demise in 1948. The most actively sought after Weller line is Hudson pottery, which was produced during the twenties. Many pieces made at that time were signed by notable artists who hand painted birds, animals, and plants on the semimatte glazed backgrounds. Two different marks used by the firm are illustrated here.

tion you are going to be able to make an accurate appraisal of the value of any antique within your field of interest.

The advantages of this information are obvious, for you will be able to spot, say, a piece of Weller pottery that has either an obscure mark or no identification mark at all, an unsigned Fox print, or even a rookie Willie Mays bubblegum card. In cases such as these, the dealer many times will not have the knowledge or have taken the time to research or recognize the Willie Mays card as being far more valuable than those of his teammates, and, as a result, will often have it priced far below its actual market value.

Locating Shops and Sellers

Finding all the antiques shops in a given area, whether in your own locality or someplace on your vacation itinerary, is not always as simple as just letting your fingers do the walking. Many small, new, or part-time shops do not advertise and these are precisely the ones you do not want to miss.

Discovering a new shop or one whose owners haven't kept up with the rapid changes in the market is like stumbling into a gold mine. Inside, you can find pieces that either haven't been correctly identified or still bear price tags from ten years ago. You'll have trouble containing your enthusiasm as you pile the counter with dusty Depression glass and pine pieces in their original milk paint (and the dealer will almost always apologize—"I meant to get that bench stripped, but I just don't seem to have the energy I used to.").

Since it fits so neatly within their budget, most of these shops depend on word-of-mouth advertising. The best way to find them is to ask. If you start your browsing in one of the larger shops that advertise in the phone book, casually ask the owner before you leave for the names of other shops in the area. You'll find that people in the antiques field, unlike those in many other businesses, are usually more than willing to help guide you to their competition. The feeling generally is that no two shops have identical merchandise, so they are not actually in head-to-head competition. And the friendly dealers will have the attitude: "Just because I don't happen to have what you need, is no reason why I shouldn't help you find it somewhere else."

You also should make it a point to ask station attendants, drugstore clerks, and anyone else who appears to have lived in the area for a while. Often they will know someone selling a few antiques from her back porch or basement who gets but a few customers a week.

"Mary, down the street there a ways, she goes to them auctions all the time. Heck, she's got a whole shed full of old furniture and junk out back. Hey, Sid! Mary back from the vet yet?"

Shops such as these often have sleepers (no, not their spouses) and steals that are waiting for someone like you to come along and recognize them.

Antiques dealers are a notoriously independent bunch, but most are now joining forces and finances to have area directories printed and distributed. If you don't see any flyers displayed in the first shop you enter, ask. It may be that the last one was picked up just a few minutes earlier or that they are being kept behind the counter. Check with the owner to see how current the information is, for some old shops may have closed or some new ones opened since anyone got around to having the directories updated.

Choosing which shops, either from the phone book or area directory, to visit first will probably be determined by your available time and their advertised hours. If one particular shop of interest to you is definitely off the beaten path, it may be a good idea to call first to make sure someone is going to be behind the desk that day. Antiques dealers, especially those with small, in-home shops, enjoy the flexibility their vocation allows and won't hesitate to close up shop in the middle of the day to dash across town to check on the Tuckers' garage sale, an afternoon auction, or a sudden fire call. Rather than drive twenty miles one way only to find that a shop is open by appointment only during the planting season, call first and save the gas and your time.

The Best Time to Buy from Dealers

While most people simply go antiquing whenever the mood strikes them, if you put just a little thought into choosing the best time for you to buy from antiques dealers you can quickly negate much of the advantage their years of experience gives them over most of their customers.

Consider what happens, for instance, when you wander into a busy antiques shop about ten o'clock on a fine, sunny Saturday morning. Business has been good all summer, evidenced by the fact that the dealer hasn't received a single overdraft notice from the bank. Much of the merchandise is fresh from several auctions she has recently attended. People will be anxious to be out moving around on a fine day like this, and she can expect to do several hundred dollars worth of business. It's early, but you're not even her first customer of the day. For weeks you have been searching for a Globe Wernicke five section stacking oak bookcase and, naturally, she has one, but it is priced slightly above its full retail value. Ask yourself, if you were the dealer right then, would you feel pressured to accept any less?

Flip ahead several pages on the calendar and the scenario might look like this: cold weather has set in and the forecast is for colder still. It's four o'clock on a dreary Wednesday afternoon and the only set of footprints in the snow leads up to the mailbox, which is brimming with sweepstakes entry forms, a new overdraft from the bank, and this month's utility bill. As she looks around her shop, all the dealer sees is merchandise left over from last summer—and she's sick of looking at it. She's spent another day alone in the shop and she's thinking about closing up early, but then she hears you come crunching through the snow and up the cracking steps, stomping off the stubborn white stuff, unwinding your scarf, and wiping the steam from your glasses. As your eyes adjust to the light you scan the room and over in the corner, a little dustier than before, sits the same stacking bookcase, priced a little more reasonably than last summer, but still more than you want to pay. Ask yourself, what are the odds *now* that she'll be more flexible on her price?

Negotiating with an Experienced Dealer

Negotiating purchase price with an experienced antiques dealer requires a little more finesse and a good deal more patience than it does with the weekend yard saler. Selling is how antiques dealers make their living and selling something at a loss takes money right out of their pocket. Most will either have detailed records or the memory of a Mississippi River steamboat pilot; they will either know or find out how much they paid for an item purchased months or even years earlier. They also know about things like restoration and transportation costs, sales help, utility bills, and shop overhead, so they will not be inclined to sell something at any price just to get rid of it.

And while you may have gotten away with some outrageous

offers at yard sales, don't expect the same tactics to work on an experienced antiques dealer. A brash offer of $50 for an early Victorian walnut sewing rocker marked $195 won't do anything but label you as a bargain hunter wasting the dealer's time. Customers such as these are one reason why more and more dealers are refusing to negotiate the sale of any of their antiques. Some see it as being unprofessional and argue that since people don't normally walk into grocery stores and expect the owners to lower the price of their steak on request, they shouldn't at antiques shops either. These dealers will tell you—politely, we hope—that they have marked their antiques at what they feel are fair and reasonable prices and that they do not, as some dealers will privately admit, purposely mark up an item so they can later lower it in order to satisfy a buyer without sacrificing their profit.

The major weakness in their argument is that antiques, unlike food and clothing, are difficult to price. You can't, as some retail merchants do, simply mark up each item a certain percentage of the purchase price, for a Tiffany lamp discovered at a yard sale for $200 may actually be worth in excess of $2,000. If the dealer systematically attempts to mark each item up 100 percent of the purchase price, then, theoretically she should sell the lamp for just $400.

How Much Is It Worth?

So how much is it actually worth? Six different dealers may give you six different opinions and all could be considered appropriate. Antiques, not unlike commodities, fluctuate in price according to what the market will bear. Our dealer may have a Tiffany lamp she has marked at $2,800, but cannot be positive whether, in her area and in its present condition, it is actually worth $3,600 or only $2,200. Thus, it should not be considered totally unprofessional for a buyer to want to pay what *he* feels it is worth. If a buyer from New York has seen a similar lamp sell at Christie's six months earlier for $4,800, he's going to be happy to pay her $2,800 to take it back with

This double signed Tiffany lamp sold for more than $50,000 in 1984 (not unusual for Tiffany lamps of this style and quality). The combination of dark leaves, yellow flowers, and the trunklike base make it a classic in the Art Nouveau style.

him, but the buyer from Stillwater, Oklahoma, who knows that his customers won't pay New York prices will be inclined to question the dealer's price.

Behave Like a Professional

As long as the negotiating is handled in a professional manner, it certainly should not be demeaning to either the buyer or the seller. As for the argument that negotiation does not take place in other businesses, antiques may just be ahead of the rest rather than behind. Customers are learning to question the prices of appliances, homes, television sets, cameras, even computers, and are discovering that increasingly salespeople are more willing than they expected to sacrifice some of their commission in order to make a sale.

Your bargaining tactics with an experienced antiques dealer start the moment you walk in the door. In fact, they start with the *way* in which you walk in the door. As Bill Cosby would say, "Be cool." Don't come rushing in, cash dripping from your pockets, looking like a starving man come face to face with a twenty-foot-long buffet bar. Waving your tax refund check over your head or wearing your Visa card around your neck may get you good service, but it won't get you any great discounts.

If shopping downtown or out at the mall has accustomed you to having salespeople descend on you the minute you walk through the door, then brace yourself. Some antiques dealers have to be aroused, interrupted, or pried away from a restoration project before they will so much as give you a "Can I help you today?" This is not to be interpreted as being rude or inconsiderate; most will be aware of you the minute you walk through the door, and while they may not drop their varnish brush to come rushing out from the back room, they may just want to give you time to acclimate yourself to the surroundings and to browse awhile.

Although they may not be standing by your side, most dealers will watch for telltale clues that identify serious buyers. Little things, such as your partner screaming from across the room, "I've found it! I've found it!", or announcing, "If you like it, buy it. You've still got all of your divorce settlement money left" may cause the dealer to drop his pipe clamp, but

it certainly isn't going to go very far in getting him to drop
his price.

Don't Weaken Your Bargaining Position

Even what would appear to be more subtle moves can also
weaken your bargaining position. If you ignore nearly everything else in the room, huddle over one piece for twenty minutes, lift it, touch it, brush it, fondle it, cuddle it, take its
measurements, balance your checkbook, ask if they take
MasterCard, or begin to disassemble it, even the not so astute
dealer may have figured out you are interested in it; perhaps
he may even feel you have made up your mind. In this instance be assured of but one thing: not only is his price going
to remain firm, but he's kicking himself for not marking it
higher in the first place.

Be a Leisurely Browser

To give yourself a fair chance against these seasoned vet-
erans, browse leisurely. Walk past the item that actually interests you most. Make it a point to pick up and inspect several
items, some of which may arouse in you no more than just a
passing interest. When asked, don't be too specific in your
description of what you're looking for. Even though you came
ready to buy an oak four drawer file cabinet identical to the
one the dealer has over in the corner, answer, "Well, we're
turning an extra bedroom into a study, or we're looking for
something to go with our desk." Then let the dealer suggest
the file cabinet and lead you to it.

How to Use a Partner When Negotiating

If you are working with a partner, agree ahead of time on
who is going to play the devil's advocate. Both of you oooh-
ing and aahing over it makes the dealer's job easy—and costs

you money. Remain cool as he points out the fine points. Let him give you his speech, for when he does, he's investing time in you—and the more time he invests, the more apt he is to make adjustments later to save the sale.

When he's finished, the devil's advocate takes over. Either your friend or, if you are working alone, your alter ego is going to need to raise some questions: "Has the lower handle been replaced?", or, "That's a pretty bad ink stain in the top isn't it?" Rarely will a hundred years of use leave an antique in perfect condition, but every flaw should be considered in relationship to the price—and considered aloud and in front of the dealer. *Asking* rather than announcing these flaws is crucial, too, for it forces the dealer to admit aloud that, yes, the handle is new and, yes, that is a bad ink stain on the top. When he realizes that you spotted the new Heirloom Brass hardware or know that the ink stain in the top is permanent, he will be more apt to adjust his asking price accordingly.

And even though it may be clearly marked, ask the dealer what his price is. That gives him the opportunity to say, "I was asking three hundred and ninety-five dollars, but, considering the ink stain, I'd take three hundred and seventy-five today." You, though, have determined by inspecting this one and comparing it to others you have seen, that you don't want to spend more than $325 for it. There is still a $50 difference in the two opinions.

Whatever you do, don't put your partner on the spot by turning and asking, "What do you think, dear?" This is no time to start a tiff in front of the dealer. If you really don't know what you or your partner thinks about the piece and the price, then tell the dealer you'd like to think it over and walk out of his hearing before you level with one another.

Knowing When the Dealer Is Ready to Bargain

At this point you have determined one important thing: the dealer is willing to bargain. *But* he is still $50 away from your price. Talk about it, walk around the room again, but don't even get close to the item for a while. Let the dealer think that you may not be all that interested. Make him work for that sale. He knows you are nibbling at his hook and he doesn't want to let you slip away. Think about it, then reply with something like, "Well, I don't know. Three seventy-five is more than we have to spend. If it was three hundred, we'd take it."

You really don't expect the dealer to take your first offer and he won't, but you make it anyway. And you make the amount less than what you are willing to settle at. And don't feel deceitful. Chances are he's doing the same thing. Now you both know where the other stands—and hopefully you'll end up somewhere in between.

A Bargaining Scenario

Here is where an alert partner can really come in handy. Lines such as "Maybe we should go back and look at that other one again" or "Sara, we can't afford that much" tell the dealer he is about to lose a sale if he doesn't do something quick.

"Just a second. Let me check my books and see just what I have in it." He'll disappear in the back for a few seconds, not to see how much he gave for it (you both know he already knows that), but to give both himself and you a few more minutes time. Take advantage of it to exchange thoughts with your partner and to decide if you've changed your opinions on the piece or the price.

"I can come down to three hundred and fifty, but that's as low as I can go."

We're getting close and now is the time for some decision making. If you sense that this really is his lowest offer, you may decide to take it, but before you do, put him to the test and see if you can negotiate for something other than money.

Here are some options: "We'll meet you halfway—three twenty-five," or "What about three twenty-five and we take it with us right now?" or "We could go to three hundred and fifty—but only if you deliver it," or "We were going to put this on our charge card, but would you consider three twenty-five if we paid in cash?"

The Magic Power of Cash

CASH.

That magic four letter word.

The more people write checks and lay down plastic money, the more powerful crisp, green cash becomes. While the antiques business has traditionally not been prone to bad checks, it certainly has not been immune to them either. And while plastic money may be convenient for the customer, it is a convenience the retail merchant must pay for—to the tune of some 5 percent of each sale. It doesn't take a genius to figure that 5 percent of $350 is $17.50—and the accompanying paperwork is more than enough to eat up another $7.50. Give an antiques dealer the choice between $350 in either the uncertainty of a check or the hassle of plastic and $325 in crisp, green, spendable cash, and you've just saved yourself $25.

A friend of mine with limited willpower and an affliction for mechanical banks had been in one particular shop several times looking at a bank from the late 1800s. The marked price was $250, but my friend claimed he couldn't afford to spend a cent over $200 for it. After his third trip in three days to see the bank he finally decided he was either going to buy it or never go back again. He first withdrew four new, crisp, fifty-dollar bills from his dwindling account, then he emptied his wallet and pockets of every bit of cash and change and inserted the four fifty-dollar bills, left his checkbook and credit cards at home, and marched back into the shop.

After more preliminary conversation about the bank and the price—which the dealer, tiring, no doubt, of my friend's indecision, had dropped to $225 by that time—Bob leveled with him.

"Look," he said earnestly, opening his wallet and spreading the four fifty-dollar bills before the dealer, "I've only got two hundred dollars to spend and I'm going to buy a bank with it today. Either sell me this one for two hundred or I'll go over to Charlie's Collectibles and buy his Stevens.''

The dealer took a long look at the four fifty-dollar bills lying in front of him, sighed deeply, and said, ''The bank's yours.''

When asked what he would have done had the dealer refused, my friend confessed, ''I'm not sure—but I had another twenty-five dollars stashed in my glove compartment just in case.''

6

Buying at Antiques Shows and Flea Markets

Estimating the number of antiques shows and flea markets that are held each year or the number of full-time, part-time, and first-time dealers who come, set up, and sell everything from Barbie dolls to Boston rockers would be a task to drive a statistician to drink. Add to that the tens of thousand of buyers who will drive miles out of their way just for the opportunity to dig through, inspect, compare, and purchase antiques and collectibles from twenty to two hundred dealers set up in a school gymnasium or asphalt parking lot, and you'll begin to understand how popular antiques shows and flea markets have become.

Why?

Convenience—and great bargains.

First, the antiques shows.

The Difference Between a Show and a Flea Market

Generally, what distinguishes an antiques show from a flea market (also called "swap meets"—a term dating from the Depression, when people would trade unneeded items with

one another simply because they could not afford to buy them
new. The term "flea market" has been traced back to France,
where at one time flea-infested clothing and bedding was sold
in open air markets) is simply the quality of the merchandise.
While flea markets generally have an "anything goes" policy,
antiques show promoters attempt, with varying degrees of
success, to restrict the merchandise in their shows to that prior
to a set date (such as 1930 and earlier).

How an Antiques Show Operates

While it is not uncommon to hear veteran antiques dealers
complain about being unable to find any good buys at major
shows and sales, that is not entirely the case. To understand
how to go about finding and negotiating some great deals at
a show, however, it is important that you first understand what
goes on before, during, and immediately after a show from
the standpoint of the exhibitors. Every show has a beginning,
a middle, and an end and once you know what is happening,
has happened, and is going to happen to those people who
have paid a promoter a fee just to be able to set up and sell
their wares, you will be in a better position to know how to
negotiate your own good deals.

So, put yourself in the shoes of a show dealer and imagine,
if you will for a moment, what you might go through during
the course of a three-day antiques show:

Thursday A.M.: You've got the car and trailer cleaned out,
gassed up, and parked next to the house. The packing and
loading process is about to begin. Breakables are carefully
cleaned and wrapped; larger pieces of furniture are disman-
tled. You decide to put a quick coat of varnish on your walnut
Victorian sewing rocker. The trailer begins to fill with furniture and heavy boxes while the back seat of the car is reserved
for especially fragile items.

Thursday P.M.: The trailer is nearly full—except for the
walnut rocker, which refuses to dry. The change bag, price
tags, touch-up kit, toolbox, Thermos, and extra clothes are

collected. You doublecheck the route on the map and go over the show contract details one more time. Instructions are left for the babysitter. You move the still wet walnut rocket next to the stove overnight.

Friday A.M.: Up at six. Suitcases go in the back of the trailer. The rocker is still tacky, but goes in anyway. By seven you're on the road, watching the clock, the gas gauge, and the low left tire on the trailer. The show opens at four and you plan to arrive around one. Someone forgot to fill the Thermos.

Friday P.M.: You pull in precisely at one, along with three vans, a U-Haul, and two station wagons. A security guard informs you it will be about thirty minutes before you can back up to the loading dock and unpack—unless you want to carry everything two hundred yards to the door. You set the walnut rocker out in the sun to finish drying. At two-thirty you back into the loading area and three burly fellows start loading your show items onto carts. You scramble to keep them away from the boxes in the back seat as a large woman wanders over and sits down in your walnut rocker. You park the car and trailer, dash back to your booth, push everything you brought inside it, and glance at your watch. Three o'clock. The large woman and your walnut rocker have disappeared. The dealer in the next booth offers to help you set up. Empty boxes and wrapping paper fly in all directions. The show promoter stops by to pick up a check and nervously studies her watch.

Friday, 4:00 P.M.: The show opens with a throng of people pushing down the aisles. Before you can hide the last empty box and kick the extension cords out of sight your booth is filled with customers. You make your first sale, then your second, and third. It's a buying crowd. Two hours later the pace begins to slow and your legs begin to ache. You turn to sit down for the first time in six hours and realize the walnut rocker is still missing. While your neighbor keeps an eye on your booth you track it down. Five hours later you catch yourself nodding off in the all-night restaurant next to your motel.

Saturday A.M.: The show opens at ten; you arrive after a quick breakfast to tidy up your booth, make a few changes, and settle down for twelve hours of sitting, standing, and chatting with customers and neighboring dealers. Morning sales are brisk, but the Saturday afternoon doldrums eventually roll in. You pass the time by picking lint off your walnut rocker.

Saturday P.M.: The show closes for the day and sales have reached your break-even point. Sunday will be crucial. Dinner across the street and then back to the motel for some badly needed sleep.

Sunday A.M.: Customers are already lining up outside the doors when you arrive. The weather forecast predicts a cloudy and cool day. Perfect. The after-church crowd are basically lookers, but a young couple buys your pine corner cupboard and glassware sales are steady. No one even sits in the walnut rocker.

Sunday P.M.: Midafternoon sales slow and, as the show draws to a close, dealers begin to get fidgety. Some early lookers return and the conversations between dealers and customers grow longer. The promoter scurries around making sure no one starts packing up before four.

Sunday, 4:00 P.M.: The show closes and the work begins again. Packing boxes come out, drivers jockey for positions around the loading dock. Furniture is squeezed onto dollies. What took all Thursday to load is packed in two hours on Sunday, including the walnut rocker. Shortly before seven you slide out onto the highway and head toward home. Anticipated time of arrival: ten o'clock. Someone forgot to fill the Thermos again.

Timing—the Key to Successful Buying at Shows

Once you get a feel for what goes on before, during, and after an antiques show, you will realize that the key to successful buying is *timing*. Rarely will you discover a great steal sitting unrecognized at an important antiques show; when a

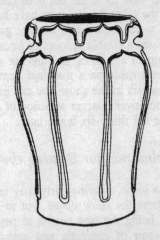

The Grueby Faience Company, founded in 1894, produced high quality art pottery, often in a unique green matte glaze with leaves and flowers in relief, until 1910. Today its work is among the most highly sought after by collectors of art pottery. Signed examples such as the 12-inch high earthenware vase illustrated here sell for more than $2,000.

dealer comes to a show she packs her best merchandise—and she knows every piece inside and out. And even if there were an unmarked piece of Grueby art pottery hiding behind a $35 price tag, you can be sure one of the other exhibitors will have snatched it up while you were still waiting outside for the front doors to open.

Arriving early in a show's tenure will give you the best selection of merchandise to choose from, even if the possibilities of finding a once-in-a-lifetime steal are slim. There always seems to be a dealer from Omaha or Ontario who makes it a point to arrive early on Thursday night, is the first to set up Friday morning, and then spends the day wandering from booth to booth watching the other exhibitors unpack their merchandise. Once in a while, especially if he spots something of interest to him (such as a rookie dealer with an underpriced punched tin pie safe), he will offer his assistance moving a table, taping down an extension cord, or steadying a step ladder. Who, then, could insist that he wait until the show opens when he innocently asks the price of the pie safe?

The dealer from Omaha, however, and any other early arrivals who spent the last hour before the show opened scouring the other booths may have had to pass on several items that were good deals, but not great steals. They, too, have invested a sizable amount of money on this show without yet taking in any sales and are not about to spend money they haven't made on a marginal item. By being one of the first customers in the show you can give yourself the opportunity to look over a larger selection of antiques than what is going to be left thirty-six hours later.

Techniques for Beating the Crowd

To some, arriving early may mean leaving home at about the time the show opens, but to others it means more even than being the first person to pay his two-dollar admission. One pair of energetic and enterprising young dealers convinced a local show promoter to hire them to help the exhibitors park their vehicles, unload their merchandise, and set up their booths. Not only did they get paid by the promoter, but the older dealers were so impressed by their industriousness that the two young men received a number of generous tips. What they enjoyed the most, however, was the opportunity to make a discreet inspection of nearly everything that came into the show even before the dealer from Omaha could check it out. They each made several good buys that, when sold several days later, netted them several hundred dollars for about four hours of work that afternoon.

Once when I realized that a major show I planned to attend was going to start at the same time I needed to be seventy miles away for an important auction, I took a slightly different approach. I called the managing editor at one of the regional antiques publications and offered to shoot several pictures and interview some of the exhibitors at the show for his paper. Needless to say he was understaffed, overworked, and thrilled not to have to cover it himself. He made a phone call to the promoter and two hours before the show officially opened I strolled through the loading area with my 35mm camera and notebook in hand and my checkbook in my hip pocket. Whenever I spotted a booth or a dealer with a piece of particular interest to me I stopped, introduced myself, asked to shoot a few pictures, took some notes, and more than once bought the piece. The line outside the front door was already fifty yards long an hour before the show was scheduled to open when I strolled back out through the loading dock door, my film shot, my interviews made, and my arms loaded with some excellent buys.

A case of illegal entry? Not entirely, since the articles, photos, and interviews did appear in print, but I have heard of buyers who use a 35mm camera, a notebook, and an imitation press card (how many people know what a legitimate press card looks like?) to get themselves into a show before it opens. One notorious local dealer, who formerly exhibited at several shows each year, made it a point to arrive a couple of hours before a show was to begin and stroll brazenly through the loading dock doors. No one ever really knew from year to year whether or not she was exhibiting (nor did anyone really care), so rarely did anyone ever question her, but once word spread among the dealers that Bertha was around, most refused even to talk, much less to sell to her before the show began. However, she still managed to get a free preview of the merchandise.

How about another ploy used by those intent on being the first in the door? I was doing an out-of-town show one weekend and had arrived early enough to set up my booth a few hours before the front doors opened. As I stood outside the loading area sipping on my fourth cup of coffee, I noticed a young man standing by the row of dealer cars and vans. As I watched, an out-of-state van screeched to a halt and what was obviously a late exhibitor jumped out and frantically started unloading boxes onto the sidewalk. The young man watched for a few seconds, then approached the late arrival with a sympathetic "Car trouble?"

"Yeah," the dealer moaned. "Blew a radiator hose on the interstate. Took me three hours to get it fixed.

"Well, here, let me help you with those. I'll get you a cart."

And with that the young man sprang into action. He immediately went up to the security guard posted at the loading dock door, asked that he get them a cart, and dashed back to help the dealer pull the rest of his boxes out of the van. Together they loaded the cart and, with me close behind, pushed it past the guard into the exhibition hall to the last empty booth. Within minutes the young man had helped him unload his merchandise, had returned the cart to the guard (and made it a point to thank him before he rushed back to the booth), and had earned the lifetime gratitude of the dealer.

It was still an hour before the show was to open and it was evident that security had been doing their job: everyone in the exhibition hall except our good Samaritan was wearing an identification badge. I judged it would only be a matter of minutes before he was stopped, questioned, and escorted to the door. As I watched he frantically scanned the floor and tables for any unattached badges, but, finding none, hit upon another solution. He picked up two empty boxes from the dealer's booth, stuffed them full of crumpled up newspaper, and slowly started up the aisle. Even without a badge he looked so much like an exhibitor in search of a trash can that he was free to roam the hall, talk to dealers, check out the merchandise, and, on more than one occasion, make an early purchase. The last time I saw him the doors had just opened, the crowd was pressing down the aisles, and he had just tossed his two empty boxes in a trash can on his way out the back door.

Whether you decide to attempt an early entrance or wait until shortly after the show officially opens, do not expect the exhibitors to start dropping their prices the moment you express an interest in something of theirs. Even just an average show can bring several hundred people past each booth and no experienced exhibitor is going to start sacrificing his profit to make a sale to the fourth person to stop by. If anything, expect some prices to be even higher than what you might find in a shop. Antiques show dealers depend on impulse buying, thus they know that a few extra dollars tacked onto the price of a Seth Thomas schoolhouse clock probably won't cost them a sale. Those few extra dollars multiplied by the number of sales will go a long way toward paying their motel bill.

If You Like It—Buy It

Nevertheless, don't let that stop you from engaging an exhibitor in a conversation over a particular item. As always, the more time you can get the seller to invest in a transaction, the more apt he will be to reduce his price to salvage something from it. Ask about it, talk about it, point out its flaws, make an offer and perhaps even get the opportunity to counteroffer; just don't expect miracles. In shop or out, dealers are tough. When you sense that they are at their lowest figure, act. Either buy or pass, but don't make the mistake of dawdling over one piece when there are thousands more to check out.

And—if you like it, buy it. Unlike what happens in a shop on a slow day, bargains won't wait even a few minutes at a show. As experienced show dealers will tell you, interest produces interest. A brass Aladdin lamp can lie untouched for hours on a table, but just as soon as someone shows an interest in it, three other people standing nearby will suddenly want it. You won't have to wait long to see it happen: one customer will spend nearly thirty minutes holding, turning, inspecting, and talking about a piece on a dealer's table while, unbeknownst to her, another customer is quietly absorbing every word and action. At the end the first customer hesitates, either legitimately undecided or, in a badly timed attempt to coax a few dollars reduction out of the dealer (who has been aware of the second customer the entire time), sets it back down, and announces, "Well, if that's the best you can do, I'll just have to think about it some more." She won't have had time to even get to the next booth before the eavesdropper will have stepped up with a "I think I will take that brass lamp, please."

Waiting for the Dealer to Start Discounting

Like opening night, Saturday morning is also full of hope and optimism for the show exhibitors. For us, then, it is a time better spent on the yard sale circuit. Any great deals left undetected by the other show dealers will have been spotted by the Friday afternoon collectors, so we can no longer consider ourselves to be early arrivals, yet Saturday is far too early to be able to expect many of the dealers to start making substantial discounts. Do some yard sales, wash the car, mow the lawn, check out a few shops, but stay away from the show. If you don't, I'll guarantee that sooner or later you'll end up buying something on Saturday that you could have bought far cheaper on Sunday.

Closing Day of the Show—a Great Time for Bargains

Sunday. The last day of the show. The day when the motel bill comes due, the laundry pile has grown higher than the bed, and the expense bag has grown considerably thinner than the sales bag.

Sunday. The day when the kids call from home wanting to know how to get grape jelly stains out of the couch.

Sunday.

Buyer's day.

Unlike the frantic immediacy associated with opening day, Sunday afternoon's pace is far more leisurely. Either you checked out the merchandise on Friday afternoon and know exactly what you are interested in and where it is located, or you go in knowing that there are no great steals that someone a step faster may snatch up. *You* are calling the shots as you stroll up the aisles—and now you aren't just studying the antiques. Each exhibitor's expressions and actions will tell you what kind of a show it has been for her. Stop, pick up a piece at random, and see how long it takes for the exhibitor to come swooping down on you. If her opening line is "I can do better on that," you know it's been a slow show. If she's too busy thumbing through her MasterCard receipts to notice you, be prepared for a tough bargaining session.

No show, however, is ever totally fantastic for every exhibitor. For the dealer who happened to bring the right merchandise for that particular crowd, it could have been the most profitable show of the season. For the dealer across the aisle who guessed wrong and tried to sell $3,000 rolltop desks in a city that four months ago experienced a major factory shutdown that paralyzed the entire economy, the same show was a disaster. Finding a dealer who has had a miserable show will be easy: look for a booth without any empty spots, a dealer who hasn't smiled in three days and price tags that have been crossed out and marked down in a last-ditch attempt to make a major sale. It she has what you want, chances are the two of you can get together on a good price.

Be Friendly—Don't Antagonize the Dealer

As always, approach each dealer in a friendly manner. Antagonizing a tired dealer about her high prices will only get you thrown out of her booth. Ask how the show has been for her, sympathize with the amount of work both ahead and behind her, and compliment her on her selection of antiques. Friendliness won't cost you a penny—and it may even save you a dollar or two.

As you turn the conversation toward the particular piece you are interested in, don't rush to point out its flaws. Give the dealer the opportunity to reevaluate her price as the two of you talk; only when the time comes for you to question her price or to make your own counteroffer should you politely draw her attention to the hairline crack along the lip of the pitcher or the replaced spindle in the back of one of the chairs. If you have been both friendly and respectful, chances are that the exhibitor will settle for less profit on Sunday afternoon than she would have Friday evening, if only to avoid having to both pack and transport the piece back home.

"Do you do your own repair work? That's a fine new turning to the furthest chair. I bet you were disappointed when you found out you were going to have to replace it."

"Have you really done this entire show by yourself? You must be awfully tired when it comes time to start packing up. [Pause] You know, I've often thought about getting a really good Persian rug for my bedroom. How firm is your price on the red one with the worn fringe?"

How to Play the Waiting Game

If there is no one else standing around waiting to grab it, you can play the waiting game with the dealer. Three hours from now he's going to be on his way back to Madison, Wisconsin, never to see you or your checkbook again. If you are serious, dawdling at the end of a show is permitted. The dealer's mind is on the trip home, the packing and unpacking ahead of him, and the motel bill he just paid with the last of his expense account cash. You may well be his last serious customer of the show; if so, he may be anxious to close on a positive—and profitable—note. Don't press him for a discount; play the coy mistress and let him coax you into a sale with a price that is sure to please you.

Closings bring to mind one particular spring show. It had started out strong on Friday evening, with brisk sales and the promise of more to come on Saturday and Sunday. But all that arrived on Saturday and Sunday was eight inches of snow from a freak April blizzard. Tons of snow fell, blocking streets and barricading parking lots. By late Sunday afternoon, those of us who still remained could hardly remember what a customer looked like—and, much to their delight, the few hardy souls who did brave the wind and snow found bargains galore awaiting them. Rather than a solemn, dignified antiques show, they walked into what looked more like a charity bazaar, as dealers cut prices drastically in a desperate attempt to thaw out their frozen assets.

Flea Markets Are Everywhere

Now, for the flea markets.

It appears that on any given weekend, regardless of where you might awaken, you can find either an indoor or outdoor flea market within a day's drive. And while the booth fees at major antiques shows threaten to reduce the number of exhibitors each year, the number of flea markets, flea market sellers, and flea market buyers continues to grow. In more than one instance, drive-in theaters and shopping mall parking lots have become Saturday and Sunday afternoon flea markets with only a fifty-cent charge per vehicle— whether you are coming to buy or to drop the tailgate on your station wagon and sell.

You've Got a Good Chance of Finding a Silk Purse

Naturally, purists might find the variety of merchandise at flea markets slightly shocking, as they may well be forced to step over a ripped lawn chair, move a box of apples, and dig through stacks of old *Playboy* magazines in order to pull out a Civil War copy of *Harper's* magazine priced at a quarter. But here, more so than in the air-conditioned comfort of a Holiday Inn antiques show, your chances of finding a silk purse tucked in amid a hundred sow's ears are multiplied. While some of the exhibitors will be experienced antiques dealers with a thorough knowledge of their merchandise, others will barely be a step above yard sale merchants who still think the Depression glass they are practically giving away was so named because no one likes it.

The Two Key Rules for Flea Market Buying

In the flea market manual there are but two rules: (1) the early bird gets the worm; and (2) don't buy before you haggle.

Once you have set your sights on a major flea market, start preparing yourself for a day's work—and a day's fun. First, plan to arrive early. If the gates open at six A.M., be there at five. In fact, you might do as many experienced antiques dealers do and pay the set up fee required of all sellers just to get in the night before. The experience alone of an all-night setup, buy, sell, and trade, anything-goes-before-the-gates-open-at-dawn flea market is worth the $10. Either way, be prepared for several miles of walking, gradual and sudden changes in the weather, and, naturally, finding some great deals. A good pair of shoes, loose, layered clothing, and an empty knapsack will all go a long way in making sure that you don't have to cut your day short to soak your blistered feet, change clothes, or work your way miles back to your car every time you buy something.

Travel Light at Flea Markets

A word of caution: flea markets are no place to take kids, pets, out-of-town guests, surly spouses, aging grandparents, or new neighbors. They are for antiques addicts, foolhardy fanatics, and heat-crazed collectors. If they can't whistle their way across the Sahara, leave them at home in front of the air conditioner. Either find a perfect partner or go it alone.

The Flea Market's Fast Pace

Unlike antiques shops and shows where the negotiating process might stretch to an hour or so, the pace at a flea market is much faster and far more direct. Rather than hundreds of customers, we're talking about thousands. Rather than taking thirty minutes to engage the seller in a detailed conversation, we're lucky to be able to get him down to our end of the table. Find something you like, inspect it, let him know you are interested, then ask if he can do better on the price. If he's busy, be prepared to get a gruff "no." Then you either pay his price or set the item down and move on. If he's not, then the two of you may get to play "let's make a deal." Don't, however, make the mistake of haggling over 50¢ on a $5 item. Your time and his integrity are both worth more than that. Pay it, take it, and leave. Bigger fish await you downstream.

Find Out about the Treasures Not on Sale

Few of the booths, vans, and card tables you encounter at a flea market will justify more than a quick once-over, but when you do find that one seller with several pieces of early Wedgwood stacked below her table, make it a point to strike up a conversation with her. It may well be that she purchased an entire twelve-piece setting from an estate the previous day, but only had room today to display a few pieces. Your best buy of the day may be made that night when you drive over to her home to see the collection of items she didn't have room for at the flea market.

Don't Forget to Use Your Business Card

If you are browsing through a flea market in or near your home base, carry several business cards with you to give to the sellers you meet. The majority of them will not have full-

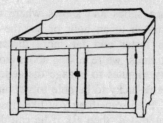

As one noted authority has written, "Drysinks are probably the most often faked, altered, and reproduced form of antique country furniture." The importance of being an astute buyer will become painfully clear if you ever attempt to sell a questionable piece to a veteran antiques dealer.

time shops, but instead depend on flea markets, regular yard sales, and private transactions to dispose of their merchandise. "Glorified pickers" one dealer who buys from them on a regular basis calls them, sellers who can become dependable sources for you year round. Treat them like the professionals they are, keep your haggling to a friendly minimum, and buy from them whenever possible. They will soon move you to the top of their list of persons to contact when they find a legitimate pine drysink, a pair of signed pewter candlesticks or an autographed copy of *The Adventures of Huckleberry Finn*.

7

Buying at Auctions

"One forty-seven going once. Do I hear one forty-eight? One forty-eight? Won't someone give me one forty-eight? I've got one forty-eight. Now one forty-nine. Do I hear one forty-nine? Come on, folks, we all know this lamp is worth two hundred if it's worth a dime. One forty-nine is a steal. Do I hear one forty-nine? One forty-eight going once. Are you going to let this young lady get away with this beautiful lamp for only one hundred and forty-eight dollars? Why, last week I sold a lamp not half as pretty as this one for a hundred and eighty dollars. A hundred and eighty dollars, mind you, and all I'm asking for this beauty is one forty-nine. One forty-nine. Who'll give me one forty-nine? Do I hear one forty-eight fifty? Just fifty more cents, folks. The price of a cup of coffee. A lamp for the price of a cup of coffee. Think of it. One forty-eight going once. One forty-eight going twice. You're going to be sorry in the morning, folks, when you realize you let this beautiful lamp—why, I wouldn't be surprised if it turned out to be made by that Tiffany guy—get away from you for just one hundred and forty-eight dollars. Do I hear one forty-eight fifty? One forty-eight fifty? This is your last chance, folks. One forty-eight going once. One forty-eight going twice. . . .

"SOLD."

Market Value

That simple, one syllable word. It leaves behind it one person happy, one person frustrated, six people uncertain, and a hundred more anxious for the auctioneer to move on to the next item. As much a modern American institution as the yard sale, the auction is where appraised value, insurance value, investment value, and hoped-for value all give way to the only value that has any real meaning in the antiques world—market value.

Gather anywhere from thirty to three hundred people, an inventory of assorted antiques, collectibles, and "junque," an auctioneer and his staff and in a few hours time you will quickly learn just how much pressed back oak chairs are bringing, what a Sleepy Eye pitcher really will sell for, or whether the people in your area are more interested in oak, walnut, mahogany, or pine.

The great attraction of an auction is the opportunity not only to participate in determining the value of an item (and in the process refusing to bid signifies as much as making the final bid), but to come away with an antique for far less than you would have had to pay for it in a shop or at a show. Nothing in the antiques business is as unpredictable as auctions and nowhere else will you find happenings as strange. Shop dealers pull their hair out trying to understand why a table identical to one priced in their showroom for $200 will sell at a Saturday afternoon auction for $350, but when they decide to run their table through the same auction house the next week it only brings $150.

So what makes the difference?

People.

Auctions bring together a cross-section of people who would give a budding writer enough characters to rival a Dickens novel. Auctions have an attraction not unlike gambling, but here your only ante is your time. If you like, you can bid on every item and just as long as yours is never the last bid, it won't cost you a dime. The gambling lure brings out the unemployed, the elderly, the young, the wealthy, the dealers, the housewives, the students—anyone who is aroused by the risk and opportunity to pull out the steal of a lifetime from beneath everyone's nose.

You Can Beat Retail Prices at an Auction

There are several different types of auctions which the antiques buyer can attend in hope of finding items going for far less than their actual retail price. If you intend to specialize in a particular type of antique, such as stereoscopes and stereoscope cards for Hoosier-style oak cupboards, then some auctions may not appeal to you. Be forewarned, however— the strangest combination of items can show up unexpectedly and the person who is there when that happens is the one who can take advantage of it.

I remember a rather common household auction where the tools were stacked in the rear of the yard, the glassware and linens on tables around the house, and the furniture and antiques in the front yard near the street. As is standard practice at such auctions, while the crowd was still arriving and inspecting the glassware and furniture out front, the auctioneer started selling the tools in the rear. In the midst of disposing of rusty rakes, picks, and shovels—some of them still inside the garage—the auctioneer suddenly realized that an old oak icebox the owner had been using for storage hadn't been moved out to the yard with the other furniture and antiques. Surrounded by old men and boys more interested in tools than antiques, he couldn't get the attention of the dealers or the buyers out front, nor did he sense he could get a good bid out of the crowd around him. Pressed on the icebox by a sole astute dealer, he was forced to sell it then and there; normally it would have brought in

The Indiana-originated Hoosier style cupboard was produced by more than
a dozen different companies between 1900 and 1950. Each touted its own
features: flour sifter, swing-out sugar canister, recipe holders, spice jars,
metal bread drawer, cutting boards, pull-out porcelain top, even ant-proof
castors. Golden Oak Sellers Company and Hoosier Company brands remain
among the most popular today.

excess of $500. That day, in that garage, and in front of that disinterested crowd, he could only raise the dealer's final bid of $150. As the lone antiques dealer stood smiling beside his steal of the day, the auctioneer could be heard swearing under his breath as he pulled his crowd along the rest of the line of tools.

The Different Kinds of Auctions

While the household auction (sometimes referred to as an estate auction) is perhaps the most common type of auction, it is by no means the only type in existence. In rural regions, farm auctions are becoming all too common and while once prosperous farmers used to present tough competition for the city antiques dealer, today they are keeping their hands firmly entrenched in their bib overalls. While machinery generally dominates the traditional farm auction, hard-pressed farmers are also including old furniture and unneeded household items in an attempt to raise badly needed cash. Even though the sale bill may only list farm equipment and tools, a few pieces of old furniture always shows up and, amongst a gathering of farmers and neighbors with their own barns and sheds full of "old stuff," go quite cheaply.

True antiques auctions attract large crowds primarily because the auctioneers make it a point to advertise them widely. They are generally held indoors, where the public can sit on the chairs provided while they wait for their items to come up for sale, make use of the restroom facilities (attend an outdoor farm auction on a cold day in March when the coffee does more than just warm the soul and you'll come to appreciate indoor plumbing), and find nourishment at the concession stand.

Growing in popularity today is the local auction house or consignment auction, as it is often called. Auctions are held on a regular basis—every Thursday night or on the second and fourth Sundays or every month, for instance—and the auction-eer, through his contacts and consignments, assembles a col-

Oak iceboxes—a standard feature in nearly every turn of the century home—are still being salvaged from garages, barns, and basements and turned into storage cabinets, bars, and linen closets. Though constructed from durable oak, they were nevertheless susceptible to wood rot in the back legs due to too many melting pan overflows. Painted iceboxes and those with missing hardware pose difficult and costly restoration problems. While larger models provide more storage, space-conscious buyers are paying premiums for smaller, easier-to-move ones.

lection of antiques and household goods to be auctioned off to the highest bidders.

The Presale Inspection—It's Crucial

No matter what type of auction you decide to attend on a given day—household, farm, antiques, or consignment—crucial to your successful buying is the presale inspection. Sale ads for antiques and community auctions generally list the times at which the merchandise can be inspected, but at household and estate auctions you must arrive a few hours before the sale begins to be able to inspect anything you might want to bid on. At many of these auctions, you'll find that pieces are still being moved into position or unloaded as the auction begins, while at the auction house you can often stop by during your lunch hour the day before or the day of the sale to see what is to be offered at the evening or Sunday afternoon auction.

Take Notebook and Pencil

In either case, go with notebook and pencil, for it is not unusual for a potential buyer to discover that she has more than just a passing interest in a dozen or so items. As you inspect each item, make note of chips, cracks, flaws, stains, and any other conditions that have a direct bearing on its value. A hairline crack in a small vase can't be seen from the back of the room, especially if the auctioneer happens to be holding the flaw away from the audience, but you will be sure to notice it when you get it home or show it to a potential buyer.

As you assess the condition of each piece, determine exactly what your top limit will be. Then *put it in writing*. If the vase is worth no more than $75, note that fact. Three hours and a hundred of pieces of furniture and glassware later, you might not remember which vase had the crack and just how much you thought you would pay for it. While latecomers who didn't have an opportunity to inspect it might drive the bidding past $75, don't let them unnerve you. Flip back to your notes, remind yourself of the condition of the piece, and keep your hand in your pocket when the man four rows up tops your bid of $75.

The Number System

Most auctioneers and auction houses today use what is called the "number system" to record bids. After you have seen what merchandise will be offered at the sale and have decided to stay, find the table where one of the staff members will be assigning numbers to the bidders. You may be asked to provide identification when you register and, if you are from out of state and the auction is one involving items worth several hundreds if not several thousands of dollars, a bank letter of credit. When the auctioneer takes yours as the final bid, you will show him your number rather than shout out your name. The clerk will enter on the sheet that will eventually go the cashier, "Small blue vase—Lot #145—$67.50—Bidder #314." When you are ready to leave, you simply approach the cashier, show her your number, pay for and pick up your purchases. If you leave before the auction is over and have paid for your purchases or made none, be sure either to destroy your bidding card or take it with you. Careless bidders who drop their card on the floor or simply toss it in a trash can could be contacted a few days later with a bill for several hundred dollars worth of antiques that someone else bought and removed from the premises using their card and number.

Even though you make it a point to arrive early at an auction, don't be surprised or discouraged to see scores of cars surrounding the auction site. Chances are, you will be equally surprised to discover that despite the seemingly large number of cars, you have been assigned a relatively low bidding number. Half the people at most auctions never make a bid, nor did they ever intend to. They come to visit, watch the crowd, enjoy the action, and, sad to say, poke through their recently deceased neighbor's belongings. One lady I stood next to at a household auction openly declared that the stepladder scheduled to be sold that day was actually hers. She had lent it to the deceased six months before—but she still had to pay $15 to get it back.

As you walk past the rows of parked cars surrounding the site of an auction, you will probably hear someone lamenting the presence of several antiques dealers at the sale—as evidenced by their cars, trucks, or vans with their business names on them. What so many people outside the trade don't realize is that they have nothing to fear from an antiques dealer at an auction. Here's why:

Antiques shop and show dealers within any area are highly competitive today, largely due to the fact that more and more people are comparison shopping before they make a purchase from any shop or show. Dealers, therefore, cannot simply pay whatever is necessary to take a piece away from an auction and know that they can show a profit from its eventual resale. Their time, transportation, restoration, and advertising costs, plus any other overhead, must be covered by their profit margin. If they cannot buy a curved glass china cupboard at far below retail value, they cannot afford to buy it at all.

Limited Overhead Gives You an Advantage

It has been determined, that most antiques shop dealers cannot pay more than 50 to 65 percent of the retail value of an item and expect to show a profit after expenses. Thus, if you are buying a piece strictly for yourself and not concerned with immediately reselling it, or if, unlike the shop proprietor, your overhead expenses are being held to a bare minimum, you have no reason either to fear or be intimidated by the antiques dealer standing next to you. While you know you can pay up to $400 for a good oak Hoosier cupboard, the dealer next to you knows he can only go as high as $250 and still show a profit when he finally sells the cupboard six months later.

You, however, are neither the private buyer who makes one

or two purchases a year for his or her own pleasure, nor are you the antiques dealer with a two-thousand-square-foot showroom to maintain. In fact, you are the envy of both these types. You have more savvy than the private buyer and less overhead than the dealer, thus you can afford to pay a little more than most full-time dealers and with the confidence lacking in the private buyers.

Keep this final thought on antiques dealers in mind when you are at an auction: if you are where they are, then you must be in the right place.

Study the Auctioneer's Chant

Other than antiques dealers, the only other aspect of auctions that occasionally intimidates new players is the auctioneer's chant. Every auctioneer has his or her own particular style of auctioneering that should be studied early in the sale before any of the pieces that interest you are put up for bids. Most antiques and estate auctioneers have a delivery that is more easily understood than the stereotypical livestock auctioneers whose chant sounds almost like an alien language to an untrained ear. Remember—it is to the auctioneer's advantage, not disadvantage, that you know exactly where he is in the bidding and do not become confused or discouraged. Why, then, do auctioneers even use a chant? To force you to listen closely to him or her, and thus keep you involved in the action.

Determine the "Jumps"

You will want to determine early in the sale what each particular auctioneer's "jumps" are. That is, whether he is taking $2.50 jumps (going from $5 to $7.50 then to $10), $5 jumps (more common in medium-priced items) or $10 or $25 jumps (found most often in early bidding on expensive items). Most auctioneers are flexible according to the piece for sale, but some will not deviate from their set jumps. Thus if the auctioneer is asking for a raise of $5 from $70 to $75 and you bid $71, he may refuse it.

Familiar Auction Terms

In addition to the auctioneer's chant and jumps, there are certain terms you should be familiar with:

So much apiece, take all: This is most commonly used with sets of antiques (such as glassware, chairs, and table leaves), where you will be bidding on just one of them, but your final purchase price will be the last bid times the number of pieces. For instance, if a set of four walnut parlor chairs is up for bid and the auctioneer announces at the start of the bidding that they will be sold "so much apiece, winner take all," and the final bid on the one chair held up is $75, then the bidder will pay a total of four times $75, or $300, for all four chairs.

Choice: This means the final bidder has his choice of the items up for sale. It also generally means that you will have the option of taking any number of them, from one to all. Thus if the same chairs were sold "choice," you could take any one of them for $75 or any combination at the price of $75 each. The bidding then starts over again for any remaining pieces.

In situations involving "choice," the importance of early inspection cannot be overstressed. I was once at an auction where two very similar Victorian oak beds with six foot tall, heavily carved headboards were for sale. The beds were beautiful and had attracted a good deal of attention before the sale. Set side by side, they made an extremely handsome pair.

I was only interested in one of the beds, however, one which, while it was not quite as fancy as the other, happened to be a standard width and length and would accommodate a modern boxspring and mattress. A careful measurement had revealed that the more ornate of the two beds was too narrow for a standard boxspring and would require the extra expense of a custom-made one.

The auctioneer announced that the beds would be sold as "choice," meaning that the final bidder would have his or her choice of the two or could even take both. I had set my top limit and was understandably disappointed when a middle-aged couple topped my last bid and won their choice of the two beds. I started to turn away when to my surprise they both pointed to the ornate but undersized bed. An alert friend of theirs frantically tried to explain their mistake to them, but it was too late. The auctioneer had restarted the bidding for the remaining bed, which I was able to buy for $20 less than the first.

As the crowd moved on down the line of furniture being sold, the four of us were left standing beside our purchases. After a few minutes of muffled conversation and some additional measuring, the couple and their friend walked over and asked if I might consider swapping beds. I couldn't help but smile sympathetically as I declined, thanking my lucky stars that I had pulled the tape measure out of my Kit as I climbed out of my van that morning.

Jumping bids: This is a psychological ploy used by bidders to discourage other interested parties from remaining in the contest. Let's set the scene: an auctioneer holds in his hands a fine Amish quilt made in the late 1800s. The bidding is progressing steadily at $5 jumps and he is currently asking for a bid of $150. You had determined early in the sale that you could go up to $225 for the quilt and still show a profit for it after you had sold it to a collector in Chicago. Rather than simply make the next bid and let the momentum continue to build, you "jump the bid" to $200. The idea behind the move is to squash any hesitant bidders before they get too involved in the bidding—and attached to the idea of owning the quilt.

Call-ups: In the past auctioneers were not very receptive to the idea of letting the buyers have any input on the order in which the items were sold. By tradition auctions started with less expensive items, holding the finer pieces until last when supposedly the crowd was the largest. It was also hoped that along the way a buyer who was waiting for a piece that would be sold toward the end of the sale would buy or at least bid on something else she had spotted.

When auctioneers began to see their crowds dwindle as they dawdled over tables and junk, the light finally came on. A few of the brighter auctioneers began turning to the antiques and collectibles earlier in the sale and started interspersing the furniture and better antiques with the more mundane merchandise in order to hold the crowd and build interest. Some, to avoid losing good bidders to other auctions, instituted ''call-ups'' where a person could request that a particular piece be put up for sale as soon as possible. The auctioneer would pause occasionally, ask the crowd if there were any ''call-ups'' and, if there were, turn the bidding to that item.

One problem with call-ups is that they identify you as being interested in a particular piece and may inspire some real or imaginary competition. But if you have set a limit and refuse to overstep it, you don't care who knows you are interested. The great advantage is that it permits a bidder to call up three or four items he is interested in, make his bids and perhaps a few buys, pack up his belongings, and be off to other projects—or auctions.

Consignments: To help strengthen what would otherwise be a mediocre sale, auctioneers will often take pieces on consignment and sell them along with the other furnishings being offered the public. These consignments generally come from private individuals who are disposing of part of their collections, full- and part-time antiques dealers wanting to generate some cash, and from the auctioneer himself who still has a few items left over from his last auction. There is nothing unethical about consignments at a household or estate auction, but most auctioneers will indicate both in the advertisements and at the beginning of the sale that consignment pieces will be included in the auction.

The problem consignments present for the buyers is that in many cases the owner or a friend of the owner may be in the

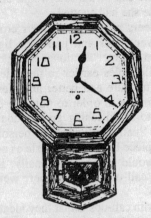

Despite a flood of recent reproductions, authentic New Haven schoolhouse clocks (c. 1890) still maintain their value at more than $200. Today's buyer, however, must inspect the back and works of any clock of this type closely, looking for signs of modern craftsmanship. In any event, insist on a receipt guaranteeing the authenticity of any antique clock you purchase.

crowd making sure that the piece does not go too cheaply. Auctioneers will insist that they won't take bids from the owner of the consignment piece, but it is obvious that it would be impossible for them to know if a particular bidder is acting on instructions from the owner. Most experienced buyers, however, aren't thrown by the possibility that one of the bidders may be ''running the bid up'' on them. ''If I think it's worth eighty dollars to me and I can get it for that,'' a clock collector snorted when asked about the practice, ''I don't care who makes the last bid or any of the other bids. I set my limit and if he pushes the bid past it, then he just bought his own *%#!%#*! clock back.''

Minimum or *Reserve:* Many times an auctioneer or auction house will permit the owner of a consigned antique to set a minimum bid which the piece must reach in order to sell. In major auction houses where catalogues are printed for each sale, these items, but not their reserve bid, will be noted. Auctioneers generally do not appreciate reserve bids, for invariably there will be a moment of awkward silence and suspicion when it is announced that despite the final bid there will be no sale on that item. Reserve bids are designed to protect and thus to encourage consignors to entrust their antiques to the auction house or auctioneer, but it is always the auctioneer and not the owner whose reputation suffers when too many buyers find their bids rebuffed.

Shill: A person planted in the crowd by an auctioneer to keep the bidding going on items that threaten to sell for less than their full value. Occasionally the shill will actually have been instructed how much to bid; at other times he will watch the auctioneer for a signal. Some auctioneers are even blatant about their shills, assigning them a number and "selling" them an item they did not even bid on. Pieces sold to a shill usually end up being sold privately by the auctioneer or appear at another of his auctions in the future. Ethical? Certainly not. Realistic? You had better be.

Buyers' pool: Also called a "buyers' ring," it is a conspiracy used by a group of buyers, generally big dollar antiques or art dealers, to hold the bidding down on key items in order to increase their profits. Here's how it works: three to five or more dealers who would normally be bidding against one another agree before the auction which one is going to "buy" each key item and what the top limit will be. When that item comes up, the other dealers lay off the bidding, hopefully permitting the designated buyer to come away with the piece for less than normally expected.

Afterward the buyers' pool gathers and the members hold their own private auction of the pieces that they had bought earlier. In most cases each ends up paying far less for a piece in their private auction than they would have paid had they been battling openly. Auctioneers and consignors are the ones who suffer at the hands of buyers' pools, but unless they know the individuals involved and have watched them operate at several sales, they can do nothing to stop the practice.

A buyers' pool isn't going to have a drastic effect on you as another bidder; in fact, it might enable you to come away with a good deal if your set limit happens to be slightly above that of the designated bidder. Serious buyers' pools are generally found only at major antiques and art auctions if anywhere, although they do function in smaller and much simpler forms at many household and estate auctions.

Once you come to recognize the dealers and collectors in your area you'll begin to notice that they often have their heads together and their pencils scribbling before the sale. You may also notice that they are not bidding against each other on several of the antiques you would normally expect both of them to want. What has often happened is that they have compared notes on what pieces they are interested in and have agreed not to bid on certain items in exchange for the same courtesy from the other. Again, the practice drives auctioneers mad, but it shouldn't have any negative effect on you.

Imaginary Bids

"Where's the bid? Where's the bid?" Every bidder at one time or another is convinced that he or she has been the victim of the auctioneer pulling imaginary bids out of the crowd. Wedged in a crowd of forty or four hundred people, it is impossible to know exactly who it is that you are bidding against, but it is only a foolish and very dishonest auctioneer who will make it a practice to pull bids out of the air to push the price higher and higher. Eventually people will catch on, word will spread, and his reputation will be ruined. If you suspect it is happening to you, the best thing you can do is to drop out of the bidding immediately.

Don't Worry about Bidding Signals

Writers of situation comedies such as "I Love Lucy" and "The Dick Van Dyke Show" enjoyed building plots around one character who accidentally buys an expensive painting or nude statue by getting something in his eye or talking with her hands—both gestures being interpreted by the auctioneer as being bids. Besides making us laugh, what these episodes did was to convince an entire generation that if we didn't sit as stiff as tombstones at an auction, we would be trapped into buying something we didn't want.

While a discreet buyer might bid simply by touching his nose with his finger, nodding his head, touching his ear, or raising his finger, experienced auctioneers know how to differentiate between the serious bidder and the casual observer at their sales. You aren't going to be entrapped into paying several hundred dollars for a worthless piece of junk just by being yourself, but you should realize that an overanxious auctioneer's assistant may momentarily interpret you waving to a friend as a bid. Consider how your actions might be interpreted and save yourself the embarrassment of having to explain to the auctioneer and the crowd that you really did not intend to buy the four-foot long velvet painting of the female nude.

The Psychology of Auction Bidding

"Bidding," an old-timer once told me, "is like playing the banjo. It can be the easiest thing to play or the toughest. Just depends on what kind of music you like."

If you like simple music and simple bidding, all you have to do is raise your hand at any point when you want to get in on the bidding. Position yourself in such a way that you can see the auctioneer and he or one of his spotters can see you. Make your first bid plain and obvious, for this is no time to be timid. After you have attracted their attention with your initial bid, don't worry about getting lost; they'll keep an eye on you.

If the auctioneer is asking for a bid of $20 on a piece of cut glass that you have inspected and determined is worth up to $36 to you, either raise your hand, or, if you choose, yell out "Yes." He will immediately announce to the crowd that he has his $20 bid and is now asking for $25. If he gets it from someone else, he will turn back to you, looking for a bid of $30. You can make it either by raising your hand again, or, since he is now looking directly at you, simply nodding your head.

If you want to slow the bidding down you can counter with a bid of $27.50, but if the auctioneer knows he can find a $30 bid in the crowd he may elect to ignore or reject it. This infuriates some bidders who insist that it is the auctioneer's obligation to take *any* higher bid; auctioneers feel it is their responsibility to get the most money possible from a piece for their client, and may justify rejecting a smaller jump for that reason.

Assuming that the auctioneer takes your bid of $27.50, he will then turn his attention back to the other bidders, still looking for a $30 bid. If he doesn't find it, the piece of glassware will be hammered down "Sold" and he'll ask for your number. To make sure that the clerk, who will be standing with clipboard in hand near the auctioneer, records your number correctly, hold it up for him or her to see and also shout it out clearly. If you wish, the piece of glass will be handed back to you or you can have them set it on the table with the other pieces that have been sold.

The real test of your willpower comes when the auctioneer gets a rival bid at or above your set limit and comes back to you for the next bid. You are going to feel as if everyone within thirty miles is staring at you, waiting to see if you are going to stay in the bidding or drop out. Those who can't look the auctioneer in the eye and say "No, thank-you" invariably wake up the next morning with a car full of overpriced antiques and a checkbook that won't balance.

The auctioneer may joke with you, tease you, tempt you,

prod you, cajole you, play upon your ego, play with your pride, even plead with you, do anything he can to get just one more bid out of you. Like a fickle lover, once he has done so, he'll turn his attention to the next bidder, leaving you to stand alone, wondering if you made a mistake.

If you did, you can only hope that his other bidder is just as weak as you were. If the other bidder succumbs to the auctioneer's outpourings, you'll feel as if you have just received a death-row reprieve from the governor. Your auctioneer and all his attention will be right back in front of you again, and if you falter this time, you deserve whatever fate befalls the weak of heart at an antiques auction. This is where your notebook will help stiffen your resistance; study your notes, double-check your set limit, then look right at the auctioneer and shake your head "No." Don't take his disappointment too seriously. Auctioneers don't hold grudges and the next time you show a spark of interest in an item that he has up for bids he'll be back like a persistent lover with all his affections (or is it affectations?) for you.

Different Auction Bidding Techniques

Once you grow confident about the basics of simple bidding (that should take twenty minutes or so) you may want to experiment with a few tactics that dealers and collectors employ in an attempt to knock down a piece for less than its full retail value. There are several different styles and techniques of bidding plus variations on each. Choosing the proper one for each situation is as important to you as it is for a baseball catcher to know what pitch to call for each batter his pitcher faces. Sometimes the techniques don't work, just as a pitcher's best fastball will oftentimes sail out of the ballpark when delivered up against the league's best long ball hitter, but you haven't got as much to lose compared to what you have to gain.

Jumping the bid, as we discussed earlier, is one very effective way of discouraging novice bidders. For the procedure to

work you must be able to see whom you are bidding against
and know just when to employ it. If a couple is bidding against
you and you sense that one of them suddenly thinks they
should drop out of the contest, but the other is starting to fall
prey to the auctioneer's hype, jumping the bid may be enough
to eliminate them. While they might otherwise have continued
indefinitely at $5 jumps, suddenly being faced with a $20,
$30, or even $50 increase may be enough to knock them out
of the bidding.

The obvious disadvantage to jumping bids is that you erase
the possibility of getting the piece at a lower price. Perhaps
the couple was going to drop out anyway; perhaps no one else
would have raised the bid. In this case, then, you cost yourself
$20, $30, or $50 you would not have had to spend. On the
other hand, you might have kept the couple from getting
caught up in the emotion of the bidding or might have pre-
vented someone else from later joining in and running the bid
up beyond your limit.

One variation of jump bidding, which is generally done
toward the middle or end of the bidding on a particular piece,
is employed as soon as the auctioneer puts the antique on the
block. Normally the auctioneer first asks for a high opening
bid near or even over what he expects to eventually get for
the antique; naturally, though, he accepts a far lower bid to
start the bidding. For instance, he may ask for an opening bid
of $400 for a square oak table, but when no one in the crowd
responds he will take a local dealer's offer of $50. From there,
he will work to take the bidding up to and past the $400 mark
at $25 and eventually $10 jumps.

Presuming, of course, that you have set $500 as your limit
on the table, you may be able to shock the crowd and scare
off all of the competition if you shout out, "Three hundred
and fifty dollars!" (Always shout jump bids; it helps intimi-
date others.) You will hear the crowd literally gasp as everyone turns to try to find who has started the bidding out so
high. And while you might think the auctioneer would be
pleased with such a fine bid, it actually makes it difficult for
him to gain any momentum in the bidding. Even if he can

Almost an American institution, the square oak table was a common sight in nearly every home at the turn of the century. Before chasing bids much past $200 or $300, make sure that the fifth leg is still intact and that all of the original leaves are included. Ornately carved legs, quarter sawn lumber, fancy aprons, molded lips, and a smoothly functioning set of extenders will distinguish a "Cadillac" model from an ordinary square oak table.

coax another bid out of the crowd, he won't have room between your bid and the value of the table to get someone else deeply involved in the bidding. If that happens, the table, which you had decided you could turn around and sell for $700, is yours for only $350. The worst that could have happened is that someone still might have joined in and topped your opening bid, but as long as you do not exceed your limit of $500, you haven't lost a penny.

Keeping the square oak table as our example, you could approach the bidding with yet another technique. What you are going to do this time, however, takes the nerves of a paid assassin. You have inspected the table and determined that, as the finish is in excellent condition, the table has four fine leaves with it, and all five legs are highly carved, you could pay $500 for the piece and sell it to one of your clients for $700 tomorrow. This time, though, you stand silent and let the other buyers warm up the bidding.

As the price of the table rises above $250, the early bargain hunters drop out until at $400 there are only two left. At $425 one of them falls aside and still you have not made a bid or even shown any interest in the action. The auctioneer scans the crowd, looking for one more bid, extolling the virtues of the table, encouraging the early bidders to get back in again. The one bidder left shifts nervously from foot to foot, but the auctioneer is determined to get one more bid.

As no one speaks, the one bidder left begins to sense that the table is his and, just as soon as he does, a strange thing happens: he begins to wonder if he went too high. After all, he thinks, no one else in this crowd of three hundred people was willing to bid $425 for it. Could he have missed something? Maybe the leaves are from another table? Is it veneered? Doubt and fear begin to take root.

"Four hundred going once. Four hundred going twice."

The auctioneer pauses, hand in air. . . .

"Four hundred and fifty dollars!" you shout.

The would-be buyer is stunned. He doesn't know whether to be relieved or enraged. The auctioneer jumps back to action. "I've got four fifty. Give me four hundred and seventy-five. Four hundred and seventy-five."

The would-be buyer can't. He wasn't ready for a $75 increase. At $400 he thought maybe he had a good deal, but he had his doubts; at $475 he can't be sure. He shakes his head and turns away.

"Sold. For four hundred and fifty dollars."

Two factors made this tactic work. First was the element of surprise. Second was simultaneously jumping the bid. You calculated that if you only bumped the bid to $410, the other bidder probably would have recovered enough to come back with a bid of $425 to get the table. You, then, would be faced with a bid of nearly $450—and the possibility that, once the shock of a new bidder was over, he would have been firmly back in the bidding. You would have ended up making the $450 bid anyway, with a good chance that the man might come back with yet another $25, pushing you to your limit. But by planning two bids ahead and sensing that the man would not go from a bid of $400 to $475 *and* by using your own form of shock treatment, you bought the table for $50 under your limit—and with only one bid.

Once in a while you can wear out your competition using just the opposite tactic. As soon as the auctioneer asks for the first bid at a reasonable starting point, make it. And make it loud and clear. Undoubtedly someone else will then respond, at which point you immediately and clearly make the very next bid. You don't exceed the auctioneer's jumps. You simply respond to each competitor's bid with an immediate and confident raise. Soon everyone will realize you are determined to buy the piece and, hopefully, will become discouraged. Each time the auctioneer receives another bid, he'll turn to you. Don't hesitate. You know what your limit is, but you want to give everybody the impression you have no limit and you're going to buy the item regardless of who is bidding or what it is going to cost you.

The idea, of course, is to dissuade any potential buyers from joining in and to convince those who started early to turn their attention to the next item. If the technique works for you, then ten, twenty, or even thirty bids later you may have gotten the piece for less than your notebook had said you could pay.

The disadvantage of this particular tactic arises if you ever run up against someone who has decided she is going to run the bid up against you. The risk she runs, though, is that you may decide at any moment to drop out, leaving her literally holding the bag. If you sense that someone is doing just that (whether it is the auctioneer or another buyer), but you are still below your set limit, wait until just the two of you are left, then hesitate when it comes your turn to bid. Her smug attitude will turn to panic when you make her suffer through a few moments of realizing that unless someone else bids, she just bought a walnut bedroom set she really didn't want. Before the auctioneer marks it sold (presuming you still want the set and it is still below your limit), make the next bid. If your competition was only trying to run the bid up on you, she won't be heard from again.

If you run into someone who more than once is running the bid up on you and you want to teach her a lesson, all you have to do is reverse tactics. While she thinks she is actually running the bid up on you, the truth is that you're aware of what she is doing and are, in a sense, doing the same to her. This, by the way, is an auctioneer's delight. When you sense that she might be feeling a bit too smug, drop out. One look at her face and you'll know whether or not she got caught.

The other problem you might encounter by using this tactic too often is a dishonest auctioneer. If he senses that he could run up the bid on you even if no one else will, he may start pulling bids out from the back of the crowd. You really have no way of knowing whether or not someone back there is actually bidding against you, for if asked, the auctioneer will point to one of his shills. If you suddenly drop out and the auctioneer is stuck with the piece, you won't know it. He'll disguise it well, assigning the sale to one of his shills' numbers. If he thinks you have caught on, however, he'll be more careful the next time.

Auctions—an Excellent Source of Reasonably Priced Antiques

All things considered, auctions are an excellent source of reasonably priced antiques. Many times you will hear antiques dealers complain that pieces are going higher at an auction than they are priced at their shops. Many times that happens. Stand someone outside in the hot sunshine for five hours waiting for one piece to be sold, force him to watch nearly a hundred other people pick it up, turn it over, criticize it, laugh at it, take notes on it, taunt him with uncertainty over its value, and by the time the auctioneer is ready to take a bid on it he will be tired, confused, nervous, and possibly determined not to walk away empty-handed. This is the person who is apt to let his emotions take control of his checkbook and will end up paying twice what the antique is actually worth. (And that's why later we will sell some of our own purchases at auction.)

You'll soon spot this type, just as you will the family members waging a bidding war over grandma's good Dresden, the antiques dealers taking notes together, the neighbors nosing through their deceased friend's belongings, the young couple setting up housekeeping, and the tall, dark stranger who shows up at all the auctions and stands alone at the back taking notes. Only he will be of real concern to you—and that's because he read this book, too.

II

SELLING ANTIQUES

8

Where to Sell Your Antiques

If your progress in the antiques business has kept pace with your reading, you may already be experiencing a problem common to most antiques dealers and collectors: your purchases are threatening to overrun your home.

When It's Time to Part with Some of Your Purchases

Most of us currently in the antiques business began by buying pieces that we either liked or wanted to add to our collection. Later we discovered that several things were happening. First, our tastes were changing. When we were younger, many of us fell in love with ornate Golden Oak beds, spoon-carved chests of drawers, and double pressed back chairs. Now we find ourselves coveting our neighbor's pine drysink or his walnut sideboard. Second, several near duplicates were showing up in our collections. Rather than just one set of Hoosier cupboard spice jars, we had purchased four—and three of them were doing nothing but sitting in a box. And, finally, we were finding antiques and collectibles that we neither fell in love with nor needed for our private collections, but they were such

Along with the Eastlake style of the 1870—1890 era came a machine carving commonly referred to as "spoon carving." Most commonly found in oak furniture, spoon carving was, at least to Eastlake admirers, viewed as superior to the applied trim used on buffets, dressers, wardrobes, and beds. Furniture manufacturers today are still incorporating spoon carvings into their designs, although this effectively eliminates them as a definitive clue to the age of any piece.

good bargains we simply could not pass them up. So we bought them.

The result?

The garage is full, the attic floor is sagging, the living room looks like an antiques shop, and the trunk of the car has everything in it but a spare tire. And there's another auction scheduled for Saturday.

The time comes for every antiques addict to begin to part with some of the antiques he or she has collected. While family heirlooms and personal favorites, no matter how bizarre, should always remain safe and sacred, many of your other pieces can be sold with two noble and attractive motives: more space and more money.

More space will permit you to better display those antiques you have decided to keep, and to store the ones you are going to buy next week. More money pays for little things like college tuitions, groceries, cars, microwave ovens, riding lawn mowers, and vacations. And, of course, more antiques.

The Secret of Success in the Antiques Business

The secret of success in the antiques business is no different in principle from what it is in the stock market, farming, or appliance business, but with an added twist: buy low, sell high—*and* sell quickly. While prices in the antiques business seldom fluctuate as dramatically as they do in the stock market, unlike stock certificates, antiques are not always easy to store. A hundred shares of IBM will fit into an envelope; six Duncan Phyfe chairs and a matching mahogany table can fill a small room. And while a phone call is all it takes to liquidate one hundred shares of stock or a thousand bushels of corn immediately, six chairs and a table can't always be sold on short notice. So buy low, sell high *and* keep your cash available for the next deal that comes along.

Just as in buying antiques, every outlet for selling them has its inherent strengths and weaknesses. Fortunately for us, we have more than half a dozen major means of selling antiques. And any one of them can be selected to best dispose of each antique we wish to sell. Only a few near-sighted dealers stick to only one or two methods; the successful ones employ nearly all of them at one time or another.

Two Dilemmas in Selling Antiques

Before we go into them, however, we need to discuss the two dilemmas that face anybody who decides to sell either one antique or a hundred. The first involves setting a price on each piece. Theoretically, you determined the fair market value of each antique before you bought it. Realistically we both know that many of the antiques you have for sale were given to you or bought so long ago that their value has changed significantly. Others you bought so cheaply that you didn't have to worry at the time what their precise value was, you just knew it was far more than what you were paying.

Use Antiques Publications to Help You Price Your Antiques

The solution to this problem certainly is not original, nor is it particularly creative. One way you can keep abreast of the market is by reading the classified ads and articles in the current antiques publications. Antiques have become so popular that we now have more than eighty local, regional, and national publications to choose from. Here again, your local library may subscribe to a few of the major ones, such as the *Antique Trader Weekly*, the *Maine Antique Digest*, the *Newtown Bee*, or *Antique Week*. Sample copies of others, including local and regional publications, can be ordered and studied to see if they warrant the price of a yearly subscription. Read the articles, columns, and advertisements closely, especially for information on current collectibles that have not yet made their way into price guides. If you stumble onto an early 1920s child's pedal car at a farm auction where everyone is more interested in the price of a six bottom plow than they are in an antique car for children, you might be able to pick it up for $50. Not only will one of the antiques publications be able to educate you through one of their articles on such cars, but the classified ads will reveal who else is trying to sell them, how much they are asking, and, many times, who else is looking for one. And no price guide can do all of that.

How a Good Price Guide Can Help You

What a good price guide can do, however, is tell you what similar such cars—or glassware or weather vanes—*have* sold for in the recent past. And if one similar in design and condition to yours sold last year at Skinner's for $825, then you at least know that yours is worth closer to that than the $50 you gave for it.

As we mentioned before, antiques shops, shows, and auctions will also keep you current in your pricing. If you have a set of eight beautiful mid-Victorian walnut chairs with burled backs and caned seats, each in mint condition, and a local dealer has a similar set priced at $200 apiece, you have a very good idea of what yours might be worth. "Might" is a very important word, however, for if she has had them on her floor for two years with nary a nibble, then it could well be that $200 each is pushing the market past its limit. An area auction with six just such chairs advertised will give you an even better idea of the current demand and the market value for such chairs. Keep your notebook handy and keep scribbling. Next week when you drive across town to look at a set of early hand-carved, hand-painted duck decoys you'll recall that a collection of very common decoys—each much newer—sold for twice as much as he is asking for these.

When to Bring in a Professional Appraiser

In the case of potentially valuable, unusual, or unique items, however, especially any that may have been the target of reproduction artists (scrimshaw, rugs, paintings, and early American furniture have been recent victims), it will pay you to bring in a professional appraiser to assess the age and value of such pieces accurately. His $25-an-hour fee will seem like a tiny investment when he reveals that your Queen Anne maple lowboy picked up at a southern Ohio estate sale actually predates the Revolutionary War and is worth more than $7,000. Finding an accurate appraiser is like finding a kind dentist; you'll develop both a loyalty and a dependency equaled only by that reserved for your antiques restorer.

To Restore or Not to Restore

Which brings us to the second of our two pricing dilemmas: to restore or not to restore? That is the question.

Restoration work, be it on a pine drysink or an unsigned oil painting, is sure to create controversy. On one side we find the purists who insist that by its nature *any* restoration work is a negative factor in determining the value of a piece. Extremists on the opposite side believe that each piece should be returned to the condition it was in the day it left the workshop of the craftsman who created it. One, then, will be aghast at removing even the buildup of wax and dirt from the arm of an old rocking chair; the other will have the wax, dirt, *and* the original finish stripped off an hour after he gets it back to

Made as a companion to and not a substitute for a highboy, the lowboy
(1700–1810) is also generally not as wide as a standard highboy.
Stylistically, it can be found in William and Mary, Queen Anne, and
Chippendale furniture. The primary woods are generally hardwoods such as
maple, cherry, birch, or walnut, while woods used for drawer sides and
bottoms will most often be a softer pine or poplar. Pieces that have not
been refinished or that bear original labels will bring premium prices.

his shop. As you might imagine, neither is entirely wrong or
right. Both have valid points to be made, but neither has the
proper solution to every problem.

Invariably, when someone learns that I ran an antiques restoration business, I am asked: "What kind of finish do you
use?" My answer is always the same: "I use them all." Just
as you would never think of using the same finish on every
piece of furniture you own, regardless of its age or condition,
you should never practice just one restoration approach to
every antique you buy. A solution to its problems, no matter
how unique or common they may be, can be determined only
after each piece has been individually analyzed.

Take, for instance, the argument regarding original finishes. To state that every finish, regardless of its age or condition, should be left alone would be as practical as insisting
that every finish, regardless of its age or condition, should be
removed and replaced with a superior one. A finish is applied
to furniture for two reasons: to protect and enhance the beauty

of the wood. If a finish is fulfilling both of its duties, then it should be left intact; if, however, it has either darkened to the point where we cannot even distinguish what kind of wood it is covering or if it has deteriorated to the point where the wood is no longer protected against moisture, dry air, or daily use, then some degree of restoration must take place to insure that the antique will be preserved.

It is the degree and quality of restoration that determine whether or not the value of an antique will be affected.

Refinishing Is a Last Resort

At this point it is crucial that we no longer equate "restoration" with "refinishing." Restoring the finish on an early Pennsylvania Dutch wardrobe (sometimes referred to as a "kas") might involve a light cleaning with mineral spirits followed by a thick application of paste wax to protect both the aging original finish and the wood beneath it. Refinishing such a piece would imply that the original finish was completely removed and a new finish applied. It should be obvious that refinishing is only to be done as a last resort, the final option in the range of restoration choices. It should never be undertaken lightly, for once the original finish is removed—even if the same type of finish is to be applied afterward—the patina of that old finish cannot be replaced by anyone or anything except time.

Restoration techniques, ranging from a simple cleaning to a complete refinishing, are the subject of another book. We are concerned here with the business of selling antiques and must decide with each purchase how much restoration work needs to be done (if any) and who should undertake the responsibility for it: ourselves or the buyer?

How Much Restoration Is Needed?

From the standpoint of the seller we have at least two major factors to consider. First, how much expense will the restoration work add to our purchase price? Second, how much restoration work will have to be done before the piece will sell?

Antiques dealers operate from a variety of philosophies regarding restoration work. Many simply buy and sell "as is." If they buy a wobbly chair, they sell a wobbly chair. They may get only $30 for it, but if they paid only $10 and invested nary a cent more, then they made a profit of 200 percent on the sale. If they had paid someone else $20 to reglue the piece, they would have to wait until yet another person is willing to pay $50 for it, just to make the same amount of profit.

The problem with this approach, however, is that fewer and fewer customers have either the time, space, or equipment to make even the simplest of repairs or do the easiest of restorations. Twenty years ago more people were doing their own restoration work; unfortunately most of it was "refinishing" or, worse yet, "antiquing" or "modernizing" (that's when someone has cut down a round oak table to turn it into a coffee table). Professional antiques restoration shops were few in number. Today, every major city supports several fulltime restoration shops, as two paycheck families find that, while they still would like to do their own restoration work, they simply do not have the time to do so.

The end result is that the number of antiques dealers with a shop, barn, or garage crammed full of broken chairs, chipped glassware, and badly worn tables is quickly diminishing. Today the trend is growing away from "as is" and getting closer to "room ready." The modern customer no longer has the time to take long jaunts to the countryside and wander about in search of a faded antiques sign strung on a barbed wire fence leading to a chicken coop full of waterstained furniture. What we are finding more and more of are antiques shops in convenient locations with clean, repaired merchandise carefully displayed and ready to be bought, packed, and taken home to be used that same day.

Restoration That Sells

How much restoration work do you do before a piece *will sell*, yet not venture over that invisible line where it then becomes difficult *to sell*?

With those types of antiques that are difficult to restore with any degree of inexpensive success, such as china and glassware, you are better off avoiding pieces that are in poor condition to begin with. A chipped Mettlach stein may be offered to you well below its listed price (that found in a price guide) of $200, but what are your chances of finding a collector who is willing to buy either a damaged piece that has to be repaired or a piece that has already been repaired? Most serious collectors, you will find, prefer to wait until they discover the same piece in undamaged condition. The one exception to this rule, of course, comes in extremely rare or one-of-a-kind antiques that maintain a high value even after extensive repair.

In the field of antique furniture, however, we have greater leeway in deciding how much restoration work to do ourselves, how much to hire a professional to do, and how much to leave to the buyer. That decision, however, is going to have a great impact on the amount of profit we show after the sale is made.

First, regardless of whether your buyer be a friend, a stranger, a dealer, or someone in the crowd at an auction (and I know a part-time dealer who one time sold a set of chairs through an auction only to get home and discover that his wife had been the one who bought them), you are going to want them to be *clean* when you present them. A minimum amount of soap and water and a maximum amount of elbow grease can turn a box full of dirty plates into a sparkling set of Royal Copenhagen. A pad of #0000 steel wool and a jar of mineral spirits can turn a black, gummy piece of furniture into a lovely, hand-carved early Victorian sewing rocker. In each case, the simple removal of dirt and grime in such a way as to not affect the finish will increase both the antique's attractiveness and its value.

A thorough cleaning not only makes a piece of antique furniture more desirable, but it will also enable you to assess the condition of its finish. If the original finish is intact, a final buffing with a rag and lemon oil may be all that is necessary to ready it for a sale. If the finish is worn or weakened, an application of paste wax will both protect and strengthen it.

Restoration That Will Kill a Sale

The one aspect of furniture restoration that will certainly kill a sale is an obvious need for repair work. Few customers have the necessary equipment and training to reglue a chair properly, turn a new spindle, cane a seat, or patch a piece of chipped veneer. If you do, you can pick up some real bargains in your travels, make the repairs yourself, and turn an attractive profit afterward. If you don't, the cost of paying a professional to make the repairs necessary to ensure a sale may push the price beyond the limit of practicality. Until you are either in a position to make these repairs yourself or feel comfortable estimating what they will cost at your favorite restoration shop, be extremely cautious in buying "as is" antiques. A collection of antiques waiting in your garage to be repaired can very easily tie up $1,000 or more of your money.

Venturing beyond cleaning and simple repairs, though, is like wandering out into a minefield. Not only will you be tying up your money in extra restoration costs, but badly damaged pieces will also make heavy demands on your time and energy. Add to that the fact that overrestored antiques rarely bring as much as those which needed only minor restoration and you will wonder why you ever bought the set of stacking oak bookcases without doors (you heard there was an old cabinetmaker over in Springdale who could make them, only it turns out he passed away a year ago); the waterdamaged buffet (no one ever warned you how difficult it is to match new

The popularity of Golden Oak furniture pushed its production past the end of the Victorian era into the twenties, but much of what was produced toward the end was of inferior quality. Elements to watch for in a superior oak pressed back chair are (1) "double" pressed back slats, (2) turned spindle backs, (3) a caned seat, and (4) a three-rung style base.

quarter sawn oak veneer to old); or the walnut table with the warped top (George Grotz made it look so easy in his book).

The Rule on Restoration

If it is clean, if it works, and if it looks good, don't refinish it. Keep the price down, sell it, and sell it quickly. Money makes money easier than you can.

WHERE TO SELL YOUR ANTIQUES NOW THAT YOU'VE BOUGHT THEM

So where are you going to sell all of these clean antiques you now have stacked in your basement and garage?

Private Sales

One means is going to be through private sales. With a
relatively small inventory it would be premature for us to consider opening up a shop or even hitting the show circuit. A
few inexpensive classified ads in the local papers will cost far
less, will enable us to start building a customer list, and will
teach us some important lessons in selling antiques. Our goal
is to sell as much as possible with as little overhead as possible. Private sales to individuals and collectors may just be
the best means of doing so.

Selling at Yard and Garage Sales

A second possibility is through yard and garage sales. As
you will learn in a subsequent chapter, organizing a multifam-
ily neighborhood yard sale is not much more difficult than
setting up your own individual sale, but can attract hundreds
more people and thousands more dollars. Whereas private
sales are generally a one-on-one situation with only one or
perhaps two antiques involved in each transaction, a yard sale
will give you a sense of what it's like to operate either a booth
at a flea market or a minishop. A yard sale does have a few
drawbacks, but I have devised ways to counter them, which
I will describe a little later.

Selling to Antiques Shop Dealers

As you gain experience both buying and selling antiques
and come to know and be known by your area antiques shop
dealers, you can turn some fast money "picking" for them.
Dealers who have chosen to be tied down to regular shop
hours or a rigorous schedule of road shows always seem to
be short on inventory. Once you come to learn the types of
antiques each of them wants to buy, what condition they expect them to be in, and what percentage of the retail price

they are willing to pay, you can add yet another dimension to your antiques sales.

Selling at an Auction

Auctioneers are another group of professionals you will come to know and quite possibly utilize in your antiques sales. And while you will most likely never have enough merchandise or a reason to hold your own auction, individual pieces can be taken to local auctioneers. If the piece warrants it, you can even ship it to one of the major auction houses to be put up for sale. As you have learned through your own auction experiences, more risk is involved in selling an antique through an auction than anywhere else, but it is also possible that a piece will inspire a higher bid at auction than you could have negotiated through a private sale or to an antiques dealer.

Selling at Flea Markets and Antiques Shows

If the time comes that your inventory and schedule permit it, you may want to test the waters at a flea market or antiques show. While you will find that flea markets are far more informal and easier to prepare for than an antiques show, they also tend to attract fewer "big money" buyers. Quality furniture and expensive glassware, fragile books and valuable collectibles are better saved for a major area antiques show than hauled to an outdoor flea market where they will be pawed over by a horde of curious pleasure seekers. Either type of event, however, will give you more exposure and more opportunity to sell a greater number of items than any other means of disposing of your antiques and collectibles.

The Antiques Mall Option

Finally, for those antiques addicts who are determined to become full-time or even full-time part-time antiques dealers, we have the antiques shop or antiques mall option. While the traditional antiques shop must confess to a growing number of disadvantages when compared to almost every other means of selling antiques, the antiques mall concept has managed to solve the majority of them. Both are viable options for us to investigate and consider, because the majority of our customers have been trained to buy their antiques through the more traditional means.

The following chapters will explore each of these possible methods of selling your antiques, examining the advantages each has to offer, and the subsequent disadvantages that must be dealt with. Remember: each antique is different from all others and deserves to be sold through whichever means will bring you the most money in the least amount of time.

9

Selling Antiques Privately

One of the easiest yet most profitable means of disposing of the antiques we want to sell is through the private sector. The very same people who drive hundreds of miles each year to shops, shows, and auctions—and who spend thousands of dollars once they get there—are also available to us for private sales.

We just have to get them before they get to their cars.

Reaching the Private Buyer

The advantages of private sales are obvious to every part-time antiques dealer. You sidestep the overhead of a full-time shop, the pressure of a three day show, the unpredictability of a yard or garage sale, and the 10 to 20 percent commission paid to an auctioneer. We won't claim that selling privately does not have its disadvantages and its inherent expenses. Neither, however, approaches the hassles or the costs incurred by any other means of selling antiques.

Print Ads Work

When you are ready to sell one or several items directly to the public, you first have to let people know (1) exactly what you have for sale, and (2) how they can go about seeing and hopefully purchasing your merchandise. The most commonly used means of publicizing your wares is through the newspaper. Regardless of whether you utilize the local daily paper or one of the area weekly giveaways, experience has proven that print ads work. Antiques dealers, auctioneers, collectors, and even those people with little more than a passing interest in antiques read the antiques section of the classified ads religiously and don't hesitate to pick up the phone when they come upon an item that interests them.

Study the Classifieds Before You Write Your Ad

Your first task will be to find which papers in your area are the most widely read. Study their ads carefully, compare rates, and perhaps even call up a few of the numbers in the papers to find out from the advertisers what kind of response their ads generated. Even though classified ads are a bargain when compared with display rates, there is still no sense in throwing away hard-earned money. Once you have determined—both through research and through your own experience—which papers produce the best results, you can eventually reduce your advertising costs through an ad contract with those papers . In return for guaranteeing that you will place a minimum number of ads over a specified period of time (three months, for instance), the paper will offer you a reduce rate per word. Ad contracts may not be ideal for everyone, but if you find that private sales are your best means of selling antiques, then such a contract can save you several hundred dollars over a period of just a few years.

How to Write Ads That "Pull"

Before you sit down to pen your first ad, however, study those found not only in your local papers, but in national antiques publications as well. Seasoned dealers have much to teach you about neither wasting nor scrimping on words when you prepare your ad. And so do the amateurs.

Compare these examples, for instance:

> For Sale: Old walnut Victorian loveseat made around the Civil War. Needs to be reupholstered and refinished. Been in family over hundred years.
> Call 333-3333 after 7:00pm.

While the ad does get the message across, it has several flaws. Compare it to a second example selling the same antique:

> **ANTIQUE LOVESEAT.** Circa 1860. Hand-carved walnut. Original finish and upholstery. Family heirloom. $300. Call 333-3333 evenings.

As you can see, the second ad wastes no words, but nothing is left out. It uses bold print to emphasize the item being sold, not just the fact that something is for sale. It also accents the positive aspects of the piece, "original finish and upholstery," rather than the negative, "needs to be reupholstered." Notice, as well, that it also includes the price, which, while reducing the total number of calls, will also screen out almost all of the time-wasting bargain hunters.

You must make several minor decisions in writing an ad. For instance, do you include your name? If you want to remain an anonymous dealer for the time being, no. When you are ready to "go public" and begin establishing a reputation as a dealer in antiques, include it.

Should you include your work phone number, your home number, or both? That will depend on the type of job you

The Victorians both enjoyed and appreciated upholstered furnishings, as evidenced by this walnut sofa. The crest across the back was designed to be removable. Finding a buyer for just such a piece will mean matching her taste with the fabric on the sofa, for having it reupholstered would be considered an expensive and risky investment.

have and your relationship with your boss or supervisor. If they frown on private calls, do not include your work number. On the other hand, if you are self-employed or in a somewhat executive situation, you may be able to. Otherwise, include with your home number the hours the buyers should call. If you don't, you risk permanently losing several potential customers who have grown angry and frustrated trying to reach you during the day when in fact you don't even get home until six thirty in the evening.

Taking Potential Buyers' Calls

If there is a good chance that a potential buyer may be calling your home at a time when another member of your family is there but you are not, make sure that everyone is well instructed in taking a complete and accurate message. Provide preprinted notepads with spaces for vital information: name, address, phone number, time, message, who will call back. If you are considering leaving your family an information sheet on the antique for sale next to the phone, forget it. A dealer who did so had three different family members talking with three different potential buyers one afternoon—and two of the three sold the same antique to two different people. As you can imagine, he had a good deal of explaining to do—and at least one apology to make.

And what about price? As the seller, you are almost obligated to start the negotiating by stating the price you are asking, but you don't necessarily have to do so in your ad. If you want to wait until you have had a conversation with a potential buyer in which you can give a more detailed description of the piece before stating the asking price, then by all means do so. If you are a good salesperson or the piece has special qualities that the ad did not have room to describe adequately, it may be to your advantage to discuss the attributes of the piece with each potential buyer before the question of price is brought up.

The greatest disadvantage of excluding the price in your ad is that you will receive far more phone calls from persons, especially antiques dealers, hoping to find a great steal. Once they realize that they are not going to be able to snap up a square oak table for $50, they will immediately lose interest in it, but you have still had to spend time talking with them on the phone. Meanwhile, a serious buyer may have gotten discouraged when all he got was a busy signal.

Including the price in the ad will reduce the number of calls, but when the phone does ring, chances are the callers will be serious buyers. What they will want to know is not the price, but further details and, if they like what they hear, where and when they can see your antique. If your ad and your phone description have been both honest and accurate, you stand a very good chance of making a sale to one of your early callers, since they have already indicated just by the fact that they responded to your ad that your price is not out of line with their expectations.

Set an Early Appointment to Show Your Piece

When a caller does express an interest in your piece and indicates he would like to make arrangements to see it, don't delay. Set an appointment for the earliest time possible; the prospect doesn't care if your house is a mess or the only thing you have clean is a pair of running sweats, he wants to see what you have for sale. So, if at all possible, get him over to your home that same evening. You don't want to seem pushy or you may risk scaring him away, but at the same time he has indicated to you that he is ready to buy a table—and it might just as well be your table as somebody else's. Let him mention at the office tomorrow that he is going to look at a square oak table next Saturday morning and Millie, Herb's secretary, is going to bubble, "Why, our next door neighbor is moving and they have a square oak table they want to sell *real* cheap!"

Your next ad might as well read "LOST: One Sale."

Make It Easy for the Customer to Find You

Once the two of you set a time to meet, give him clear and specific directions to your home and not just a street and house number. Be prepared to direct him to your house using easily sighted landmarks. When asked, many people will hesitate to admit that they do not know where a particular street is; they figure that they can always find it on their map—which they discover too late someone has borrowed and failed to return to the car. Then they must stop for additional directions, find a phone to call you, or give up and go home.

Make sure you give him a description of your house or apartment building as well. If you live in a house, and the customer is coming at night, tell him you will leave a porch or yard light on—then do it. I once ended up ringing the wrong doorbell simply because every time the father turned on the light, one of the kids would turn it off. Their neighbors had

no visible house number, but they did have a similar house—
and a porch light that was on.

You will, no doubt, recall the number of times that, as a
potential buyer, you arrived for a scheduled appointment
only to discover the seller acting as if he or she were completely unaware you were coming. As a seller don't be like
the lady I once met who, when I stepped through the doorway, literally started flying around the house grabbing bikes,
toys, and newspapers as if I were a fashion editor from
Better Homes and Gardens dropping by to do a photo layout
for the fall issue. On her third lap around, she swept unfin-
ished homework, dirty dishes, and a confused cat into the
arms of a bewildered child, pushed them behind her, then
turned and announced, "Here's the table. How do you like
it?"

Once the dust settled and the kid and his cat grumbled into
the kitchen to salvage what was left of their homework and
dinner, I rather reluctantly looked the table over, but I certainly was feeling more like a paid repossessor than a professional antiques dealer.

How to Show Your Antiques to a
Private Customer

When you set up an appointment with a potential buyer,
show your family the courtesy of alerting them to the fact
that someone will be arriving shortly to see the antique you
have for sale. Perhaps you can prevent your teenage son
from walking into the room in his underwear or your seven-
year-old daughter from choosing that particular time to announce that Jimmie next door just told her where babies
come from. Since you are in the business of selling antiques
and not your family's possessions, we will assume that you
will not have to clear the dinner dishes off the table when
the buyer arrives.

Ideally you should have the piece or pieces for sale in a
room separate from the rest of the family. It would be uncom-

fortable for both your family and your customer to attempt to transact business over the noise of the television or the stereo. If possible, display the pieces in the garage, basement, or spare room, away from all the rest of the household activity. And don't give the buyer the impression that you have been actively using the piece. If it is a dresser, for instance, remove all the off-season clothing and old blankets you had temporarily stored there. Put yourself in the place of the buyer and you'll realize how awkward you would feel pulling out a drawer only to discover it still contained someone else's clothing.

Make Sure the Item Is Clean and Attractive-Looking

Rather than apologize for the dust that has settled on the item or for the minor scratch it got when you tried to unload it yourself, take the time before the buyer arrives to wipe it down with a soft rag and lemon oil and to touch up the scratch with a little wood stain. Rather than force the buyer to try to imagine what it *could* look like, show him what it *does* look like. Little things like cleaning the glass, putting a bag of cedar chips in a musty drawer, removing the old newspapers, wiping out the inside of a vase, or putting new wire on the back of an old picture frame take but a few minutes of your time and could put several hundred dollars in your savings account.

Make sure that the buyer has both adequate space and light to inspect the piece properly. Leaving an old unicycle hanging from the rafters in your garage with only a single sixty-watt bulb illuminating the entire room will not go far in convincing a potential buyer that the unicycle is in excellent condition. Haul it down out of the rafters, clean it up, display it in the middle of the room bathed in plenty of light, and the buyer will be less suspicious and more apt to take it with him.

Bargaining with a Private Customer

Not only will a good cleaning, a few simple repairs, and a well-lit display help turn a serious looker into a cash buyer, it will also erode most of his bargaining position. You won't be hearing such lines as "Well, I guess if it were cleaned up. . . ." or "Let's see, I'll have to get all that old dirt and grease off and then see about that missing bolt. Considering that, you'd take twenty dollars less, wouldn't you?"

Instead of being on a weak defensive what you'll be saying is, "You wouldn't believe the shape it was in when I bought it. It was covered with dirt and cobwebs and had been stored out in a barn for years. I had to wade through a barnlot full of cattle, climb up a broken old ladder the farmer was holding, and knock off a couple of pigeons just to get it down. Took me half a day to clean it up and the other half to clean me up."

Who, then, is going to expect you to knock $20 off the price after hearing that?

Bargaining from the standpoint of the seller involves just as much psychology as it did for you as a buyer. You know what your customer is trying to do, namely, get you to lower your price. As the seller, you are now attempting to do two things simultaneously: (1) convince the person with you to buy it, and, (2) convince him to buy it at your price.

How to Figure Your Asking Price

You should determine your asking price long before any potential buyer arrives. Your inventory notebook will remind you how much you paid for the piece and what you had to invest in time, materials, supplies, or parts to restore it. All of this translated into dollars and cents represents your break-even point. Anything you get above that is clear profit. Sell for less and you will show a loss. Sell for less very often and you'll become just another small business statistic.

Figuring your break-even point is the first step in arriving at an asking price, but not the last. If your asking price is too high, the piece simply won't sell—at least not very quickly. Make it too low and you are merely taking cash out of your pocket and putting it in someone else's, namely the buyer's.

Standard pricing formulas, however, rarely work in the antiques business. Assume for a moment that you have two identical pressed back chairs. One was a yard sale "steal" for $10; all you had to do was glue a loose rung, touch up a few nicks and scratches, and wipe it down with lemon oil. Total investment: $15. The other you spotted at an auction, paid $40 for, then had caned. Total investment: $65.

If your formula called for a 100 percent markup, then, you would sell the first one for $30 and the second one for $130.

Make sense?

Of course not.

Observation and experience tell you that similar chairs are selling for $75 to $90 in the local antiques shops, so for you to sell one of yours for $30 and the other for $130 would be ridiculous.

You want to sell your chairs quickly, so if the area market value is around $80 (as evidenced by the shops you have browsed in and the auctions you have attended), you decide to price yours at $75 apiece. Sold separately, you would show a profit of $60 on the first chair and $10 on the second.

So why did you spend $65 on the second chair?

Individual pressed back chairs might be selling for $80 each, but identical pairs are bringing closer to $100 apiece. You were willing to pay almost market value for the second chair because you knew that, with the one you had at home, it made an identical pair—raising their value from $80 apiece to $200 for the pair.

In the end, then, you invested $80 in two chairs which you later sold as a pair for $200. Net profit: $120.

Are you rich?

Not yet, but you're $120 richer.

Keeping the chairs as our example, you have determined

that, as a pair (and you would be a fool to sell just one of them and reduce the price and desirability of the other), your break-even point is $80. Market value of the pair is $200, but your working capital is low right now, so you're more concerned with making a quick sale than holding out for the full $200. Instead, you advertise the pair for $195—which sounds like a lot less than $200.

One of your first callers is a young couple furnishing their apartment who were given an oak drop-leaf table by one of their parents and are looking for a pair of pressed back chairs to go with it. You and they both know that they didn't have to pay anything for the table, so financially and psychologically they can afford to invest in a good pair of chairs. The price seems fair to them, but the crucial question is going to be, "Do the chairs match the table?"

You realize as soon as they arrive that this couple is smart—they brought one of the table leaves to check the color match. You also realize that they are serious about buying chairs. At this point, you can't do anything about the color of the chairs; if they are either too dark or too light, and neither they nor the table is going to be refinished, then there will probably be no sale. You would be doing both the prospective buyers and yourself a disservice if you convinced them that the chairs would either lighten or darken in time (depending on what they wanted to hear) or that they did match when actually anyone without a seeing-eye dog could tell that they didn't.

If the chairs and the leaf match, then the sale price is all that is left to settle. Since in this instance you chose to list the price of the chairs in the ad, chances are you are about to clinch a sale. They know what your asking price is and they know that the chairs and the table match. Just as important, they know that if they don't buy these, they will have to start their search all over again. Even if you are determined to take no less than $195 for the pair, chances are pretty good that you will get it. If, after some discussion regarding the chairs, they ask if you will take less, you may be able to lock in a profit of more than $100 by dropping your price as little as $5 or $10.

Now while some antiques dealers will adamantly cry that reducing a set price demeans the professionalism of the trade, remember this: until a time comes when someone can prove that they can accurately determine the real market value of every antique to the last dollar, who is to say that your pair of chairs is not actually worth $180 rather than the $195 you had hoped? In this instance, if you don't budge and if for that reason your prospects decide not to buy the chairs, then you are going to have to invest more time and possibly even more money in the sale of these two chairs. Three months and several more ads later you may find yourself with two chairs priced as low as $175—and still with no buyers in sight. Dropping your asking price but a few dollars could have saved that first sale—and cost you less than what it eventually cost you to keep the chairs.

The Seller's Number One Rule: "The best time to make a sale is when you have a buyer."

Assuming that your original price of $195 is not chiseled in stone, you might reply, "For a hundred and eighty-five, the chairs are yours." Or, better yet, "Well, I've got a lot of time and money invested in them, but I'll certainly listen to your offer."

Both replies do more than fill up empty air space. The first is important because of the ending—" . . . the chairs are yours." Suddenly the buyers realize that all they have to do to become the new owners of the chairs is to say "okay." Up to this point, the chairs have been yours, but suddenly they can start to envision them next to their table.

Let the Buyer Make an Offer

Giving the buyer the opportunity to make an offer has several distinct advantages. The most obvious is that the buyer's offer may in fact be more than you intended to settle for. Perhaps you know of a walnut table that you can buy that afternoon for $150 and sell tomorrow for $300, so you are prepared to take as little as $160 for the chairs just to enable yourself to buy the table and make a quick additional $150 within the next twenty-four hours. Rather than reveal that, you let them make an offer. If it is too low, explain in a pleasant manner how (a) you have too much invested in the chairs to simply give them away, and (b) the chairs are worth far more than the amount that they are offering. If their first offer or a compromise price are still above what you are willing to accept, you've just made a sale.

Perhaps more important, however, is the commitment that making an offer places on the buyer. If you had said, "Okay, I need the money. I'll let you have them for one seventy-five," the buyer still could counter with "Well, we'll have to think about it." Or, if he or she was fast enough to catch your slip when you indicated you needed the money, they could counter with even less than that.

If you give the buyer the opportunity to make an offer, though, and he replies, "Well, we didn't want to spend more than one seventy-five; would you take that?", the decision-making roles are reversed. Now you are the one thinking it over. If you agree to accept their offer, it would be both unusual and awkward for the customers then to say, "Well, we'll have to think about it." They made an offer; you accepted; the chairs are theirs. If they suddenly have second thoughts, be quick to explain that the sale price of $175 is only good right now; if they walk out the door without the chairs, the price returns to the original $195 and stays there.

If the Offer Is Too Low

If their offer is too low, then you can genuinely look perplexed, scratch your head, moan, groan, or even chuckle if you can do any of these things without insulting your customers, and decline their offer. Rather than risk losing a sale with a simple "No," however, it is wise to compromise and make a counteroffer.

"One fifty is just too low for two matching pressed back chairs. I can sell them to a dealer at that price and they'd still make money on them. No, I can't take that, but I would be willing to let you have them for one eighty."

Naturally, the game of offer, counteroffer, countercounteroffer can go on forever—or until one of the participants drops out or the two agree on a price for the item.

Formalize the Sale with a Receipt

As soon as a final price is reached, two things must happen. First, the buyer must pay the seller the agreed upon amount and, second, the seller must provide him or her with a receipt for the purchase. Since you are the seller, you should have a simple receipt book close at hand to record the sale for both parties. I once saw a dealer spend ten minutes looking for his receipt book, during which time the couple had a hurried conversation in private and changed their minds. The dealer emerged from beneath a pile of papers with receipt book in hand just as they quietly closed the front door behind them.

While your buyers are writing out a check or getting their cash together, you should be writing out a description of the piece on the receipt. Indicate the amount paid and figure the state sales tax. Then ask for their name, address, and phone number, all of which you should include on the receipt for your records. Most receipt books—you can purchase them at office supply stores—make carbonless copies, so that both the buyer and the seller can leave with identical receipts in case any questions should arise later.

Should You Take a Check or Insist on Cash?

Small purchases are most often paid for with cash, which naturally you as the seller prefer. However, as most people do not carry large amounts of cash with them, you can expect to be accepting personal checks on a regular basis. This can be a problem, as all retail merchants can attest, for sooner or later you are bound to have one of these checks returned to you by the bank with "Insufficient Funds" stamped on it.

The only way you can be sure never to risk accepting a bad check is to insist on payment in cash only. In other words, the buyer will have to take his check to the bank, cash it, and return with the money. Not many dealers do this, however, because they fear that, asked to make the extra trips to the bank and back again to their home, the customer and the sale will be lost. If you plan to stick to a cash-only policy, you should either indicate this to all potential buyers when you speak to them over the phone or expect to lose some sales.

Getting a Deposit

If you feel that the number of increased sales will offset the risk attached to accepting checks, then you will need to make some quick character judgments as you and the buyer conclude each sale. If you feel uneasy about the person or persons involved, do not hesitate to institute a cash-only policy. Politely inform them that you will hold the piece until they return with the correct amount of cash. Set a time for their return and, if possible, get a deposit of anywhere from 10 to 25 percent of the purchase price in exchange for a detailed receipt. Naturally, you will sign this receipt to assure them that the piece will await their return. It is not unusual to accept a check for either the deposit or the full amount so long as both it and the antique remain with you until the buyer returns with cash. At that time, you simply trade the check for the cash and the antique becomes theirs.

As a general rule, the farther away from you the customer and the bank upon which the check is drawn are, the more difficult it will be for you to collect on a bad check. For that reason, many businesses accept personal checks only from accounts at local banks. Making sure the check has the buyer's current address, phone number, and social security number on it isn't going to put any money in his or her account, but it may help locate them in the event the check fails to clear the bank.

In days of tight money, you can expect to be asked if you have a payment policy. Naturally, you do—one payment, cash, please.

How Large a Down Payment?

Wouldn't it be nice if it were that simple?

Since it isn't, you should think about what you will say when asked that question. Dealers and merchants have different policies, but the most common seems to be a sizable down payment (no less than 25 percent, and more if you can get it), the balance within a specified time (no more than ninety days and only that long if it is a sizable amount), and no possession until the amount is paid in full.

Some dealers have been known to let the customer take the antique upon receipt of the down payment, justifying it by stating that they trust the customer and need the space or that they will insult the customer if they don't let them leave with it. My own opinion, however, is that once the customer has the piece in his or her possession, the incentive to pay for it is decreased significantly. As long as they have partially paid for it, but cannot yet enjoy it, they are going to want to get the remainder of the money together so they can take possession. I once had a woman buyer put $75 down on an unsigned, yet original nineteenth-century oil painting; she had asked to be able to make two additional

$75 payments the first of each of the next two months. I agreed, we wrote the terms on the receipt and both signed it, and I carefully stored the painting away in the back room, only to have to get it back out at five minutes before five that afternoon when she came rushing in with the rest of the money. She had gone home, decided where she was going to hang the painting, and realized that she could not wait forty-five more days for it. I stood and watched as she counted out crumpled fives and tens from her "mad money" stash until she had the amount needed to take her painting home and hang it on her wall.

As you might expect, the larger the down payment, the smaller the balance due and thus the easiest—and faster—it will be for the customer to save up the balance. With only a small down payment, you risk having the customer change his or her mind and never get around to coming back for it. During this time, you cannot continue to advertise it, yet the bulk of your investment is still tied up. That is why you want to get as much as possible as a down payment and specify precisely how long you will hold it for them. If the due date passes with no explanation, call the buyer and explain that according to your contract, the next payment is now due.

When the Customer Wants the Deposit Back

Once in a great while the unusual will happen. For whatever reason, the customer will decide that he no longer wants the antique and ask for his deposit back. You, then, have a dilemma to resolve. Most merchants feel that in such a case the deposit is forfeited to them and that they can feel justified in keeping it since they have missed other opportunities to sell the item while awaiting the balance of the purchase price. By explaining this to the customer, you may inspire them to come up with the rest of the money, so as not to lose both the antique and their money, or you may incite them to riot. You wouldn't be the first antiques dealer, however, to return a deposit to a fuming customer simply to quell a burning rage, avoid litigation, or keep them from dragging your reputation through every gutter in town. So long as you still have the antique, you haven't lost anything except some time when the piece could have been on the market. It is a tough decision and one that you can justify either way—and may have to.

Do keep in mind one safety precaution: as long as you keep the piece in your possession until it is totally and safely paid for, chances are you won't end up the loser.

How to Negotiate Delivery Terms

If your buyer wasn't cunning enough to negotiate delivery into the purchase price, you may be asked as you are handed the money if you will deliver the piece. Flushed with euphoria and with nine twenty-dollar bills in your hand, you blurt out, "Sure, no problem, I'll bring it over."

No problem, huh?

Not until you find out that your buyer lives seven miles away, works until six, has a class at seven, rents a third-floor apartment, and can't help with the moving because she has a bad back. Then you can subtract from your profit the cost of gas, wear and tear on your vehicle, time away from your work or your family, payment for help loading, unloading, and carrying the piece, and, eventually, a trip to the chiropractor for your own bad back.

Naturally, you can't limit your customers to those who have vans and strong backs. Most people have no ready way of picking up a roll-top desk or a walnut wardrobe, so must rely on others more suited and prepared for such work. If you fall into this category, then you may wish to rent your services in delivering your buyer's new purchase. If not, do her a favor and have on hand the business cards of one or two delivery services that you would safely recommend.

If you are going to undertake the delivery of a large piece, figure your cost just as a professional furniture mover would.

Include the number of miles to and from the buyer's home, time involved, and extra labor. Tell the buyer how much it would cost for you to deliver the piece and let her decide whether she will hire you or contract someone else. It may seem cruel to sell someone a large piece of furniture and then let them worry about delivery, but I have had too many dog bites, too many sore muscles, and too many trips around the block looking for a missing house number or nonexistent parking space to continue to offer free delivery. Think of delivery as a separate business: you are selling antiques; if customers want you to deliver antiques as well, then think as a professional furniture mover would. If you don't, you'll either go broke or get broke—or both.

You may face a problem, however, because the buyer may assume that you are going to deliver the item for free. Furniture stores have offered "free" delivery for years and the public has come to expect it. They don't realize that the charge for delivery has already been factored into the price of the item. They actually paid for their "free" delivery when they bought the sofa.

Furniture stores are able to do this in part because they sell and deliver dozens of pieces of furniture each and every day. In addition, they tell *you* when they will deliver your item so that they can make several deliveries in the same area on the same day. Your volume does not approach theirs, so single deliveries at the customer's convenience are costly. Explaining your situation to your buyers will generally relieve you of the responsibility of providing free delivery; giving them a solution to their problem—e.g. the name of a reliable delivery service or offering yourself for hire at a reasonable and fair rate—will keep you from losing any present and future sales in relation to delivery.

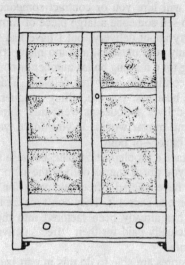

While Victorian pie safes were often made from undistinguished soft-
woods, their pierced tin panels appeared in attractive patterns. Watch for
advanced stages of rust and problems with hinges and hardware. Walnut
examples command premium prices. Some pie safes can be found with two
drawers above the doors or with punched tin panels in the sides. The panels
permitted ventilation while preventing flies from feasting on freshly baked
pies.

Building a List of Clients

Once all of this process—the display, the bargaining, the
payment terms, and any delivery—has been completed, make
sure you and your buyers part on good terms. You want to
make your next sale to them. If they liked the antique or
antiques they just purchased from you, chances are they will
want to see others you will have for sale later. Before your

conversation comes to an end, ask what pieces they might be looking for in the future and note in the "wanted" section of your notebook any that they mention. They may also be able to tell you about friends who are currently looking for particular pieces and, if you were to buy something similar in the next few weeks, you might even be able to make your next sale without the added expense of advertising. You are, in effect, building a list of clients.

Given a good antique for a fair price today, your satisfied customers will contact you first when they next begin looking for yet another piece. And soon, when you leave home on a Saturday morning for a day of antiques buying, you will already have a list of items that your faithful clients will be waiting to buy.

10

Selling at Yard and Garage Sales

Yard sales are great!

Why?

Where else can you get rid of almost all your old junk, dusty inventory, and half-finished refinishing projects, clean out the garage, basement, and attic, dispose of your outgrown clothing, even get rid of your old car—and make several hundred dollars as well?

But even though yard sales are great, there is one kind of event that is even greater—GIGANTIC YARD SALES!

Think about it for a moment. During the peak yard sale season you flip open the local paper to the special section reserved for yard sale advertisements and what do you find?

Dozens of similar sounding ads for similar looking sales.

What catches your eye? What ad gets circled regardless where it is located? Which sale goes to the top of your list?

THE GIGANTIC NEIGHBORHOOD YARD SALE!

So ask yourself: how much more work could it take to organize a neighborhood yard sale than it would to do my own?

Not much.

And if you play your cards right, your only task will be delegating tasks to your neighbors who want to get in on the act. Ron across the street is an ad copy writer; Jean next door has a flair for making signs; Tom and Wendy have lived in the neighborhood longer than anyone else and know everybody up and down the street.

The key to any successful yard sale is people. Hundreds of people—with thousands of dollars to spend. If you are just another individual household yard sale stuck over on Yewel Street, how are you going to convince the hundreds of people reading the yard sale ads that your sale is any better than the forty or fifty other sales going on that same morning.?

But—if you organize five, ten, twenty, or even fifty households into one gigantic neighborhood yard sale, combine your advertising costs, and write lots of large, flashy ads, you'll have nearly every person who reads the yard sale ads scrambling to be the first one to your gigantic sale come Saturday morning.

How to Organize a Gigantic Neighborhood Yard Sale

So how do you organize five, ten, twenty, or even fifty households into one gigantic yard sale?

With lots of planning.

First, sit down over coffee with a couple of your immediate neighbors and bounce the idea off them. Outline the advantages of holding a neighborhood yard sale: larger and more numerous ads, more buyers with more cash, less work for each individual involved, extra cash for vacations, a new lawn mower or other item they crave, and fun. If they like the idea and feel enough families in the neighborhood would be interested, take the next step: decide what boundaries your neighborhood yard sale should follow. Sketch out the area so that each of you is sure which homes and apartment buildings would be included in the sale.

Setting the Date

Together you should then pick out a weekend that appears to be the best for the majority of the neighborhood. Naturally you will want to avoid conflicting attractions, such as home football games, county fairs, traditional travel holidays, and major street repair work. Select a weekend far enough in advance so that most of your neighbors won't have already made plans for it and so that they have enough time to clean out their garages and basements in preparation for the horde of buyers that will descend on them.

Many individual yard sales start on Friday afternoon, but you will find that most of your working neighbors will both want and need Friday night to get ready for the early Saturday morning rush. Friday night, in fact, may become a bit of a festive holiday as neighbors become friends helping yet another neighbor move a player piano, try to start an old riding lawn mower, or start picking at the old four-string banjo dragged down from the attic. Fire up a couple of charcoal grills and ice down some refreshments for what for some people will be almost an all night marathon of "clean it out and tag 'em."

Don't Limit a Gigantic Yard Sale to Just One Day

At the same time, if you and your neighbors are all going to do this much work, don't limit yourself to just one day. Advertising a Saturday and Sunday gigantic yard sale will bring people from miles and miles away on both days. And, if the worst happens and it rains Saturday morning, you still have Sunday in which to save the sale. Moreover, those neighbors who have Saturday conflicts can throw open their garage doors Sunday morning to catch the second wave of buyers.

While you can set the days of your yard sale, the one tough problem you'll face is setting your times—or at least getting any of the buyers to pay attention to them. Serious yard salers will begin to drop by on Friday afternoon while everyone is setting up, others will be waiting outside your door at six the next morning, and the laggards will still be stopping by at six that night. Your neighbors, however, will need to know the parameters of the sale; thus your committee must establish hours for your sale, for example, eight to four on Saturday, eight to three on Sunday.

How to Estimate Your Advertising Costs

The next stop on your list is estimating your advertising costs. Your group should be able to list the most important papers in your area and a quick phone call to the classified advertising department of each will enable you to figure the approximate cost of each ad. By studying other ads, you should be able to plan the size your ads will be and figure the cost of each. Plan to run the ad two weeks in advance of the sale in each of your papers so as to maximize the results. Remember: advertising is crucial to the success of your sale. This is neither the time nor the place to cut costs. One good buyer can pay for all your advertising costs within minutes of the sale's opening—but only if he knows about it.

The single greatest advantage of a neighborhood yard sale will become evident when you divide your projected advertising costs by the estimated number of participants. At just $3 per household, twenty yard sales will generate $60—and $60 will buy some very large classified ads! Set a fee and don't worry about having money left over. The more you generate, the larger and more frequent ads you can run.

Putting Your Neighborhood Organization Together

All of this information—the dates and times of the sale, the area included in the sale, the advertising fee, the names of the persons on the organization committee, and the date of the organizational meeting—will need to be communicated to the people living in the area your sale will include. The easiest and most effective means of communication is a single sheet flyer that you and your friends can distribute to your neighbors. At the top of the sheet give them all of the vital information they need. At the bottom leave space for each participant's name, address, phone number, and a list of the major items they anticipate having for sale. Ad writing will be simpler and more effective if you know, for instance, that your sale will include a washer and dryer, two sets of barbells, an exercise bicycle, two square oak tables, several sets of maternity clothes, old picture frames, a broken riding lawn mower, a 1974 MGB, and a four-string banjo.

The Organizational Meeting

The lower half of your flyer can serve as a registration form which, along with the advertising fee, can either be dropped off at the home of one of the committee members or brought to the organizational meeting. The meeting will serve several purposes:

(1) you can explain to your friends the advantages of a neighborhood yard sale;

(2) you can encourage each household to be creative in its own display, using banners, flags, and costumes to attract customers and to make the event fun for everyone;

(3) you can recruit volunteers for sign making and traffic control (recommend that each family park their vehicles outside the sale area so as to leave more parking spaces for customers);

(4) you can announce that one or two charities have been asked to come by after the sale closes on Sunday to pick up any items that did not sell and that are not going back up into the attic;

(5) you can encourage families to set up craft and concession stands if they so desire;

(6) you can distribute an information sheet entitled "Yard Sale Tips" to each of the participants (more on that later);

(7) you can answer questions.

Preparing and Placing Your Ads and Flyers

Afterward the committee and any volunteers can begin writing and placing yard sale ads in the newspapers. A driving tour of the surrounding streets should be taken, noting where and what type of directional signs should be displayed. Appoint a volunteer to supervise the making, hanging, and removal of signs (this final job is most important if you do not want to find a member of the police force at your door on Monday morning).

With the lists of items submitted by the participants, ad writing should be rather easy. Invest in bold print for your opening words: GIGANTIC NEIGHBORHOOD YARD SALE. That is your eye catcher and it is important, because if it doesn't work, then none of the readers are going to get to the important information. Under your banner headline, list the location, days, dates, and times: Saturday & Sunday, May 23 & 24, 8AM—4PM.

In your list of items, start with those that are likely to attract the most people. Naturally words like "antiques," "old books," "used clothing," "tools," "furniture," "glassware," and "plants" are crucial, but then so are specifics: Edison Victrola, complete set of Dickens' novels, maternity clothing, auto mechanics' tools, brown corduroy sofa, Heisey glassware, African violet starts. If the mood strikes you, don't be afraid to drop in a bit of humor—"baby crib (used six times, never again)"; "exercise bicycle with heavy duty shocks"; or, "golf clubs, used once, three slightly bent."

Your objective in advertising is threefold: make them

Highly figured quarter sawn oak and mahogany veneer were used in the construction of crank Victrolas. While records were stored behind the lower doors, the smaller pair were opened and closed to control the volume from the speaker behind them. The value of these old Victrolas is determined to a large extent by the condition of the veneer, and any missing mechanical parts. In the event that restoration is necessary, care must be taken to protect any and all labels on the machine, for they are essential in determining the history and value of the Victrola.

(1) read your ad,
(2) remember your ad,
(3) respond to your ad.

If your ad stands out, so will your sale.

**GIGANTIC NEIGHBORHOOD
YARD SALE**

700–989 Gilbert St.
OVER 23 HOUSEHOLDS!!!

Saturday & Sunday
May 23 & 24
8A.M.—4P.M.

Thousands of items: antiques, 4 pressed back chairs, baby furniture, riding lawn mower, cornet, new set of encyclopedias, free kittens, Simmons hideabed, wrought-iron lawn furniture, Depression glass, plants, men's clothing all sizes, oak bookcases, garden tractor, left-handed bowling ball, Billy Beer cans, postcards, new groom's collection of early *Playboy* magazines, all sizes of bicycles, old picture frames, lamps, paperbacks, mirrors, pottery, free coffee, thousands and thousands of items, concession stand.

"If you need it, we got it."

Many of your neighbors will never have held their own yard sale before now and a few might not have even been to one. Providing all of them with a list of yard sale tips at your organizational meeting and discussing these tips as a group can go a long way to insure that everyone has a successful and profitable sale. Some of the points you might want to consider for discussion are examined below.

SUCCESSFUL YARD SALE TIPS

(1) If you have not been to a yard sale in recent months, *go to several before* you hold your own. Pay close attention to their layout, how the merchandise is displayed, what condition it is in, how clearly it is marked, how well organized they are, and your general impression of each sale. Make a note of what you think they did right and what they did wrong and remember what you saw later as you plan your own yard sale.

(2) *Walk through your entire house and take inventory of all the items you plan to sell at your sale.* Next to each indicate anything that needs

to be done to it before the sale, such as reglue the arm on the rocking chair, wipe out the Crock Pot, straighten and scrub the rust off the golf clubs.

(3) *Decide where you are going to hold your sale.* A large garage offers protection from the elements and prevents people from rummaging through your house. Large porches also work well. If neither of these is available, consider renting an open tent or a dining fly for the weekend. Remember that electricity must be readily available to demonstrate appliances and lamps. Plan how to attract buyers to your particular house. Banners, balloons, humorous signs, costumed sales personnel, an unusual or highly desirable item placed prominently in the front yard—any of these can draw in a prospective buyer who might otherwise have strolled on down the street.

(4) *Start preparing your inventory several days before the sale.* Wash and fold clothing, touch up furniture, hose off the lawn mower, clean up the tools, wash glassware, and dust off your antiques.

(5) *Pricing nonantiques items involves two considerations:* (a) how much would it cost new, and (b) how good is its condition? Naturally, if you price something too high, you will still be stuck with it at the end of the sale. If you price it too low, it will sell quickly, but you will have sacrificed too much profit. To help figure your price on an item, start at 25 percent of what it would cost new today. If it is in poor condition, work down from there; it it is in excellent condition, try pushing the price up.

(6) *Pricing antiques may require expert advice.* It

is better to have a $300 oak dresser accurately appraised for a $20 fee than to underestimate its value and let it slip away for only $75. Your committee will be able to help you appraise it or give you the name of a professional antiques appraiser.

(7) *Make sure every sale item is clearly and securely tagged.* If you are the only one who knows that the oak dresser is going to be priced at $300, you can be sure someone is going to want to buy it just as soon as you run off on an errand. Most of your items will be handled several times in the course of the sale, so affix your price tags and stickers firmly to keep them from either being lost or switched.

(8) *Remove from the sale area any items that are not to be sold.* If, as in the case of large ladders or a tool bench, they cannot be removed, cover them and plainly mark them NOT FOR SALE. If you don't, you risk having your teenage son sell your good tennis racket to the first person who waves a twenty-dollar bill under his nose.

(9) *Arrange items by types.* Put all of the tools together, all of the clothes together on one or more tables or racks, set the furniture together, display all of the books in one area. To save time tagging, put small items on tables or in boxes marked ''Anything In Here For $1.00'' or ''Everything on Table 50¢.''

(10) *Be prepared for the early birds.* Regardless of the advertised starting time, they will be pounding on your door or sifting through your merchandise while you're still trying to rub the sleep out of your eyes. As either a family or a neighborhood you need to decide how you will handle these early birds. One side will claim that

the time to make a sale is when you have a buyer and will urge that early birds be tolerated. Others may sometime in the past have been one of those who waited to arrive at the appointed time, only to discover that the best merchandise had been plucked out by an early bird thirty minutes earlier. They, too, have a good argument on their side: if you post an opening time, then you should abide by it. You and your group will have to decide which policy you will follow.

(11) *Before the sales starts have the following on hand.*

    (1) a tape measure,
    (2) assorted paper bags,
    (3) newspapers for packing,
    (4) several cardboard boxes,
    (5) an extension cord for demonstrating appliances.

(12) *Arrange to have small children and all loose pets out of sight and preferably out of mind.* Neither can ever be a positive factor in a sale. Just when you have nearly convinced a middle-aged man that no one has ever truly lived until he has experienced a kayak ride in your son's leaky boat, your Irish setter will corner a pesky kid, your three-year-old will fall down the steps, or the phone will ring. Call in your parents, in-laws, or a friend to babysit, pet-sit, and house-sit while you conduct business.

(13) *Have plenty of help on hand.* One person cannot successfully run a yard sale by him or herself. If you have to break away from one potential sale to make change for another, then assure someone else that the lawn mower *does* work, and to point out to yet another that the chairs

are sold as a pair and not individually, by the time you get back to your first customer, he will be gone to the next house. If you don't have a responsible child or spouse, pull in a friend from outside the neighborhood who also has items to sell. Join forces to decrease headaches and increase sales.

(14) *Appoint one person at each house to be responsible for the change box.* While the other sales people should have carpenters' aprons and small change on them as they move around helping customers, one person will sit at a table near the front of the sale area to do nothing but take money, make change, keep an eye on all of the customers, and handle checks.

(15) *Money—Have plenty of change on hand.* If you have a supply of twenty to thirty one-dollar bills, $10 in quarters and $10 in dimes and nickels, by pricing items in increments of 25¢, you will find it simple to make change. Make sure everyone working the sale knows how to make change. Run a practice session with your children; you may be amazed to learn that they don't know what to do when someone gives them $1.15 for a 65¢ item.

(16) *Handling checks.* A few yard sales now post "No Checks" signs, but unless you want to eliminate almost all of your major sale items such as a $100 refrigerator, a $200 walnut table, or a $75 set of dishes, you had better think that decision over carefully. Bad checks can be difficult to collect on, but you will minimize your chances of getting stuck if you:

a. take one-party checks only;
b. accept local checks only;

    c. accept checks only for the amount of purchase;

    d. write the buyer's driver's license number and the number from a major credit card on the checks;

    e. ask that they wait until after their bank opens to pick up items paid for with a check for more than $500 (or whatever limit you want to establish.)

(17) *Learn to study your crowd closely.* Stand near the edge and watch for customers who are hesitant to ask for help, who might be tempted to slip something into their purse or, more often, who might switch price tags or slip a $10 item minus its tag into the $1 box. No one wants the embarrassment of a scene, so take precautions:

    a. affix price tags securely,

    b. keep sale area open and well lit,

    c. encourage your sales help to move around and talk to their customers.

If you do spot someone who might be in the midst of considering or attempting an illegal act, rather than shouting, "Spread 'em, dog breath!" as you leap across the table with a loaded pool cue, simply walk up and engage them in a pleasant conversation about the piece whose price tag they have just "accidentally" rubbed off. Looking them right in the eye will give them the message—and you don't risk ruining your sale with an unpleasant encounter. Alert one of the organizers with a good description if there is any chance this person is going to another house in the neighborhood.

(18) *Half or three quarters of the way through the sale, start marking down items that you don't want left over.* Leave the original tag in place

so that the later or repeat customers can see what
a good deal they are getting. Be bold with your
markdowns; put a sign on your golf clubs: ''My
wife says either they go or I go—Make an offer
on either.''

(19) *Dealing with leftovers.* If you plan to have another sale, like the item too much to part with
it for less than it is marked, or plan to send it
over to your son's new apartment, pull it back
at the end of the sale. Goodwill Industries, the
Salvation Army, or a local charity will pick up
any remaining items. After that it's time for the
garbage man.

(20) *Have fun.* Yard sales aren't meant to be a chore.
The secret to having a grand time Saturday
morning is simple: good planning. The person
who an hour into the sale is out of change, is
still sticking price tags on items, has a screaming child standing in the doorway, a dog in heat,
and a husband at the car wash isn't having fun.
And she probably isn't making any money.

Good Planning Will Make You a Lot of Money

Plan ahead, delegate duties, then check up on everyone,
and when Saturday morning rolls around, you'll push the but-
ton that opens your garage door, your help will move tables
and items out onto the driveway, your change table will be
set up and manned, and while you're sipping a cup of coffee
and watching the cars start pulling up front, you'll smile as
you realize you are going to get rid of a lot of junk and make
a lot of money and having fun doing it.

Gigantic Yard Sales Work Only Once a Year

The neighborhood yard sale is a grand way to turn a simple
idea into a huge, gala, money-making success, but it generally
won't work more than once a year. You, however, aren't
interested in yard sales just to clean out your basement every
spring. For you they are an inexpensive means of selling the
antiques and collectibles you have bought from individuals,
dealers, and auctioneers. For you, once a year isn't enough.

Your family, your neighbors, and your city officials will
tend to get annoyed, though, if you begin holding weekly or
even monthly yard and garage sales out of your home. Astute
customers, too, will learn to spot addresses that keep appearing in the yard sale advertisements. They will label you a
nondealer dealer and will begin passing by your house hoping
to catch a sale where the seller might not know the true value
of her merchandise. Soon your customer and cash flow will
dwindle, and your neighbors and family won't be talking to
you—but some city official will be.

How to Set Up a Roving Yard Sale

What you need to do is to set up a roving yard sale. For
every recognized antiques dealer in town you can find a half
dozen individuals like yourself who enjoy buying and selling
antiques, but who do not want the extra responsibilities and
overhead associated with a shop.

Where do you find them?

The same places they would find you—at yard sales, auctions, and flea markets.

Watch for familiar faces and don't hesitate to go up and
introduce yourself. Obviously, standing in the midst of an
auction or a giant flea market the two of you won't have any
problem finding something in common to discuss. Then or
later you can bring up the subject of yard sales and, if you
feel he or she would be receptive to the idea, suggest that the
two of you organize a sale. Hopefully, he has not held one at

Although to the novice most duck decoys may at first glance look alike, astute collectors can not only identify what type of bird each was modeled after (a canvasback drake in this instance), but also the region it was made for (Delaware River Valley) and, more rarely, the carver. That helps explain why some decoys are tagged with prices of several hundred dollars. Experts urge that any restoration work be postponed until approved by a qualified collector, for the value of an improperly restored decoy can plummet far below what would have been obtained had it been left alone.

his home in recent months, so your first sale can be at his address, but even after you have held yard sales at each other's homes, you can call on other part-time dealers or friends who would like to host a yard sale and offer them an exchange: they provide the location, you provide the organization and you all provide the merchandise and share the costs. They get rid of their household items with a minimum of hassle and you reduce your inventory without drawing attention to your new business.

The only disadvantage to such an arrangement is obvious: you need to transport your antiques from your home to the site and back every time you hold one of your sales. Let's hope you won't be trying to sell a player piano or a set of rare Hummel figurines at a yard sale. Experience will soon teach you which items are both easy to transport and to sell. Trying to sell anything else to a yard sale crowd is simply a waste of time, space, money, and energy.

If you and a partner set up a regular yard sale arrangement, you will soon have the duties clearly delegated and easy to handle and will find your setup takes less and less time each sale. Saturday morning you and your partner (if you have plenty of help) can slip away at separate times to catch a few yard sales of your own. I once saw a new dealer pick up an oak parlor table at one sale for $20, drop if off at his own sale a few minutes later, and have it sell for $60 before he even got back from his next stop. That, dear reader, is both fun *and* profitable.

11
Selling to Antiques Dealers

If you have the knack for buying, enjoy going to auctions, sifting through flea markets, and double parking at yard sales, but would rather not undertake any of the headaches associated with selling antiques to the public, the antiques business still has an outlet for your merchandise. When a new furniture dealer sells his only remaining oak roll-top desk, he simply picks up the phone and orders a half dozen more. When an antiques dealer sells her only remaining oak roll-top desk, she may wait weeks, even months, before she has the opportunity to buy *any* oak roll-top desk in *any* condition.

Why?

For several reasons. First, more people are holding onto family pieces that years ago would have been sold or even given away. Instead of being thrown out, grandfather's oil-stained, mouse-chewed, cigar-burnt desk becomes the center of a family feud. Second, rather than calling in an antiques dealer, people are selling more and more antiques through their own yard sales or are consigning them to a local auction house. Antiques dealers just are not getting the same number of calls that they did ten years ago from people wanting to sell their antiques. Finally, sales, shows, and auctions have become so popular that they are drawing larger crowds—and higher prices. Add to that the fact that most are held during prime shop hours and you begin to see why so many dealers increasingly complain more about the problems they have buying antiques than selling them.

Becoming a Picker

Into the picture, however, comes the "picker," the nondealer-dealer who seems to show up at every yard sale, flea market, auction, and tag sale, checking his pocket notebook, buying a variety of merchandise, loading his van, and disappearing down the street. He doesn't own a shop, but instead chooses to sell directly to shop dealers. He is the picker—an essential cog in the antiques dealer's wheel of fortune.

All of the responsibilities associated with a shop—regular hours, deliveries, cleaning, paperwork, inventory, and much more—prevent most dealers from doing enough of what got them hooked on antiques in the first place: bidding at auctions, picking through yard sales, traveling to flea markets, and enjoying the excitement of a great steal. Instead they come to depend on a few select individuals who on a regular basis supply them with much of their inventory. And, whether the dealers know it or not—or like it—most pickers will actually be working simultaneously with several area antiques dealers.

If you want to keep a low profile, avoid the hassles of a shop, show, or even a yard sale or, better yet, want to make use of every possible means of selling antiques, including being a picker, you will want to start by studying the inventory of the major antiques dealers in your area. Later, as you come to know them, you can also buy for other part-time dealers and serious collectors, but chances are they will be at many of the same auctions, sales, and shows that you will attend. For now, concentrate your efforts on the major dealers who are having more trouble finding good quality antiques than selling them. These, too, are the same people who have the money available to buy fine antiques, simply because they also have the clientele who want them.

Don't restrict yourself, however, to just those dealers in your immediate town or neighborhood. Besides the fact that there will not be enough of them to buy all that you have to sell, you also do not want to find yourself showing a dealer a pine drysink that she had already turned down the week before. Many pickers will attempt to do almost all of their selling to dealers with shops twenty-five to a hundred miles away. Not only do they thus increase their number of potential buyers, but they also are able to bring their dealers fresh merchandise that neither the dealers nor their customers will have seen before. As you will soon learn, many antiques dealers shy away from an antique that has had too much local exposure. A dealer will cringe when a woman standing in front of an early Atwater Kent radio he just spent six hours and $70 on *after* he bought it shouts across his crowded shop, "Why, I saw this sell at the Fitzpatrick auction two weeks ago for only twenty dollars!"

Go into each shop you are studying, not as a seller, but as a buyer. Everyone, it seems, likes to talk about the antiques they might want to sell, but only when someone shows up with piece in hand and ready to sell will a dealer know she has a serious seller and not just someone out looking for a free, sight unseen appraisal. Browse through the shop noting what kinds of antiques the dealer stocks, whether she sells room ready or as is, and how reasonably they are priced. What you do not know, of course, is what she paid for and/or invested in each piece, but you can safely assume that if she has been in business for long, she is consistently averaging somewhere around a 50 to 60 percent markup on her items. On some she may be doubling her money; others may be priced at what she paid for them just to make room for new inventory, but if she has a mid-Victorian walnut dresser priced at $500, chances are she has less than $300 invested in it. If you can sell a similar piece to her at below that margin and still show an acceptable profit, then you have just found yourself a new source of income.

Victorian cabinetmakers enjoyed working with walnut, leaving us dressers with beautiful handkerchief drawers, wishbone mirrors, applied half columns, and raised panels. On occasion the top would be adorned with a marble slab, increasing both its beauty and its value. These mid-Victorian pieces have continued to remain popular with collectors in all parts of the country, maintaining steady prices at times when other large pieces of Victorian furniture have not.

Naturally, the closer a dealer sells to the wholesale price, the more difficult it is going to be for you to sell to her without sacrificing too much of your potential profit. Successful dealers with a select clientele who are more than willing to pay top dollar for a fine piece to add to their collection are our target. Find them, study their merchandise, and then talk with them. Let them know you are interested in antiques and sympathize with their problem of finding good merchandise. In a few minutes time they will be confiding in you what kinds of antiques they sell the most of, but find the least of. For one dealer it might be brass beds, for another it's walnut tables, and a third might need all the good art pottery he can find.

Pickers Must Win a Dealer's Trust—and Vice Versa

Talking money at this point is fruitless. All dealers want to buy as cheaply as they can and no one is going to guarantee you a certain number of dollars for an antique that they (and possibly you) are yet to see. Even when the time does come that you walk in with a fine Navaho saddle blanket, you are still going to have to name your price. And you'll have to continue to do so until you and a dealer have come to know and trust each other to be totally honest with one another.

You are going to have to be able to judge what his top limits are and determine both your buying and your selling prices accordingly. It matters not that you only paid $25 for it at an open air flea market; if it retails for $175, you are entitled to ask for somewhere between half and three-fourths of that when selling it room ready to a dealer.

Learn Your Dealers' Preferences

Naturally, if you are leaving responsibility for major restoration costs to the dealer, your asking price will have to remain below 50 percent of its retail value, but then you had better not have paid too much for it in that condition in the first place (if you did, go back to the section on buying antiques). Here, again, you will have to learn your dealers's preferences. If one wants to do her own refinishing or prefers antiques in their original finish, then bring them to her as you find them. If, on the other hand, another dealer likes the way you restore your antiques, you can buy the walnut dresser with the flaking finish for $50, restore it, and sell it to her for $300. All she has to do is clear a space for it, mark it at $495, and start calling those customers who have been in looking for a good walnut dresser.

A couple of Saturdays spent visiting the major shops in your area will leave you with a notebook brimming with information on each dealer. In addition to each dealer's preferences, note also their shop hours, and both their home and business phone numbers. And keep this information with you when you are out buying. I once spotted what I was almost sure was a piece of Gustav Stickley furniture at a mall show, but was unable to find a decal, brand, paper label, or a unique construction technique that would have confirmed it. The piece was priced too high to risk buying without verification, but I had in my notebook the name and phone number of a major Mission Oak dealer in New York City with whom I had done business before. I stepped to the phone, reached her at home, gave her a description of it and the measurements, and she confirmed the piece as being an early, unsigned custom-made Gustav Stickley table. I was able to get the exhibitor to come down $50 on the table, bought it, and later sold it to the Mission Oak dealer in New York.

A Picker Must Buy Carefully

As a general rule, however, do not buy anything (1) that you would only have one buyer for, (2) that you do not personally like, or (3) that you cannot afford. As one shop dealer advises, "Don't buy anything you don't like, because you just might get stuck with it."

When in your travels you do come across a piece in which a dealer has indicated he might have interest, one that you yourself happen to like, one that you know has sales potential to other dealers, and that is priced quite reasonably, then buy it.

Do not, however, immediately run over to the dealer's shop and shove your buy breathlessly in his face.

What to Do When You Make a Great Find

In this case, let's say that you just purchased an eight-piece setting of amber Depression glass at a farm auction. One of the dealers you had met several weeks earlier specializes in Depression glass and had expressed a strong interest in buying complete place settings. You have just walked away from a hayrack full of spades and shovels with two boxes of glassware that cost you only $85—and you know that in the dealer's shop the entire set will be priced at not less than $500. Before taking the merchandise to him, however, consider what needs to be done to it before it can be displayed to the public.

You bought the set wrapped in yellowed newspaper and stuffed into two old boxes that had been sitting in the attic for years. Mice have shredded most of the paper and littered all of the plates with droppings. Every dish is dirty, but although a few of the top ones were handled during the auction, luckily none has been chipped or broken.

Instead of taking them to the dealer's shop as they are, drive home and unpack the entire set. Wash and dry each piece and separate them into place settings. Locate two or three sturdy cardboard boxes and invest in the corrogated cardboard protectors glassware dealers place between plates and saucers. Replace all of the old newspaper with very thin foam rubber that will protect the old glassware in its travels. Pack the dishes neatly in the boxes in such a way that the dealer or potential buyer can easily count all the pieces. Finally, mark on the outside of each box exactly what the contents are.

What you have done is exactly what the dealer would have done had he rather than you been at the auction and bought the glassware. And by doing so, you have made your items more attractive, easier to sell, and, thus, more valuable. If he is like most dealers, he already has several boxes of glassware waiting to be cleaned and sorted before they can be displayed in the showroom—and six months from now they may still be waiting. What he does not need are two more boxes of dishes to clean.

But—if you bring him not two more boxes of dirty dishes,

Brightly colored Fiesta Ware was produced by the Homer Laughlin China Company of West Virginia in eleven different colors, with Fiesta Red the most expensive to produce and, also, the most sought after today. The simple band of rings illustrated on this disk pitcher is indicative of the company's product, which first appeared in the 1930s and remained popular until the seventies when the plant closed.

but an eight-piece place setting of amber Depression glass that is clean, packed, and ready to sell or take to a show, he is going to sit up and take notice.

Presenting Your Find to the Dealer

Rather than risk finding the dealer out of the shop when you arrive, call first, describe what you have purchased (omit the price, even if asked), and inquire if he might be interested in seeing them. If he asks what your price is, tell him you would like him to see the items first, then the two of you can talk price. Next, set up a time that is convenient for both of you to inspect and discuss the dishes.

The telephone call serves two other purposes. First, it stimulates anticipation. After he hangs up the phone he will still be thinking about the set, wondering what condition it is, what your price will be, how much his buyer will pay for it, how much he will make on the deal. As the appointment approaches, he will be thinking about it rather than something else.

The second purpose of your phone call has to do with money. The time between the phone call and the appointment, even if just a few minutes or an hour, will give your dealer time to consider the financial aspect of the meeting. He may postpone making another purchase or paying a bill to make sure he will have the money in his account to buy your set, should he like it and the price. When you give him time to think and prepare rather than walk in off the street with no warning you push the odds for a successful transaction in your favor, not his.

Be Frank about the Price You Want

We are going to assume that the dealer's first impression of your professionally packed and cleaned set of Depression glassware will be favorable. As he checks for chips and cracks, he will realize that you have taken the time to do much of his work for him. As the seller, it will be your responsibility to name a price for your set and he will undoubtedly ask you to do so. If you want to establish a good rapport with him, this being the first of many sales you hope to transact with him, now is *not* the time to be obstinate in your bargaining. Rather than starting at an amount much higher than you intend to settle for, I have found that with antiques dealers you know, want to trust and be trusted by, it is best to give them your actual price (or at least very close to it) right from the beginning. If you feel, considering your investment and the retail value of the dishes that you deserve $300 for the set, say so. Don't start at $500 and risk losing his respect and patronage. The dealer may counter with a lower offer, but it is best that you both come to realize that you are not going to play games with each other. The best relationship between a seller and an antiques dealer is one wherein both parties know that the asked-for price is honest, fair, and reasonable to both of you.

Creating Your Reputation with Dealers

If the dealer finds you difficult to work with or feels that
you have no compassion for his expenses and overhead, he
will have no incentive to continue the arrangement. By not
attempting to gouge him, by accepting less than you might if
you were selling privately, you can establish a regular clientele that over a long period of time will pay you more money
for less effort than private sales require.

Regardless of whether it is good or bad, the reputation you
earn will outdistance your legs and your vehicle every time.
If you are difficult to deal with, handle questionable merchandise, or cannot be trusted, antiques dealers are not going to
be receptive to your inquiries. On the other hand, if you develop a reputation for being reasonable, offer high quality
merchandise, and stand behind your word, dealers are going
to begin contacting you rather than waiting for you to contact
them.

Keep Dealers' Confidences to Yourself

These antiques dealers will be your regular clientele, so
make it a point to stop in at their shops often just to chat with
them regarding everything from business to their family's
health. You'll learn what items are selling, what looks to be
a growing trend in antiques and what each individual needs in
terms of inventory. For some strange reason, many shop dealers don't communicate regularly with their fellow shop-
keepers, so you'll find yourself becoming a source of
information regarding all that is going on at each shop. Be
careful, though, that you do not betray confidences. Antiques
dealers, like most retail merchants, are never anxious to make
public figures concerning pieces they have in their shops or
booths. If word spreads that your business dealings are not
always confidential, you can expect to see your sales to dealers slipping.

Convert Your Camera into a Sales Tool

You can save yourself many miles, hours, and dollars when working with dealers—especially long distance dealers and large or fragile antiques—by investing in a moderately priced 35 mm camera and flash attachment. This is another legitimate business deduction, so make sure you pay for it, your film, and your processing out of your business account. Some basic instruction from an experienced photographer friend and a couple of rolls of experimental shooting will enable you to take clear color photographs of your antiques. Invest in a rubber stamp with your name, address, and phone number on it so that anyone chancing to see one of your photographs need only to turn it over to know how to reach you; to talk to you about your antiques. Three or four photographs showing what a piece looks like from the front and sides and any important details such as inlay, a designer's mark, or a particular construction technique will enable a dealer to decide whether or not she is interested in the item without your hauling it seventy miles.

Attach to the photographs the measurements of the piece and any pertinent information (for example, "purchased from the H. M. Brooks collection in 1934 by former owner; can be verified as having been in the home of the state's first governor; an identical piece sold at Sotheby's in May 1985 for $1,350"). Such information may well insure a sale, for a dealer who might pass on a walnut barrel roll secretary might not if she were assured that it was once in a boarding house room rented by Grant Wood.

If you are mailing photographs and information to a dealer and want them returned, indicate it in your cover letter and include a self-addressed, stamped envelope. A few photographs, some detailed information, a follow-up phone call, and the next thing you know you'll be on your way to the dealer's shop to deliver the piece and pick up your check.

CONSIGNMENTS—THE ADVANTAGES
AND DISADVANTAGES

Whenever cash flow is a problem for an antiques dealer saddled with either a low inventory or a high quality, expensive antiques that she would love to have on her floor but does not feel she can afford to buy outright, the subject of consignments invariably creeps into the conversation.

For the shop dealer, consignments can be both a blessing and a burden. Technically speaking, she does not actually buy the piece until a customer buys it from her, thus she never spends any of her own money. The burden comes each time the owner calls up or stops by to see if the dealer has been able to sell it yet. And when it does sell, the major portion of the check, regardless of how much it hurts, must be turned over to the true owner, despite the fact that the customer's check for the full amount is written out to Anne's Antiques.

For the seller consignments are time consuming and, if you are working with limited capital, constraining. Let's say that you have discovered, restored, and now have for sale an ornate hand-carved walnut serving buffet. Both you and the shop dealer who often sells pieces such as this agree that it is worth $2,000. But, the dealer tells you, he cannot pay you the $1,000 you are asking for it. Instead, he proposes placing it in his shop on consignment, and pricing it at $2,000. The shop's commission will be 25 percent, and when the piece sells, you will receive $1,500 instead of the $1,000 you are asking now.

The decision here is not an easy one. You have $500 invested in the piece; you want that back plus a $500 profit. But you don't relish the thought of hauling it any farther, you cannot be sure that anyone else will pay you $1,000 cash for it, and you know this particular dealer is the best in your area for selling such pieces. Add to that the lure of a $1,000 profit rather than just a $500 one and you may well decide to place the buffet on consignment, despite the fact that your business account is now dangerously low.

Precautions You Need to Take When Consigning Your Antiques

Naturally you can choose to reduce your asking price to the dealer in the hope that the lure of a $1,250 profit on a $750 investment will coax him to come up with the cash you need. But if you decide to stick to your minimum of a $500 profit on the item and choose to place it in a shop on consignment, there are some specific precautions you need to take.

First, make sure you choose the antiques dealer and the shop carefully. If you have been in contact with the shops in your area in recent months, you will know which ones are selling merchandise and which are simply dusting the same pieces from week to week. You are going to want your piece in the shop that sells the most of what you have for sale. If you want to sell a piece of furniture, then don't consign it to a shop that specializes in glassware. If customers have been trained to come to that particular shop when they are looking for china and not chairs, odds are that it will take longer for the right person to come along, see your buffet, and buy it.

The dealer will make all decisions regarding how the piece is displayed, so choose a dealer you feel has good taste in showroom arrangement, who changes her display often, and who will not simply shove your antique into the back of the shop under a pile of moth-eaten quilts. No dealer, however, should be expected to make even minor repairs that the piece needs before it goes onto the floor, unless that was part of your agreement. Veneer chips, loose joints, and touch-ups are the owner's responsibility and should be corrected before you arrive with the piece. The dealer will take day-to-day responsibility, such as dusting and display, but should not be given the burden of improving the condition of the piece.

How to Negotiate Consignment Arrangements

If the dealer has made it a previous practice to take items in on consignment, her terms will already be set. If not (or if you do not agree with her regular terms), the two of you will need to negotiate them. Basically, the owner and the dealer agree on a showroom price tag for the piece and the percentage division. If the dealer works with a 25 percent commission and your small pine table, for instance, sells for $200, you will receive $150 while she retains the remaining $50 to cover her time and overhead. You cannot expect to receive the full retail value of a consigned piece, for if the piece has a retail value of $200 and you demanded that much for yourself, the dealer would have to tag it at $250 to retrieve her 25 percent. As a result, the piece probably would not sell.

The other terms to be determined are time and, if applicable, delivery. Many dealers specify that if the piece does not sell within a certain time period, ninety days perhaps, the price is either automatically lowered by a fixed percentage or is renegotiated between the two of you. This protects the dealer in that it keeps her showroom from becoming a free storage space for sellers and prevents her from gaining the reputation of having either stale merchandise or high prices or both.

Delivery of Large Pieces on Consignment

The responsibility for delivery of large pieces may depend on the dealer's normal policy, for if she charges for delivery of her own items, she will probably do the same for yours and take care of it herself. If the piece is unusually large or she normally takes no responsibility for delivery, then you may have to assume at least partial responsibility in the event that a sale is made to a customer who likewise has no means of moving the piece. In either case, you will want to have the terms worked out clearly and to everyone's satisfaction before the piece enters the dealer's shop.

Given the opportunity, Victorian cabinetmakers enjoyed combining different furniture functions into one piece. A perfect example is the combination desk/bookcase, commonly called, in this case, a curved-glass secretary. Space-conscious collectors still seek them out, for, as one veteran dealer put it, "being practical sells." In addition to the obvious features, the drop front opens to reveal a set of pigeon holes.

Look into the Insurance Situation

A final precaution involves insurance. Problems have arisen when antiques left on consignment have been stolen from a shop. The shopowner's insurance may not cover items owned by persons other than the actual policy holder, so make sure that either her policy covers consignments or that your household or business insurance covers those pieces you have placed in her shop. At the same time (and these things are not fun to think about, much less discuss, but it's not any easier after the fact), determine who accepts the responsibility for breakage. I know of two antiques dealers who still do not speak to each other since the curved glass in a door to a fine oak secretary was broken by a customer. Since neither was at fault and the guilty party slipped out amid the confusion, offering nothing but an apology, determining who would pay for the replacement glass caused a permanent rift.

Consider Consignments Only as a Last Resort

As you no doubt can see, consignments not only can be messy, but potentially troublesome as well. It takes clear and open communication of terms with no misunderstandings on either party's part to achieve a successful consignment. The owner of the antique must realize, for instance, that even though you might send or bring someone to the shop to see the piece you have on consignment and they in turn decide to buy it, you should not expect the shop dealer either to decline or to reduce her commission. She has spent time dusting it, extolling its virtues to other prospective buyers, and sacrificing space that could have been taken up by one of her own pieces. Consignments are time consuming and must be entered into only as a last and very carefully considered resort.

HOW HAULERS OPERATE

An advanced form of the local picker is the individual who is referred to as a "hauler." Haulers were more prevalent ten years ago when the cost of transporting antiques cross-country was far lower than it is today. However, you can still find many pickers who, rather than sell in the same area in which they buy, will stockpile their purchases until they have enough

Nearly every period and style had its own version (or versions) of a lamp table and the Victorians were no exception. This cloverleaf design was available in several different woods and with several different leg turnings. The Golden Oak style was the most popular around the turn of the century, as it remains for many collectors today.

to fill a van or truck. They will then drive the collection to a part of the country where the supply of those particular antiques is low and demand high.

When Golden Oak was still plentiful and inexpensive in the Midwest, pickers would drive around the countryside buying round oak tables, sets of pressed back chairs, iceboxes, Hoosier cupboards, stacking oak bookcases, parlor tables and china cupboards. Three days later they would be parked in Denver, Dallas, or Los Angeles, making calls on dealers and setting up appointments to show their selection of oak Victoriana. When times were good, when oak was scarce and money plentiful in the West, a hauler could arrive, make a few calls, sell his entire load, and be on his way home all in forty-eight hours.

His profit?

Anywhere from $100 to $500 per major piece of furniture.

Gradually the cost of transportation rose, the demand for oak diminished (both through legitimate antiques and convenient reproductions), and the number of haulers declined. But those who still haul antiques to different areas of the country insist that for the smart hauler, the money is still there.

"You have to do your homework," explains one dealer who splits his time between refinishing antiques, running a full-time shop, and taking two major hauling trips a year. "You can't just throw a bunch of antiques in the back of your truck, take off for Denver, and expect to make a couple of thousand dollars. A lot of haulers have come through there now and the dealers have gotten a lot smarter—and a lot pickier.''

Careful Planning Is the Key to Successful Hauling

What the hauler does is to plan his trips several months in advance. He will pick a metropolitan area where the economy is healthy and not reeling from a recession, major labor strikes, or severe layoffs. A telephone call to the circulation department of the largest newspaper in the area will get him several recent issues, which he will study to see what is being bought and sold through the classified ads. A letter and a check for $1 made out to the public library will get him a photocopy of the Antiques section from the local telephone book. He will then study his material and start making phone calls to the dealers in the area. As he talks to each he makes notes: what is selling, what isn't, how prices are doing, what they want to buy, what kind of condition their customers want, what time of year is best for them. In just a few minutes time he has a good idea of what is happening in the antiques business in that particular area and is ready to buy accordingly. If brass beds are hot, he goes shopping for brass beds; if dealers there want painted pine primitives, he finds them; and if they still cannot get enough Golden Oak, he will. As he buys, he takes photographs of important pieces and mails them to the dealers to whom he spoke over the phone.

''You can't believe how much pressure is taken off when you know you've got a thousand dollars worth of stuff sold before you even start down the road,'' a friend who is a hauler explains. ''I once had a guy in San Francisco promise to pay me seventy-five dollars for every iron bed I could bring him. I ran ads in my local papers, called every dealer I knew and went to every auction that listed iron beds. At that time no one around here wanted old beds and most of the dealers were glad to get out from under them for ten or twenty dollars. The nicer ones I paid more for, but when I left here I had nearly sixty iron beds crammed into my van—and the dealer in California wanted to know when I could get him more.''

The key to successful hauling is careful planning. Arriving at a resort area at the height of the off-season is only going to leave you staring at "Closed For The Season" signs on antiques shops. Those shops that are open will not be anxious to tie up their cash for six months while they wait for the tourists to come back. Time your arrival a month into the peak season; by then their inventory will be down and their cash flow up—and they will be more than happy to pay your prices without a great deal of haggling.

Research the Market in Other Cities

Any time you are traveling make it a point to talk to the area dealers to find out what they are selling—and buying. Hauling mahogany to a city where everyone wants pine is only going to mean that you either dump it for a loss or haul it back home with you. Let your dealer friends know exactly when you are coming and what you are bringing with you.

Use the Phone and Photos to Presell

Whenever possible, sell in advance using photographs and the telephone. And don't put all of your glass eggs in one basket. When a dealer sees your out-of-state license plates, he's likely to assume (and correctly so) that every day you spend on the road cuts into your profits, so he may try to drag the transaction out a day or so to get your prices down. To counter, before you make any stop know exactly where you are going from there. And use the competition as leverage. Then, if you run into a dealer who wants to play games, simply slam the doors to your van shut and tell him, "I've got three more dealers to see this morning. If you're interested, let's get serious. Otherwise I'm headed over to Murphy's Emporium on Jefferson Street.''

Chances are, he'll get serious.

You'll Need a Dependable Vehicle if You Travel

Two nonantique items will make your trip both easier and more profitable. The first of these is a dependable vehicle. Don't assume that just because your van has been running fine in town lately that it is ready to take twelve to fifteen continuous hours of interstate driving. Have hoses and belts checked over carefully, then pack extras for insurance. Make sure your tires, including the spare, are ready for the road—and the weather—ahead of you. And remember, a faulty exhaust system could turn a five minutes rest stop into a permanent one.

Traveling with a Partner Can Be Profitable in the Long Run

The second item you'll find helpful is a partner. Obviously, paying someone to come along to share the driving is going to cut into your profits, but if you ask among your friends, someone may be able to come along with their only expense (unless you want to pick it up) being their food. A partner and a dependable vehicle will enable you to trim two or three days off your trip, thus saving you added meal and lodging expenses, not to mention medical bills should you fall asleep at the wheel.

Turning the Antiques Hobby into a Paid Vacation

One husband and wife partnership live in Chicago where they both teach school. Three years ago they started turning their hobby—antiques collecting—into paid summer vacations. Their condominium was chock full of antiques, but they kept on buying, so they started selling to local Chicago dealers. They applied for a resale tax number, took their profits, and bought a van. Now, each spring they begin planning an extended summer trip. They pick an area they want to visit, make contact with the local dealers and begin to concentrate their buying on the types of items their research tells them they can sell there.

They may pack only five or six major items in their van, but most will have been sold via photographs before they ever leave home. They don't rush the trip, for this constitutes their summer vacation. Along the way they stop at antiques shops and flea markets, sight-see, and enjoy themselves. Once they arrive at their destination they call their dealers, set up times to exchange their merchandise for cash—and pay for their entire trip out of the profits from the sale. On the way home they do even more buying, this time looking for small pine primitives, Art Deco accessories and other antiques and collectibles to sell to the Chicago area dealers.

They arrive home three to five weeks after they started out, ahead financially, with a fresh inventory to sell, and ready to face the rigors of the classroom again.

12

Selling Through Auctions

No business, including the antiques business, can be started, managed, or expanded without taking some risks. However, if you are a gambler, if you sometimes have the urge to fly to Las Vegas, to buy a lottery ticket, or to enter a football pool, then auctions are for you. Even if you are not a gambler, the time may soon come when the antique you have for sale can reach its highest price only when held up as booty between two bidding warriors fully armed with stinging checkbooks and razor-sharp Visa cards.

As a buyer you have seen how auctions work. From under the seed corn hats of a simple farm auction to behind the tuxedos at a highly charged Sotheby's, the basic elements are the same. We have an auctioneer and his staff, we have an assemblage of bidders and onlookers, and, naturally, we have merchandise and, less evident, its owners. Up to this point you have seen how all of these elements work together, except one—the owners. Now it is time for you, the owner, to consider selling your antiques through an auction.

Even though modern architects seem hesitant to allocate much space to hallways, the demand for Victorian hall trees has not seemed to suffer. A fretwork top, applied trim, marble top shelf, mirror, and glove drawer make this seven-foot example highly desirable to bidders and buyers. Most walnut hall trees of this style were constructed in the mid to late 1800s. Buyers should be sure that the original beveled mirror has not been replaced with a nonbeveled one and that the cast-iron umbrella drip pans are still in place.

Advantages and Disadvantages of Selling Through Auctions

Like every aspect of selling antiques, auctions have both advantages and disadvantages for us to contend with. On one hand they are a quick sales method. Place a walnut hall tree on consignment in even a busy antiques shop and it may sit for weeks before it is sold. Send the same hall tree to a consignment auction and within a few hours it will be headed to a new home and hallway.

But speed costs. The auctioneer, for his time, trouble, and overhead, will deduct a percentage of the final bid, regardless of whether that final bid is above, at, or far below what you think the piece is worth. And if a blazing summer heat wave chains everyone to their air conditioners, you cannot suddenly decide to pull your walnut hall tree off the auction floor. Except in extreme cases the show goes on and sometimes the gamble simply does not pay off.

But at other times it does. Ask any shopkeeper how often a drop-front desk, Aladdin lamp, a Heisey platter or Seth Thomas clock nearly identical to one of hers sitting but a few miles away will sell far above her showroom price, and her eyes will roll. "Often enough," one confessed at an auction, "that when traffic is slow I'll bring pieces over here to sell."

Secrets of Successful Auction Selling

There are several secrets to successful auction selling, however, and you need to know them all before you start dragging your entire inventory down to the nearest consignment auction.

First, you need to understand that it is the antique, and not just you, that determines whether or not it should be sold at auction. The major auction houses where world records are set and broken on a regular basis expect and accept only those antiques that meet the highest of standards. They do not draw buyers from around the world to bid on an ordinary Victorian hall tree. Give them a signed Tiffany floor lamp, a Frank Lloyd Wright chair, or an authentic Hepplewhite table and they will pack the house for you. Ask them to sell a set of pressed back chairs and you may not even get your photographs back.

On the other hand, the same ornate walnut hall tree may not be best suited to a community consignment auction where the bidders are simply out bargain hunting. Instead, this is where your $100 I-thought-it-was-oak-before-I-stripped-it library table belongs.

An oak side chair designed by
Frank Lloyd Wright (c. 1903) for
Unity Temple in Oak Park, Illinois.
Note the leather seat and linear
construction characteristic of the
Arts and Crafts Movement of 1900–
1915. Most collectors never have
the opportunity to view in person an
original Wright chair and rarely the
opportunity to buy one. Chairs of
this type have sold for more than
$6,000.

Use the Auction That Suits Your Antique

Which brings us to the next point: select the auction according to the antique.

As explained in an earlier chapter, you have several different types of auctions to choose from, but seldom will more than one be best suited for any particular antique. Neither Sotheby's nor the weekly community consignment auction nor a farm implement sale would provide the best arena and audience for your Victorian hall tree, but a regionally advertised major antiques auction would. Rather than forcing the antique or antiques you want to sell into the most convenient auction for you, evaluate each antique as to the type of buyer it will require and match that with the auction that attracts those same customers. Pushing a $2,000 lamp through a local auction simply because the place is closer to you or because the auctioneer is your neighbor's brother-in-law will only cost you money. The qualified buyers won't hesitate to drive an extra hundred miles for the opportunity to bid on a fine quality antique and you certainly shouldn't cringe at doing the same to increase your odds of receiving as much, if not sometimes more, than the piece would bring in a shop.

Successful Auction Selling Involves Timing

A third guideline for successful auction selling has to do with timing. Every area has certain seasons or times of the year that inspire more antiques buying than others, and auctions are not immune to these seasonal differences. Only experience and personal research will reveal to you whether spring is better than fall or if the first month after the university opens finds a sudden surge in buying or if an influx of tourists pushes weekend auction prices beyond normal expectations. Even the major New York auction houses carefully study and select dates for their various departments' auctions, but in their situations another factor bears careful consideration: their competition. One house trying to improve a particular department's reputation will often select an auction date only a few weeks in advance of their competition's to try to draw away some of the money before it is spent at the more widely publicized sale.

Your timing will be more influenced by conflicting—or beneficial—functions, such as nearby antiques shows, flea markets, or cultural, sports, or entertainment events that would either decrease or increase the number of people attending a scheduled auction.

Consider any of the above quite carefully, for once you commit your walnut hall tree or Hudson River School oil painting to an auction, it would be both embarrassing and unprofessional to attempt to withdraw it.

How to Select the Right Auctioneer and Auction House

Finally, and perhaps most important, is the consideration you give to the particular auctioneer or auction house. Highly visible, well-publicized, and often criticized auctioneers are celebrities in their own right. Each has his or her own particular style, and whether it be pompous, righteous, humorous, down-home, country, urban, good ol' boy, or dignified, you can be sure to find some people cussing him and others ready to kiss his cowboy boots.

Auctioneers and auction houses, not unlike restaurants, shows, and nightspots, will go through various stages in their careers. They may be on the upswing and drawing people from hundreds of miles away, consistently pulling in a regular stream; or failing and finding their crowds dwindling with each sale. Study each auctioneer carefully, noting the type of merchandise each sells, the size of the crowd each draws, the organization each provides, the energy each exudes, and, most important, the prices each knocks down for his owners.

As you read your area newspapers and antiques publications, notice which auctioneers are consistently advertising forthcoming sales. See if any particular auctioneers or auction houses are doing more sales, investing in more advertising, and being used by more sellers than the others. Which are writing and designing ads that attract your attention and that of other buyers? A few telephone calls to former customers of theirs will give you a great deal of inside information that will help you decide which to approach.

Working Out the Financial Split

While some auctioneers will buy pieces outright to later be run through one of their sales, all generally work on a percentage basis. The major auction houses, like Sotheby's, Phillip's, and Christie's, in recent years have gone to a 10/10 system, wherein both the buyer and the seller pay the auction house an amount equal to 10 percent of the final bid. For years the auction house commission came entirely from the seller, as it still does at most regional and local auctions. But as the commission steadily rose from 10 to 15 to 20 percent to cover rising expenses, the number of quality consignments brought to the major auction houses began to waver and, in some cases, dwindle.

In order to attract higher quality merchandise the major auction houses in the United States adopted the English custom of splitting the house commission between the buyer and the seller. This "buyer's premium," as it is called, was a bitter pill to swallow, but, judging from the continuous stream of record-setting prices, has not turned a significant number of influential buyers away from the major auction houses. And while the impact on a middle-income buyer might be significant, the additional buyer's premium charge of $24,200, for instance, did not dissuade a collector from bidding $242,000 for a 1909 Greene and Greene designed desk at the June 14, 1985, sale at Christie's.

Commissions Vary from Auctioneer to Auctioneer

The commission charged by auctioneers to their sellers varies from auctioneer to auctioneer and from state to state. In almost every case, including Christie's and the local community consignment house, the size of the commission is open to limited negotiation. The more an auction house wants a piece to attract attention to a sale, draw more bidders, or enhance their reputation, the lower it will drop its seller's commission (buyers rarely receive such encouragement). Major auction houses, in fact, have been known to offer to charge no seller's commission in order to woo a coveted antique or work of art away from the other houses.

Naturally, your area auctioneers, when presented with the opportunity to sell yet another walnut hall tree or set of pressed back chairs, may not be inclined to offer you a reduction in their standard commission, but you should, nevertheless, compare their percentages, discover whether or not they are ever flexible, and weigh that in your considerations.

Study the Auction House Catalogue

The majority of the antiques dealers in the United States never sell a piece through one of the national auction houses, but that does not mean that they have never had an antique or work of art or even a collectible that could not have or did not end up in Christie's, Morton's, or Skinner's. Before discovering too late that you did, indeed, have in your possession or close to it a piece that could or should have been sold through one of the major auction houses, familiarize yourself with them by studying several of their sale catalogues. Each house is divided into major departments and each department has its own sale and corresponding sale catalogue at least once or twice a year. Christie's, for instance, distinguishes "American Paintings" from "Art Nouveau and Art Deco," assigns each a department head, a separate sale, and a separate catalogue. A letter to the catalogue subscription department at any of the major houses can give you the information you need to obtain any available copies of catalogues for recent auctions of particular interest to you and for upcoming ones.

Each catalogue is invaluable as both a learning textbook and an updated price guide. The initial section provides information on viewing times for the sale, the house's warranty and its limitations, conditions of the sale, a glossary of terms pertinent to that particular sale, and dozens of other fine points. You should never, never consider buying or selling in person

Three classic chair back styles; left, Chippendale (c. 1745); center, Hepplewhite (c. 1750); and right, Victorian (c. 1860). What every experienced dealer knows, however, is that craftsmen never bothered to read when one style ended and another began. Chairs are still being manufactured today in each of these and several other famous styles. Accurate dating comes as a result of a combination of several considerations: style, wood, construction techniques, finish, materials, history, and wear.

or via the telephone through a national auction house without having carefully studied the information provided at the front of one of their most recent catalogues.

The remainder of the catalogue provides descriptions of each lot that is being offered for sale to the public and, when the piece warrants it and the seller wishes to pay for it, either a black-and-white or color photograph. The house also provides a presale estimate of what it thinks the piece will bring. Experience will show you that even though these presale estimates are highly subjective and often more suggestive than objective, the majority of the pieces sold will fall between their low and high estimates. The exceptions, naturally, are the ones that spark the hottest debates.

Photographing Your Antiques for Auction House Evaluation

Suppose that in your buying, you have been both smart and fortunate enough to purchase a piece that you feel may warrant national exposure (and it takes both brains and luck to do so—and no small amount of guts). Your first step is to have the piece evaluated by a qualified area antiques appraiser. If he or she agrees with your conclusion that the piece merits national exposure, then you should next send quality color photographs of the item to the appropriate department chairperson at the auction house or houses that according to your research have the best track record for your particular kind of piece. Even though you will also include a detailed description, including accurate measurements, whatever history you know of the piece, and any restoration it has undergone, the importance of the photographs cannot be overemphasized. While you may have, in your exuberance and with your lack of experience, misidentified the piece, clear photographs will permit an expert to make an accurate evaluation. Blurry, distant prints could mean that what is truly a valuable piece may never be accepted by a national auction house only because you did not provide it with the opportunity to correctly identify your antique.

Before You Sign the Auction House Contract

If, upon either studying the photographs or, geography permitting, having inspected them in person, the department chairperson feels the piece is of such quality, rarity, and value to justify its inclusion in their next sale, he or she will contact you either by phone or letter with particulars on what you need to know to work with them. These include such things as the date of their next sale; the deadline by which they would have to have the piece in order to both catalogue and, if appropriate, photograph it; the house commission; insurance and transportation costs; and payment schedule. As a general rule, the more common the piece, even by their standards, the more of each cost the owner will have to pay, including the entire 10 percent seller's commission. The more desirable the piece, the more the house will be willing to lower its commission, reduce its photography charges, or share in transportation and insurance costs. Let the initial joy of having your evaluation of the piece verified by a national expert pass before you agree over the phone or in writing to anything. Each point should be carefully explained, discussed, and negotiated, including the important presale estimate and a reserve bid, before you sign the forthcoming contract and prepare to ship the piece.

What Is a Reserve Bid?

A reserve bid?

Auctioneers and auction houses dislike them, avoid them, and discourage them, but if the owner insists on having a minimum price which the bidding must surpass in order for the sale to take effect, they will reluctantly agree to it. Turn a deaf ear when the house representative tells you that a piece as valuable as yours is sure to exceed the presale estimate and that the announcement of a reserve bid (even though the amount remains confidential) will only discourage bidding. Insist on a reserve as close to the low end of the presale estimate as possible. You will get it and it will serve as free insurance against, for whatever unexplainable reason, an unexpected lack of interest on the part of the bidding audience. Buyers are a fidgety and fickle lot; let an unverified rumor race through the crowd that your piece has undergone major undisclosed restoration and it could destroy any hope you had of it even reaching, let alone surpassing the presale estimate. If that happens, the reserve bid goes into effect and the piece remains in your possession.

You Need Not Attend When Your Piece Is Auctioned

It is not necessary or recommended by the house that you be present at the sale. House policy does not permit taking bids from the owner of any piece they offer for sale and the house does not want to risk public embarrassment at finding out that the owner has inadvertently bought back his own item.

National auction houses, like local auctioneers, must rely on their reputation and any hint of unethical practices can be enough to turn buyers to other houses. Negotiate a reserve bid that will protect you, then sit back at home and wait until the results are in to call and find out the price that your piece brought.

Then go out and celebrate.

Regional Auctions and Sales

Regional antiques auctions and local estate and consignment sales seldom publish catalogues describing the items they are selling, but instead rely on sale flyers, advertisements in public and professional newspapers, and direct mail brochures to attract bidders to their auctions. Choosing the appropriate area auctioneer or auction house for your ornate Victorian walnut hall tree, however, is just as important as deciding between Christie's and Sotheby's for your rosewood Belter sofa with a presale estimate of more than $30,000.

Even though your antique will, to a large degree, determine which auction houses in your area will be best suited for it, you should still make it a point to compare reputations, techniques, commissions, advertisements, and, of course, results of competing houses or auctioneers. Generally a telephone call to the auctioneer or auction house will give you the particulars regarding forthcoming sales and standard commissions, but, again, if the piece is both unusual and valuable, test to see if the seller's commission is flexible. Since you will rarely find even a regional auction house that charges a buyer's premium, the commission taken from the seller's check will range from 15 to 25 percent. The standard 20 percent commission means, obviously, that if your cut-glass chandelier has previously been appraised at $800, it is going to have to bring $1,000 at auction if you expect to receive a check for its appraised value.

Be prepared for a wide range of reactions when you start conversing with your local auctioneers. While some auctioneers maintain a close and healthy working relationship with area antiques dealers, other auctioneers attempt to discourage them from either attending or consigning anything to their sales. At one extreme you may find the auctioneer who flatly refuses to accept consignments from antiques dealers on the grounds that the dealers or their representatives bid their pieces up to inflated values. Even if the dealer ends up buying his or her own piece back, they explain, the damage has been done because someone in the crowd will then incorrectly assume that if he consigns his similar piece to the same auctioneer, it, too, will bring that same price. When it does not, the auctioneer's reputation suffers.

Perhaps one other explanation for the rift that exists between some auctioneers and area antiques dealers can be traced back to when dealers have been buyers rather than sellers. Experience soon teaches auction goers to be on their toes; if an auctioneer lets a piece go too cheaply as a favor to someone once too often, the savvy antiques dealer in the crowd will spot it. If too many pieces sell to the same bidder at one sale and then show up at the next to be sold again, it probably will be the antiques dealer who was at both sales who will catch it. Antiques dealers can be a thorn in an auctioneer's side—and not always justifiably so. Let a dealer think he was burned by an auctioneer who in truth was not pulling bids out of the air and you may soon see him shouting out $1 raises when the auctioneer is asking for $10. Tension? You bet.

"Buy-Backs"—Good Protection for Sellers

On the other hand, you also will meet auctioneers who encourage antiques dealers to consign pieces to their sales. While small auctions rarely permit reserve bids, some auctioneers will allow consignees to bid on their own items and, if it happens that the owner's is the highest bid, will charge only a nominal fee for what are called "buy-backs." In this way the auctioneer gets the chance to sell a $1,500 curved glass china cupboard belonging to a dealer, for the dealer knows that he can sit in the crowd and, if necessary, buy it back if the bidding does not go high enough to suit him. Rather than charging the dealer 20 percent of the final bid as he would any other owner, the auctioneer perhaps only assesses a $10 buy-back fee as compensation for his attempt to sell it.

"In addition to getting some good pieces in my auctions that I might not have otherwise," one auctioneer explained, "by making those antiques dealers wait to bid on their own stuff, they always end up bidding on or buying something else. I might not sell a single stick of his furniture, but I'll bet he bought something else while he was here."

Regardless of his reasoning, buy-backs are good protection for sellers, although as a buyer you know that many times they are going to keep you from getting a steal at an auction where the owner is present. Naturally, though, your reason for taking a piece to an auction is to sell it, not to bring it back home with you six hours later, so selecting an auctioneer who is attempting either to build or salvage a reputation by offering buy-backs solely for that reason can be ill-fated. Advertising, organization, and sales techniques will go further in making successful sales than buy-back clauses.

The Auction Routine

Selling a piece through an auction is going to mean you have one long and, though not always busy, tiring day ahead of you. If the auctioneer has his own building, you can generally be expected to bring your piece or pieces to it several days in advance of the sale date. If, on the other hand, he is renting a large hotel conference room, a gymnasium, or an exhibition hall, you may have to deliver your pieces either the night before or the morning of the sale. In either case, it is your responsibility to make sure the pieces arrive safely and in room-ready condition. Take care of loose rungs, chips, nicks, and touch-ups before you leave home, for astute auction buyers will spot them immediately. And if the hinge on your drop-front desk is loose that morning, imagine what con-

The ever popular, ever present pressed back rocking chair (c. 1910). This particular model was made from ash and, without arms, is commonly referred to as both a sewing and a nursing rocker. Such rockers are still in abundance today, although many have been painted over the years. When buying, check carefully to make sure that the curved back supports (often referred to as "hip-huggers") are not cracked.

dition it—and the door—is going to be in after 137 people open and close it. If you have a fragile rocker, don't hesitate to place a ribbon across the arms or from the top to the front of the seat to keep people from sitting in it. A tasteful note explaining that there is nothing wrong with the rocker and you would like to keep it that way will be appreciated by serious buyers.

Always leave roll tops tied in an open position with a note indicating that the roll does work. Some quirk in human nature makes people who have no intention of ever buying a roll-top desk want to run the roll up and down a couple of times. Multiply that by 137 and you will know why professional antiques refinishers are always busy repairing the canvas on the backs of rolls that were bought at auctions.

The Presale Viewing Period

Staying near your antique during the presale viewing time is generally not recommended unless you need to protect it or are unsatisfied with either where it is sitting or the auction house security. If either of the latter are a problem, locate the auctioneer or the manager and get the situation corrected immediately. If you have not seen your antique in the several days that have elapsed between the time you dropped it off and the morning of the sale, make it a point to swing by the auction location at the beginning of the preview. You may discover, as one owner did, that the leaves to your round oak table have accidentally been assigned to another table. Have your touch-up kit in the car, for you may discover a new nick or scratch that could hold the bidding down if not corrected before the bidders start making their notes.

If you are going to be present during the auction, either to keep your piece from going too low or to bid on another one, keep an eye on your antique. Do not, however, be tempted to approach the couple who has spent several minutes inspecting your roll-top desk. Identifying yourself as the owner is only going to convince them that the desk is not going to sell cheaply and they may leave. One dealer with a flair for acting enjoys assuming the role of the wandering expert, stopping as if by accident next to her furniture and commenting on its fine points to anyone who happens to be showing an interest in it. It is a difficult role to act, however, for if overplayed, will backfire and cast suspicion on both you and your furniture.

If you have information that might influence either a bidder or the value of the piece, such as some significant history behind the piece or an indication of an important designer or builder, type this information on a notecard and attach it to the piece before the preview. Even information which you might take for granted, e.g. "quarter sawn oak, circa 1880, dovetailed drawers," can help educate and thus encourage prospective bidders.

Once the Auction Starts

Once the auction starts you will be able to judge whether it is a buying or looking crowd and whether pieces are tending to sell high or low. As the sale progresses keep an eye on the auctioneer and his staff, especially between items. A little grin, a wink, or quick nod between them can tell you that they are pleased with the way things are selling. A raised eyebrow, a helpless shrug, or a hint of impatience can signal trouble. Hopefully as the crowd settles in, warms up, and gets into the flow of the bidding, the smiles will replace the shrugs before your piece is brought up for bids.

If yours is a large item, such as a roll-top desk or a curve glass secretary, it may be left in its preview position and the auctioneer, at his option, may either move over to it or may remain at the podium and direct the crowd's attention to the piece on which he is about to accept bids. If space and help permit, the auctioneer may have the piece moved in front of the podium or on a stage next to him designed for displaying furniture. In either case he will either refer to a lot number assigned and attached to the piece or will give a precise description of the item so as to avoid confusion.

Should You Bid on Your Own Antiques

The decision to bid or not to bid on your own antiques is both an ethical and a practical one. If the auctioneer or auction house prohibits it, don't. He may not realize it the first time, but if you bring items to future sales, he will soon identify you. In public he may just ignore your bids; afterward he may ask that you not bring items to him again. The little you gained the first time will be minimal compared to all you have lost in future sales.

If, though, the auctioneer or the house do not prohibit the practice, you certainly would be free to bid on your own antiques. Keep in mind, however that your attempt to push a bidder "just twenty-five dollars higher," may leave you hold-

During the late 1800s the Larkin Soap Manufacturing Company offered premiums as an incentive for housewives to buy their products. Among the gifts they could "buy" were quality pieces of oak furniture that bore a large Larkin label on their backs. Today Larkin pieces still have a devout following among a dedicated group of collectors, giving an astute dealer the opportunity to profit from his knowledge of labels.

ing the bag—minus your buy-back charge. Therefore, you should decide before the sale what your absolute minimum price (reserve) will be, add to that the auctioneer's commission, and when the bidding tops that mark, keep your hands in your lap. If the piece is destined to go higher, it will; if you attempt to push the bidding beyond its market value, odds are you will be dragging it home with you, a sadder, but wiser dealer.

Collecting Your Check

All that remains for you is to collect your check. The major auction houses seem to be the slowest of your options when it comes to payments. Although the specific time varies from house to house, expect to wait several weeks before your check, minus the house commission, insurance charges, and any photography costs, arrives in the mail. Most regional and local auction houses and auctioneers have checks ready anywhere from two days to a week after the sale. Make sure you know in advance exactly when the checks will be ready and, if you so desire, make arrangements to pick it up at the auction house rather than waiting for it to arrive in the mail. If you hear persistent rumors regarding the financial stability of your auctioneer, be the first in line that morning and proceed from there directly to, if possible, the bank it was written on. If you think auctions are a gamble for you, imagine what they are for the auctioneers who ties up all of his cash and assets in scores of antiques to be run through one of his auctions. If he makes a few bad buys, has a couple of poor sales, and tries to recoup it all at one major sale that flops, that check you are holding may not be any good a week later.

Get to Know Your Area Auctioneers Well

Like your area dealers, it pays for you to get to know your area auctioneers as well. They will come to recognize, know, and remember you, especially if you are a regular at their auctions, and will be more apt to work with you when the time comes for you to sell one or several of your antiques through their sales. Auctions are always a gamble, but when you do your research, match your antique to the right auction and work with your auctioneer, the odds will definitely be stacked in your favor.

13

Selling at Antiques Shows

The time may well come in your career in the antiques business when you are ready to join that band of brave and hardy souls known as antiques show dealers. Anywhere from two to fifty-two times a year they pack up their merchandise, drive to a shopping mall, exhibition hall, or school gymnasium, set up their display, sell their antiques, pack up what does not sell, and head either for home or the next show on their tour. Though they like to think that with each show the routine gets easier, the truth is doing antiques shows is hard work.

For Big Money, Exhibit at Big Shows

Why, then, is there a waiting list of dealers wanting to be invited to do certain shows?

Money.

Big shows in big cities bring in big bucks.

Granted, the competition is keen and a dealer can invest $1,000 in booth rent, transportation, insurance, lodging and meals *and* still not get a cent of it back—*if* he comes unprepared. But if he brings the right merchandise, sets up the right display, and uses the right sales techniques, he can come home four days later several thousand dollars richer.

Mall Shows and Paid Shows

As you have observed, there are major differences in the crowd, the exhibitors, and the merchandise in the two types of antiques shows: the mall show and the paid show. Shopping malls will invite an antiques show promoter to arrange a weekend or three or four day show as a means of drawing attention—and business—to the mall merchants. No admission charge is levied and thus many of the people you find poking through the booths came not to find a blue Everglades jelly compote or a 1969 Wedgwood Christmas plate, but instead came shopping for a set of snow tires or to exchange a pair of pantyhose.

Antiques shows with an admission charge of perhaps $2 (more, the trend indicates, for a first night preview) will attract fewer lookers, but more serious collectors. There is no sense in trying to determine which is better, a mall show or a paid show, for the secret to a successful show lies in matching the merchandise to the crowd. Just as our $2,000 walnut sideboard would be better suited to a regional antiques auction than it would to a local consignment sale, so would it be better received at a paid antiques show where, proportionally speaking, there are more serious buyers than at a shopping mall show. Thus while we expect to find higher quality merchandise at a paid show, that does not imply that the exhibitors at a paid show make more money in a weekend than do those who choose to do mall shows. As one veteran dealer summed it up, "I would rather be a rich mall exhibitor than a poor show dealer."

How to Prepare for Your First Show

Your merchandise and the area or areas you specialize in will play a major role in determining whether you plan to do mall shows or paid admission shows. In either case, there are both good and bad mall shows *and* good and bad paid shows. Distinguishing one from the other is going to determine whether or not you have a profitable weekend.

Preparations for your first show need to start nearly a year in advance. The two most important tasks—choosing the right show and bringing the right merchandise—cannot be accomplished overnight. Experienced show dealers will tell you that you will do best to start with a show close to home. That way you hold down transportation and lodging costs and can still rush home when you realize that you forgot to bring a change of clothes or enough extension cords.

Do Your Homework—Study the Shows Before Deciding Where to Exhibit

Either a local or a regional antiques publication will supply you with the dates, times, and locations of upcoming shows, but now, instead of just going as a buyer, study each show from the viewpoint of a potential exhibitor. Make a chart and note on it how well the show was advertised; how well it has been attended. What are the parking conditions? What is the facility like—is it well lit; are there adequate outlets; is it clean; is it conducive to keep customers there, or is it either too warm, too cold, too quiet, or too noisy to create a browsing and buying atmosphere?

As you wander through the booths, strike up conversations with the dealers. Ask how the show has been; you will find most of them are painfully honest. If they are doing well, they will not be able to disguise it; if the pace is slow, the look on their faces will illustrate the fact. Whenever you come across a dealer who has the time and the inclination to talk to you about more than just his or her antiques, pause. Introduce yourself and your situation; tell him you are thinking about doing a show in the future. Ask his advice, both about this particular show and others he has done. While posing questions and taking notes like a cub reporter may strangle a conversation, soak in all he has to say. Ask what has been selling for him at the various shows he does, for matching merchandise with a show's clientele is critical to every exhibitor's success.

If the opportunity presents itself or if you wish to make the opportunity happen, introduce yourself to the show promoter. If this is a show you feel would be appropriate both for your merchandise and you as a first-time exhibitor, ask for details regarding next season's show. She may have a blank contract to give you to study and while her booth rents for next year may yet be undetermined, chances are that they will not vary drastically from this year's. She will probably be taking reservations from exhibitors who have been with her at this show for several seasons and thus will not be able to promise you a booth until they have had an opportunity to renew. But, then, you are not necessarily ready to commit yourself either.

Facts about Booth Rental Costs

The single most expensive item associated with paid admission shows will be your booth rent. Rent alone, though, should not be the determining factor in whether or not you do a show. While a major city show may cost you more than $500 for a ten- by-twenty-foot booth for four days, it may bring you twice as much business—and profit—than a less reputable show that only charges $250 per space. What you have to consider is the reputation of each show. Five hundred dollars may be a steal for a booth in a show that has been widely publicized, well attended, and highly successful for several years. Promoters who are attempting to build a new show, especially in a less densely populated area, will have to charge lower booth rents in order to entice dealers to their show. Compare booth rents and sizes at different shows, but give utmost consideration to both the show's reputation and the promoter's track record.

Figuring Your Total Costs and Break-Even Point

Before making your decision, add up your booth rent, your anticipated travel costs, including gasoline, motel rooms, meals, and babysitters, and any lost income while you are on the road or in your booth. That figure will come close to equaling your break-even point. Remember, though, it is not your total gross sales that have to surpass that figure, but your final net profit. If you were not able to make some good buys on your inventory, a road show is not going make them any better.

Are Your Ready to Do a Show?

How do you know if you are ready to do an antiques show?

First, you have to have the physical stamina.

Second, you have to have the inventory.

Once you have determined which types of shows you are going to do, you must begin assembling an inventory of antiques that your observations have indicated will sell well at each of them. Competition at antiques shows is keen, keener than ever before, one exhibitor claims, because these days there is less money to go around. What that means to you is that your merchandise has to be cleaner, sharper, brighter, more attractive, and more unique than not only anyone else's at the show, but in the area antiques shops as well. When a couple comes face to face with your cherry roll-top desk priced at $2,200, it not only is going to have to be better than any other cherry roll-top in the show, it is going to have to be so good, so desirable, and so unique that they will know if they walk away from it, they may never see another one like it again.

An early nineteenth-century pewter whale oil lamp. Such lamps were once both readily available and inexpensive, but the scarcity of whales by the middle of the century signaled the end of whale oil and, in 1854, the beginning of the kerosene-fueled lighting era.

Selecting the Items for Your First Show

Avoid the temptation to simply take to a show that which you happen to have accumulated. You should be selective in your buying, picking those pieces which will draw attention to your booth, which will complement one another, and which will transform a browser into a buyer.

Before a piece, whether it be an Art Nouveau lamp, a Harrison Fisher magazine cover, or a Victorian brass bed, is loaded into your van, you should see that it is room ready. Buyers at antiques shows are not looking for do-it-yourself projects. They are impulse buyers who will spot something, fall in love with it, justify buying it, and want to take it home and use it that day. Lamps should be cleaned, polished, and, if necessary, rewired; framed prints should have tight mitre joints, clean glass, and strong wire ready for a nail; brass beds should be polished, sealed, and ready to sleep in. Offer anything less and you'll haul it home with you.

During the months before a show assemble a collection of antiques that will suit the show or shows you plan to do. Even though you will have grand intentions of doing whatever restoration work is required by each piece soon after you purchase it, you will undoubtedly wake up one morning to realize that the show is two weeks away and only half of your inventory is ready to go.

You'll Need Physical Stamina

That is when the physical stamina part comes in.

Two weeks before the show you will start pushing your furniture and/or boxes into two separate areas. One is designated pieces ready to load. In the other—the larger of the two—sit those pieces awaiting your attention. After work and on weekends your friends and family can expect to find you gluing table tops, varnishing chests, cleaning glassware, and hunting for lamp shades. Depending on when your mode of transportation is available and how near or far your destination is, you will probably start loading the day before the show opens. As with every aspect of doing shows, the more qualified help you can muster, the better. But do not overlook the word "qualified." When it comes to antiques, especially moving antiques, bad help can be worse than no help at all. Pack your merchandise carefully, anticipating unplanned sudden stops, and shifting loads. Use strips of inner tube as giant rubber bands to hold dresser and desk drawers closed. You can never have enough packing blankets, but thin sheets of foam rubber also work well between pieces of furniture and are easy to store later.

There is no sense in investing several hundred or thousand dollars in a trailor, truck, or van until you have determined whether or not you are going to do more than just one or two area shows a year. Borrowing from a friend is both inexpensive and risky; truck rental companies are definitely more expensive but do not compare in the degree of guilt associated with a new ding or a small dent in the side of your brother-in-law's new van.

In either case, consult your insurance agent regarding protection for your antiques while in transit. Depending on your company, your homeowner's policy may not cover the antiques you have purchased for resale in the event someone empties your van while you are asleep inside a motel room.

Get to the Show Early

Allow ample time for both your travel and to set up your booth before the show opens, especially for your first few shows. After you have fine-tuned your packing, loading, unloading, and display skills as efficiently as an Indy 500 pit crew, you can perhaps save yourself an extra night on the road by not leaving home until the morning of the show, but inexperienced exhibitors need to arrive at the show that morning simply because it is going to take them twice as long to unpack and display their merchandise. Spend the extra night on the road if necessary to insure that you arrive rested and ready to set up your booth.

One of the crucial aspects of a successful show (assuming, of course, that you have carefully selected your show and matched your merchandise to it) that you should make a point to study at every show you attend is booth arrangement. Hopefully, you have bought and brought items that will lend themselves well to a booth setting, but simply dropping them in the closest convenient spot is not going to guarantee that anyone is going to even come into your booth, let alone buy something.

Once your merchandise has been safely transported from your vehicle to your booth, take a few minutes to calm down, catch your breath and study what will be your home for the next three days. Consider, as you mentally arrange your booth, the *visual impact* you want it to make on the people who will be passing by. Any booth, whether your merchandise is primarily composed of furniture, glassware, collectibles, or a combination of them all, has to be inviting. Make the visitor walking by *want* to come in your booth. Ooze appeal.

Attracting Visitors to Your Booth

How?

- *First, do not jam too much merchandise into your booth.* Graphic designers use what they call "white space" around key words, photographs, and artwork in an advertisement to draw our attention to it; do the same in your booth. Give each piece ample space for it to be noticed. Let people see three sides of a butternut dresser and not just the front. Make your booth look more like a well-designed display ad than an overcrowded page of classifieds.

- *Second, give the public a wide entrance to your booth.* Narrow openings dissuade people from coming into your area; easy access pulls them in to where you and your merchandise can talk with them. Many dealers like to place their larger pieces along the back of the booth, their medium-size pieces along the sides, and a low piece, such as a table or two low dressers back to back as an island in the middle. As a browser approaches the booth, she is naturally drawn in one end of the booth and can exit through the other.

- *Third, have at least one highly unusual, rare, or unique piece prominently displayed to attract attention.* Before you can talk to someone you first have to get them to stop by. You may not sell that signed Tiffany lamp with a price tag of $25,000 sitting on your island table, but if nearly everyone stops to admire it, you will get a chance to sell them something else in your booth.

- *Fourth, make your pieces look as if they were actually sitting in someone's home.* Assemble your brass bed; place a foam mattress on it with several

Three important early twentieth-century pottery marks: the initials "LCT" of Louis Comfort Tiffany (left); an early Artus Van Briggle (center); and the Grueby Faience Company (right). Works of all three are eagerly sought after by collectors.

quilts. Set an antique comb and brush set on your dresser, a vase of fresh flowers on your table, a piece of Rookwood pottery on an end table, and a live fern on your plant stand. Rather than make your customer imagine what each object might look like in her home, show her.

- *Fifth, provide plenty of light.* If you do not have any floor or table lamps to sell, bring small floodlights and numerous extension cords. Dark booths are unappealing and cast suspicion on what we both know are high quality pieces that deserve to be shown in their full splendor.

- *Sixth, make sure each item is priced and adequately described.* Most browsers will not ask the price of an unmarked item, thus never getting the opportunity to become buyers. And while a price tag of $275 will tell them how much your lamp is, a slightly large tag either typed or clearly printed "Art Nouveau Lamp, circa 1885, Brass Base, Raised Leaf Design, Original Patina" will bring the piece closer to a new home—especially if you are busy with another customer at the other end of the booth.

- *Finally, if your booth is going to look professional, then so should its exhibitor.* Bring a change of clothing for each session. Look refreshed and alert.

And smile. Greet people as they pause in your booth. Stand rather than sit. Keep food out of your booth. And do not ignore your customers. This is not the time nor the place to entertain friends or relatives. You are at work and if you expect to show a healthy profit for your efforts, then you had best thing about how you, as well as your booth, appear to your customers. If you want to be treated like a professional, dress and play the part of a professional.

Among the items that you should bring with you to a show are your business cards and a Want Book. Keep in mind that you are not here just to sell antiques this one time. Hopefully, you will continue in business for many years to come and may, in fact, be back at this same show next year. Perhaps the young couple could not afford your walnut dining room table this year, but if they leave with your business card and a positive impression, chances are that they may come back next year and if they do, make sure that they will remember you.

To make sure that you remember them and those customers who are looking for an item you do not have at this show, keep a notebook nearby in which you can record their names, addresses, and what each is looking for. Next year, a few weeks before the show, send each person in your Want Book a postcard, reminding them of the show and informing them that you will be there again. If it happens that you will be bringing a set of chairs they might be interested in, tell them so. And even if you sold them a major piece last year, send them a postcard this year. They may not be ready for another walnut sideboard, but their friends may be.

While nearly every family has or has had at one time a Hitchcock-style chair, a legitimate hand-decorated model (c. 1800–1820) would be a great find. Many of the chairs produced under Lambert Hitchcock's supervision will have his name plainly stenciled on the back of the seat. Even late reproductions of Hitchcock chairs can be of value and, although most were made from hardwoods such as maple or birch, none will be as valuable stripped down to the bare wood as they will be left in their original paint with the stenciling intact.

Utilize Services of a Part-Time Helper

As in any business, partners at an antiques show can be both a blessing a curse. If you are accustomed to working alone, do not feel that for that reason you cannot do a three or four day show. Certainly the rigor of doing a solo show will tax your stamina, but as any dealer will attest, "Nobody sells your antiques like you do." A partner will enable you to escape your booth, but when you are gone you can expect your sales to reflect your absence. Customers like to talk to the owner and no one knows your merchandise better than you. As well meaning as a partner may be, she cannot compare to you.

Better than a partner with whom you have to share space as well as decision-making power, then, is a part-time employee. When you need them most, during setup and tear-down and around meal times, you bring them in to help, but unlike a partner, they do not make the decisions. You do. Regardless of whether your part-time helper is a spouse, friend, offspring, or friend of an offspring, choose the person carefully and leave strict instructions during your absence. You need to have them "on-call" to help with deliveries, morning booth rearrangements, and running errands while you stick close to the booth to do what only you do best: sell antiques.

What to Do about Delivering Large Pieces of Furniture

Those dealers who do not sell large items rarely have to worry about delivery during an out-of-town show, but those who specialize in or carry large pieces of furniture must wrestle with the problems associated with deliveries in a strange city. No dealer enjoys making deliveries, but almost all come to expect it as a necessary part of the job. Walnut wardrobes simply do not walk or carry themselves out, nor do many urban dwellers drive pickup trucks and vans. Naturally, you do not want to immediately offer to deliver a piece when, in fact, the buyer may have planned to take responsibility for delivery himself. Save free delivery as a sales tool, something besides a reduction in price to sew up a sale.

Some dealers insist on a nominal delivery fee to cover their time and expenses, but most feel that if the piece commanded a premium price, then the hour of their time and $5 spent in gasoline after the show closes at night need not be tacked onto the receipt. What is more important is customer satisfaction, for long after the customer has forgotten how much they paid for it, that customer will still remember you and the personal service you provided. And that, more than bargain basement prices and self-service delivery, will lead to repeat sales.

What can be frustrating, though, are the logistics of a delivery. If you have a partner or on-call help available, they can either watch the booth or make the delivery for you. The advantage, of course, comes in being able to follow your customer home without getting lost. If you are working alone, however, your delivery will have to be scheduled after the show closes that day or in the morning before the next session opens. Be sure to get detailed directions, a map of the best route, and a description of the house or apartment building. If you are going alone make it clear that you will need and expect either their help or that of their friends or neighbors in bringing the piece in and setting it up.

Special Sales Techniques for Shows

Most dealers will insist that their sales techniques at shows do not differ from those they use either in shops or in private transactions, but the time restraints of a show do influence the way in which buyers approach show exhibitors. Everyone in the building knows that what you do not sell you will have to pack up and take back home with you Sunday night. Thus, you can expect many buyers, especially toward the end of the show, to test the firmness of your prices. Whether or not you become flexible in your pricing is a matter of personal preference and philosophy; what is important is sales. Sales without adequate profits, however—especially with show overhead to pay—will quickly drive you out of the business. Never feel pressured to sell at a loss or even at your break-even point at the end of a slow show; next week or next month will bring more customers, additional buyers, and anticipated profits. Your piece won't be worth any less next week, so if you have to take it home with you, do so before selling it for less than you know it is worth. Another day brings another buyer.

You have a major advantage at a paid or mall show in that the customers know that what they do not buy today they will, in all likelihood, never see again. They cannot come back next week, wait for their next paycheck, or hope that you will have a special promotion next month. That is why it will pay you—quite literally—to bring merchandise that both they and you know they would have to hunt for for weeks, months, or forever to find again. And for that reason most show dealers now accept major credit cards. Safer than personal checks, they cost you a small percentage, but give your customers instant financing—and you an instant sale.

With high quality merchandise, a visually exciting display, and a well-organized and highly attended show, slick sales techniques are never necessary. Honesty about your merchandise and sincere interest in your customer will go further in making a sale than a degree in human psychology. Telling a potential buyer all that you know about a piece and have done to it rather than waiting for him to either draw the information out or detect it will both bring that piece closer to him and you further into his trust. If the hardware is new, explain to him how you discovered the piece in a basement with the original hardware missing, but that your replacements are high quality reproductions, appropriately tarnished and consistent with the style and period of the piece.

As someone should have said, "Suspicion is more dangerous than the truth."

Sincerity can be feigned by only a practiced few, but if you set yourself in the proper frame of mind as you walk around your booth, when one of your browsers shows more than just a passing interest in one of your pieces, you can quickly learn enough about her and what she needs to create a sincere interest in her, not just as a potential buyer, but as a fellow human being as well.

Don't insult her with a brusque "I can do better than that" or "Make me an offer I can't refuse." Consider, instead, asking her a question or two about herself. "Just get to the show?" or "Has it stopped raining yet?" or "What do you collect?" avoids creating an antagonist versus protagonist scenario. Without prying or becoming too personal, find out what her special interest is, whether she is buying for herself or a gift for a friend, if she is decorating a house or a condominium. Instead of being adversaries, take it upon yourself to put the two of you on the same side with a common goal: finding for her exactly what she wants.

One experienced Midwestern show dealer contends, in fact, that eagerness to sell an antique at a show can actually work against you. "I've watched dealers try to sell a customer something the customer did not want," she explains, "then cut the price immediately. All it did was convince them that there must be something wrong with the piece. I talk with them, learn what they need, we discuss the price, I explain why it is priced where it is and then I leave them alone. For a while. In a few minutes I'll walk back over to see if they have any questions and hopefully we will conclude the sale, but if they don't want it, I'm not going to force it on them or belittle myself. Either way, I lose, because if they don't want it, they're going to come back, call back, or meet me at the door with the bad news when I deliver it."

Whether it has been a good show or not, as Sunday afternoon goes on, most dealers will begin to get fidgety thinking about the packing and the trip home. Unless you are anxious to antagonize the show promoter, the other exhibitors, and the remaining customers, regardless of how few they may be, do not give even the slightest indication you are leaving before the appointed closing time. Leave your packing boxes under the table or in the van and do not start counting your receipts. Five minutes before closing time you and your booth should appear as ready to sell as you did at five minutes after eleven that morning. If your contract states that the show closes at four on Sunday, then up until that time you should be concentrating on selling and not on getting ready to close up and go home. Failing to do so will only act as an insult to your fellow dealers and your promoter and will insure that you will not be invited back to do one of her shows again.

"Antiques shows are a marvelous opportunity for both buyers and sellers," one exhibitor commented. "They bring together more serious buyers, more serious sellers, and more quality antiques than either could get in a week of shop business."

When you are ready, then, pack it up and sell it!

14

Setting Up a Showroom

Perhaps the ultimate indication of a true commitment to the antiques business is the setting up of a showroom. Here you have gone all the way: you've stocked an inventory, rented or purchased a space, had a business phone installed, perhaps even taken on a partner or employee, and opened your doors to the public.

And it's a whole new world.

The first thing you had better realize before diving into deep water, however, is the commitment of both time and energy required to start and run a successful showroom. In the course of a single day, you will be concerned with simple house-keeping chores, dusting and cleaning, rearranging of mer-chandise, pricing, answering the phone, buying additional inventory, advertising, restoration problems, bookkeeping, in-surance, pickups and deliveries, and, we hope, talking with customers.

And while the telephone is a wonderful business tool, it cannot solve all of your problems. Errands must be run, deliveries must be made; but closing down your shop during regular business hours is not going to go far in establishing your reputation as a dependable proprietor. Your choice is simple: you either cut back on your hours, hire an employee, or plan on working after the front doors are locked.

Right along with the disadvantages of running an antiques shop, though, come the advantages. No longer must you make all of your sales in the evenings or on weekends. Whereas before you had to track down customers, now they come to you. People will respect you as an authority in your field and will seek out your advice. Families with antiques to sell will call you. And on a cold, miserable, rainy day when you are most discouraged, most lonely and most broke, a young couple will come in and, without any haggling, any hesitation or any help, buy the entire Duncan Phyfe dining room set that had threatened to become an albatross around your neck.

Two Basic Ingredients for Running a Full-Time Antiques Business

Starting a *full-time* antiques business—and, regardless of your hours or whether you choose to open a showroom in your basement, in a rented building, or in a shopping mall, that is exactly what it is going to be—requires two basic ingredients. The first is obvious—a solid knowledge of the antiques you are going to buy and sell. The second should be just as obvious but is often overlooked, primarily by the nearly 500 businesses that fold each week, and that is a firm grasp on the fundamentals of small business bookkeeping.

Bookkeeping.

Ugh.

Take it from someone who started with only a liberal arts degree in English literature and five years experience reading term papers, it isn't easy—or profitable—trying to start or run a business without a solid grasp of the fundamentals of bookkeeping. If terms such as "debit and credit," "accounts receivable," "accounts payable," "positive cash flow," "profit and loss statements," and "depreciation" are foreign to you, realize that they are the fundamental language in the world of bankers, insurance agents, accountants, Internal Revenue Service agents, and financial advisers. You can know more about Tiffany lamps than anyone else in the entire country, but if you cannot account for where your money is coming from and where and how much of it is going, then you and all of your knowledge are doomed to become just another depressing statistic.

You Don't Need an MBA to Run an Antiques Shop—but You Must Understand Business Fundamentals

You don't, however, need an MBA from Harvard to run an antiques shop. You don't even need a college degree. What you do need to handle the volume of business and additional overhead associated with an antiques shop is either successful business or bookkeeping experience or a simple accounting and/or business class from either the Small Business Administration or your local community college. These courses get right to the heart of the matter; short on theory, long on nuts-and-bolts, they can show you how to keep from becoming one of those depressing failure statistics. With their help you will quickly come to grips with the most commonly used accounting terms and business techniques and you will soon be able to balance a ledger sheet and compute payroll deductions as easily as mend a wobbly chair. Even if you plan to hire the services of a professional bookkeeper or have a partner or employee who has accounting experience, you are going to need a knowledge of the fundamentals. You must be able to understand what they are telling you, what a profit-and-loss statement means to you, what the right questions are to ask, and, most important, what the right decisions to make are.

Once you have decided that you have the two basic ingredients—a knowledge of the type of antiques you plan to handle and a grasp of the fundamentals of business—you will have even more decisions to make, but isn't that one

reason why you wanted to go into business for yourself anyway—to make your own decisions? And to profit by them?

A SHOP IN YOUR HOME

The next crucial decision regards a location for your business. You may have already decided that you are going to
run your antiques business from your home, but to be safe
you should consider all of your options before making the
decision final. Home businesses can be an excellent way to
start, especially if you have extra space that is currently
unused. If you would have to sleep four in a room or park
your car in the street, however, think twice before clearing
everyone and everything out. A business in the home is a
definite invasion of privacy and if your entire household is
not ready to sacrifice some of their privacy, then severe
problems are going to develop. It won't be the inconveni-
ence of tearing out a wall in the basement or moving in
twenty-eight boxes of antiques from the garage that will
wreak havoc on an unsuspecting family. What will disturb
you is the insensitivity of strangers tromping in at all hours,
openly criticizing everything from your merchandise to your
family cat to the color of your carpeting, poking their noses
in areas clearly marked "Private" and, in short, treating
your home as if it were a public park.

Check Your Local Laws Concerning a
Home Business

If privacy will not become an issue, if all of your family
has grown and left the nest, or half of the garage has sat
empty for three years, then starting an antiques business in
your home can be an effective means of keeping both overhead and start-up costs down. You will need to check on
your local zoning ordinances to ensure that your project does

not come to a screeching halt before it even opens when your neighbors learn that you are planning to open an antiques shop in your basement. Make sure that you will be able to comply with all parking, zoning, and sign ordinances before you move the first box or drive the first nail or you may invest several hundred dollars in start-up costs but never get the chance to start.

Legal obstacles are not the only ones that have to be hurdled when deciding where to open your antiques shop. Naturally, your own building or property will generally be the least expensive, but many antiques collectors and casual buyers are hesitant to drive twenty blocks let alone twenty miles off the main highway to check out a small shop in the garage of a private residence. Be realistic about both the number of people who will be able to find your shop and how many will just happen to drop in, for if you live on a quiet street or a road that requires a navigator's compass and a Boy Scout to find, your merchandise, regardless of how reasonable its prices and high its quality, may never have a fair chance to sell.

RENTING A SHOWROOM LOCATION

If you and your family decide that your home situation is not suited for an antiques shop or showroom, then you will have to look elsewhere. Assuming for the moment that you do not have the means or the desire to purchase a commercial property, renting will be your most realistic option. Begin by checking with local realtors and watching the commercial property listings in the classified section of the newspaper to find what's available. You will discover that the two main influences on rent are size and location, and will probably come to the conclusion that you will have to make some compromises in order to stay within your budget.

How Many Square Feet Will You Need?

First, to get an idea of how many square feet you will need, start by measuring each of the rooms in your house and visualizing which combination of rooms would be sufficient both for your present inventory and near-future expansion. Total the square footage of those rooms and you will have an idea how large or small an area you will want for your showroom. Size is relative to you and your antiques, for while one dealer may see twelve hundred square feet of showroom space as more than she could ever need, another might not even consider it.

Size alone will not determine the rent of a building, for a twelve hundred square foot area in a busy shopping mall might cost more than $1,000 a month, while a room the same size just two blocks away on a side street might rent for only $300. Be prepared to compromise in what you want and what you feel you can afford. The temptation of a larger space in a less desirable location cannot compare with a smaller space in a better location. Keep in mind that to stay in business you have to sell antiques, not just store them; you need people—browsers, buyers, dealers, collectors—and while you may think you have built a better mousetrap, that does not mean enough people are going to beat a path to your door soon enough to keep you in business.

The Benefits of Locating Close to an Established Shop

Most dealers will agree that the best thing that can happen to an antiques shop is to have another one open next door. Competition between shops has never been as large a problem as has been getting customers inside the door in the first place. Comparison shopping between antiques shops is made difficult by the simple fact that rarely will you find two identical pieces ready for easy comparison. What happens more often is that a greater number of customers will drive a little

A classic collector's showpiece: a country Chippendale highboy (c. 1755–1810). Generally five tiers of drawers are found in the upper section, three in the lower. Feet will range from claw-and-ball to simply a heavy pad. Cherry, walnut, and maple were common woods used during this period; drawer sides and bottoms were generally made from the softer and less expensive pine and poplar.

farther if they know that there are two shops in the same immediate vicinity and a great deal farther if they know that there are three or more for them to browse through.

What you may want to do is to mark on a map the location of all of the antiques shops in your area. Visit each one and determine which appear to be doing well and which are struggling. If you find one or, better yet, a number of prospering shops in one area, investigate the rental possibilities nearby. You may be able to step into a steady traffic flow if you can locate close to an established shop with a regular clientele and a large advertising budget. And once you settle details and get to know your neighbors, the two of you can combine forces by planning joint promotions, splitting advertising costs, getting more for your advertising dollar, and attracting greater numbers of customers than a single shop ever could.

Be Careful to Understand All the Terms of Your Lease

Working out the terms of a lease does not have to be difficult and won't be if you are in close and clear communication with your landlord. Make sure the building is going to accommodate all of your needs without major renovation or your start-up costs may be too large for the business to overcome. Make sure that any changes and improvements are cleared with the landlord before they are begun and also determine which of you is going to pay for them. Many times the owner will furnish the materials if the tenant provides the labor. Whatever the terms, work everything out and have it in writing before the lease is signed.

If you plan to supplement your sales income with another source (see Related Services section), or perhaps if you plan to do your own refinishing on the premises, check to see that the use and storage of flammables will not violate your lease agreement. Fumes will have to be vented and not into your neighbor's air-conditioning unit, so make sure that everyone is perfectly clear as to what you intend to do and what will be required for you to do it.

JOINING AN ANTIQUES MALL

Although it is a concept that dates back centuries, not until recently has the idea of an antiques mall spread across the country. In space conscious cities such as New York, dealers began combining inventories and sharing costs years ago, but now even in areas where rents are low and spaces abundant, antiques dealers are joining forces to battle long hours, climbing utilities rates, and rising overhead.

For the part-time dealer who feels the urge to do more than sell privately or set up at antiques shows, the antiques mall is a natural step. Unlike an individually owned shop, an antiques mall will provide you with the guidance of experienced dealers, a better location than you most likely could have afforded on your own, a low ratio of working hours versus shop hours, and freedom from worry about sales taxes (collected and paid by mall management), utilities, building maintenance, snow removal, parking problems, zoning ordinances, sign regulations, and a host of other concerns. In short, it will enable you to expand your operation, increase your income, and yet still not endanger your present job.

The Mall Concept

The mall concept is actually quite simple. First, it takes a building, which is owned or rented by the mall management. The mall management usually divides the showroom area into individual booths, either through physical dividers or imaginary walls visible only on a floorplan. The exhibitors rent the booths from the mall management and, in doing so, agree to follow a set of established guidelines regarding merchandise, hours, sales help, promotions, and shop policies.

In addition to their monthly rent, the management often retains a small percentage of each sale. In exchange for booth rent and the sales commission, the mall management generally takes total responsibility for building maintenance, utilities, promotions, cleaning, and often sales help and advertising costs.

As a mall exhibitor you rent a space much as you do in an antiques show, only you don't pack up on Sunday night. Every item is carefully tagged and, depending on mall policy, often coded if you wish to indicate to the management, the sales clerk, or another exhibitor that a lower price can be negotiated. In some malls the exhibitors take turns working the showroom; in others the management provides the sales help— and in some the exhibitor has that option, with the amount of the sales commission reflecting whether or not they wish to have the mall management provide the sales staff. If you wish to work two days a month in the mall, for instance, the commission paid to the management on each of your sales might only be 5 percent; if, on the other hand, you do not have the time to work and must rely on them to provide qualified sales help, their sales commission might be 10 percent or more of each of your sales.

Naturally, the more people you have involved in an operation of this sort, the more potential you have for problems. The policies, attitudes, and personalities of the people responsible for the mall management will have the greatest effect on these potential problems, but the personalities of the individual exhibitors will come into play as well. The most obvious problem—that of the exhibitor in charge that day trying to sell only his or her merchandise to every customer who comes in and making little or no attempt to point out the fine points of the antiques of the other exhibitors— is one that the management can detect through daily sales receipts and then correct. They—and you—can avoid that problem, however, by taking care not to have too much duplication in merchandise. Ten exhibitors all trying to sell round oak tables is going to create tension, but if one exhibitor emphasizes pine primitives, another books, one cut glass, another advertising art, one pottery and yet another English furniture, the problem can easily be defused. The small amount of overlapping that will occasionally occur should not be bothersome, for if a couple comes in looking for a Shaker rocker, the salesperson working that particular day would have a difficult time convincing them that they should buy her cut-glass cruet set instead.

Points to Consider in Choosing an Antiques Mall

Choosing the antiques mall that is right for you will take some time and careful consideration. No two malls are alike and thus it is imperative that you find the one that is best

Setting Up a Showroom

Three important art pottery marks to watch for: left, Rockwood (1901); center, Cambridge (circa 1907); and right, Roseville (1914–1930). Fortunately for both buyers and sellers of art pottery, extensive illustrated price guides are available to help us determine the supply, demand, and value of the thousands of designs produced by just these three firms.

suited to you, your merchandise, and your goals. In your selection process be sure to consider the following:

- *Location:* While at one time dedicated antiquers would rise to the challenge of trekking across miles of uncharted country roads in search of that faded ''Antiques'' sign hung precariously on a sagging barbed wire fence, the days of the Ma and Pop back porch operation are gone. Our customers are too busy and our competition too stiff for us to fall prey to the lure of an inexpensive building or a seldom traveled road. Many of today's antiquers were raised in shopping malls and, while some may occasionally get the urge to take a Sunday drive to pick up a Red Wing crock or another rug beater for the family room wall, when the time comes to do some serious buying—whether stereo equipment, a new tennis racquet, a three-piece suit, or a round oak table—they want the convenience of a shop that is easy to find, fast to get to, and provides safe and adequate parking.

  When analyzing an antiques mall location, ask yourself the following questions:

  (1) Is it easy to find?
  (2) How many cars drive by each day?
  (3) How much walk-in traffic does it generate?
  (4) How advantageous are its neighboring

businesses in attracting customers to the area?

(5) Is the neighborhood in an economic rise or decline?

(6) Does it provide adjacent parking?

(7) Is it centrally located in the area your customers will be coming from?

You can change your merchandise, you can rearrange your booth, you can train yourself to be the best salesperson in town, but you cannot easily change the location of the building you are in, so do not forget to see where your tree stands in relationship to the rest of the forest.

- *Building:* Antiques shops have been set up in former gas stations, opera houses, mortuaries, railroad depots, saloons, grocery stores, libraries, boarding houses, even, in at least one instance, a former bordello, providing evidence for the theory that location is more important than the type of building itself. Nevertheless, a successful antiques mall will require certain elements that, regardless of the structure, will be crucial to you as a potential exhibitor. Among the things you should look for in the building are:

  (1) Easy accessibility for your customers;
  (2) Convenient loading area;
  (3) More than just adequate lighting;
  (4) Well-maintained interior walls and ceiling;
  (5) Adequate temperature control;
  (6) Flexible display options;
  (7) Clearly defined exhibitor areas;
  (8) Storage for layaway items.

- *Exhibitors:* While good fences may make good neighbors, it takes more than just a clearly defined boundary to insure that you and your neighbors are compatible—and the same goes for your merchandise as well!

Note what types of antiques are being offered by the exhibitors in any mall you are considering and find out what is actually selling and what has just been sitting. Talk to the exhibitors. Are they pleased with both traffic and sales? What do they think about the location, the building, and the management? How long has each been in the mall? Who is planning to leave and why? What changes would they like to see made? And who has left and why?

Get a feel for the attitudes of the exhibitors. The world is made up of both positive and negative people and it is neither pleasant nor profitable to share a mall with the type of persons who are determined to find a dark lining in every silver cloud.

What type of merchandise is prevalent? If the mall is basically a permanent flea market selling everything from used clothes to boxes of moldy books, then your collection of Meissen is going to feel both out of place and out of price. If you need a class act with clean, room-ready, legitimate antiques, then keep searching. You may have to travel fifty miles, but if that is where the right mall, the right exhibitors, the right merchandise, and the right buyers are, then that is where you should be.

- *Management:* Despite the importance of the building, its location, and its exhibitors, the greatest single influence on the success of your business and that of the mall will be the policies and personalities of the mall management. If you are considering joining a new mall, what experience does the management have that is going to aid them in handling a dozen or more dealers? What other malls are they

modeling their policy after? How successful are
they? Are they willing to accept responsibility for
the problems that are going to arrive along with
their dealers and customers?

Study carefully each mall policy book and consider its impact on you. If you are accustomed to
selling furniture "in the rough" to do-it-yourself
refinishers, a strict "room ready" criterion applied to all furniture will either mean that you are
going to have to refinish several of your pieces or
restock your inventory. If the mall management
expects you to work the showroom one day per
week, yet your regular job is from eight until five
Monday through Friday, you had better discuss
with your family the effect your absence on either
Saturday or Sunday projects and outings is going
to have.

Established malls will be easier to evaluate,
simply because you can talk with the exhibitors
to discover what problems have persisted regarding the mall management. Hopefully, by the time
you arrive on the scene the mall policy statement
will have been fine-tuned to cover all potential
problems, a series of successful promotions will
have been set up, and the management will have
cultivated an exciting, innovative family of exhibitors.

You Will Need Policies on Hours, Display, and Security

Regardless of whether you choose to open a showroom in
your home, a rented building, or an antiques mall, you will
have several decisions to make regarding hours, policies, display, and security for your business. In a mall environment
many of these decisions will already have been made, such as
policies regarding layaways, returns, hours, and methods of

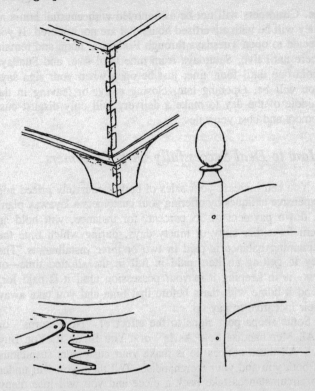

Three examples of Shaker craftsmanship: open dovetail joints on a blanket chest; a tapered finial and pegged joints on a chair post; and overlapping end fingers, riveted for extra strength, on an oval box. Irregular dovetails are an indication of hand craftsmanship, as are lathe-turned finials, rungs, and spindles. The Shakers manufactured and sold furniture from 1868 into the twentieth century, always maintaining high standards of craftsmanship and materials.

payment, but if you are going to be a sole proprietor in a solo setting, then you will need to write your own policy handbook.

Setting your hours of business may be the most difficult aspect of writing your policy, but keeping them should not be. Customers will not be as annoyed with unusual hours as they will be with advertised hours that are not honored. If you decide to open Tuesdays through Fridays at noon and remain there until five, Saturdays from nine until five, and Sundays from one until four, fine; just be open when your sign says you will be. Opening late, closing early, or leaving in the middle of the day to make a delivery will only disgust customers and cost you sales.

How to Deal Successfully with Customers

You can increase your sales of both moderately priced and expensive antiques by offering your customers a layaway plan. A down payment of 25 percent, for instance, will hold an item for either sixty or ninety days, during which time the remaining balance is paid in two or three installments. The key to getting an item paid in full in the allotted time—or less—is in keeping it in your possession until it is paid for. Send it home with them before that time and you take away their incentive to pay up.

Some shops post signs to the effect of "No Returns" or "All Merchandise Sold As Is" or "You Break It, You Buy It." All these notices do is make your customers suspicious of both you and your merchandise. Tell them you will under no circumstances take back a piece and you will lose many indecisive buyers; let a lady pay for and take a small walnut table home to see if it will match her buffet with the understanding that if it does not, she can return it the next day and you will, more often than not, clinch a sale. Telling your customers everything is sold "As Is" does nothing more than say to them, "There is something wrong with the piece you are interested in, but you had better find it before you buy it."

Build trust, not suspicion. Treat each customer, each antique, and each situation as unique. Work with your customers rather than against them, and they and their friends will be your patrons for years to come.

Arranging Your Display

There is nothing more fun, yet more frustrating, in setting up a showroom than arranging your display. Every dealer, be he a showroom or show exhibitor, has his own philosophy on how antiques should be best arranged for fastest sales. You should make it a point to study different techniques in different shops not just while you are setting up your first showroom, but any time you get the opportunity. The most important aspect of a display comes not in finding the one arrangement that will always work, but in changing your display often. Let a piece sit in the same spot for more than three or four weeks and it becomes stale. If a customer returns to find almost everything as she left it three weeks earlier, you run the risk of losing her just because nothing looks new and exciting. Every veteran dealer has had it happen: a piece can sit in one spot for a year, but move it across the room, put it in a different light with different accessories around it and a customer who has been in three times in the past three months will ask, "Why, Tom, when did this lovely cupboard come in?"

Try Recreating a Home Setting

One of the best techniques for a display is borrowed from show exhibitors who make an attempt to recreate a home setting with their furniture and accessories. If you want to sell a bed, be able to set up a bed, not just lean the headboard up against a wall. If you want to sell a table with leaves, put the leaves in, cover it with a four-piece place setting of Depression glass (it, too, will sell better on a table than stacked in a cupboard), and top it off with a floral arrangement in the center.

Most of your regular customers are going to be too busy and many too well dressed to want to dig through boxes of glassware or rooms packed with dusty furniture. If it is worth selling, it is worth displaying in a clean and well-lit environment. Successful retail merchants in nonantique fields make sure their merchandise is easy to view, free of dust, brightly lit and attractive to look at. Borrow some of their techniques and you will borrow some of their success as well.

Consider a Theme Arrangement of Merchandise

If not all of your merchandise lends itself well to home settings, consider arranging it by theme. Set aside one corner, for instance, for general store merchandise, a collection of old weather vanes, a symphony of antique musical instruments, or a convention of advertising memorabilia. Publicize a special each month for your theme corner. By deciding several months in advance what each theme is going to be, you can watch for particular items on your buying excursions that will help fill out your corner when their time rolls around.

Use Wall and Ceiling Space for Exhibits

Two of the most underused spots in almost any antiques shop are the walls and ceilings. Even if you are not in a room or space too small for your inventory, you can excite the eye of your customer with a visual splash of the unexpected. Hang baskets, stained glass windows, or weather vanes from the ceiling; use the walls for advertising posters, type trays, and other collectibles. Break the monotony of a floor-level display with color from above. A kiddie car from the early twenties sitting on our showroom floor attracted little attention until we hung it with thin wire from our beamed ceiling. As one customer commented, ''I felt like I was in the Smithsonian looking up at the planes suspended from the ceiling.'' It was up only two days before it sold.

How to Avoid Breakage and Shoplifting

Two unfortunate side effects of a showroom business are breakage and shoplifting, but in both cases a well-designed display can prevent them. Breakable items should never be placed near the edge of a piece of furniture or next to a traffic lane where a coat, umbrella, or small child can reach them. Display them, instead, in glass cases or inside glass-doored cupboards. Give your customers visual encouragement to roam about your shop without the fear of knocking something over.

What do you do in the event something does get broken? If you are at fault, if you displayed a fragile item in such a way that it is accidentally broken, then you must apologize to the customer and absorb the entire loss. If, however, the customer is careless or, even more so, if the customer permits an unruly child to almost purposely break something which you had, under normal circumstances, safely displayed, then it would not be improper for you to accept payment for the item. Such would be the case if you, upon request, removed an item from a locked case or high shelf, handed it to the customer and then she, either through carelessness or negligence, dropped or broke it. Ideally, she would offer to pay for it, but if she does not, then you may have to tactfully point out that she was solely responsible for the damage to the piece. Legally, you don't have a leg to stand on, but then neither does your Hummel figurine, and you might as well try to collect for it.

Shoplifting can be a problem, but more often than not, it is the carelessness of the dealer rather than the deftness of the customer that leads to the crime. Temptation is a wicked weapon and when you leave small, valuable items sitting next to a blind exit, you are, in effect, asking someone who came in not to steal, but to browse, to take something with them. One dealer had never had a shoplifting incident until the day she left a neatly folded quilt sitting on a table next to the front door so that she would not forget to drop it off at a buyer's home that evening. Needless to say, all that she dropped off was the $400 the customer had left earlier that day for the quilt.

You can avoid encouraging customers to become shoplifters by using several techniques. One is to greet each customer as he or she comes in the shop and to engage them in some conversation. Ask about the weather, their particular area of interest, even the local football team; the idea is to let them know that you are aware of their presence. Ignore them and you give the impression you neither know nor care what they are doing.

Following customers throughout your shop is both irritating and rude. If you arrange your showroom in such a way that large, obstructing pieces are along the walls and not out in the middle forming blind spots next to a display of smaller items, then you can watch all of your customers from any part of your shop without appearing to be Big Brother. Carefully hung mirrors (antique ones, of course) can enable you to look around corners or watch distant exits; and brightly lit displays rather than dim corners seem to dissuade potential pickers.

Roam about casually, but be aware of everyone who is in your shop, especially those who come in pairs. If one asks you to step outside to look at something in their van, request that they bring it in instead. Leaving your shop unattended, even for just a few minutes, can cost you several hundred dollars. Delay using the restroom or stepping across the street for a cup of coffee until such times when you can lock the front door or have a friend or partner watch the showroom. And if business is so good that on Saturdays you might have ten or more people in the shop at one time, then by all means hire extra help. The cost of their labor will be quickly paid for by additional sales and saved merchandise.

Discouraging Break-ins

Finally, though we hate to think about it, every shopowner must realize that by going public you are announcing to a less desirable element of society that you have assembled under one roof a collection of very valuable antiques. And unlike automobiles or even television sets, thieves know that antiques are both easy to sell without raising suspicion and difficult to trace. Again, however, careful consideration of the problem and a few extra measures can prevent a curious prowler from becoming a costly felon.

Make sure doors have strong locks, including drop bars and deadbolts. Dusk-to-dawn lights over doors will make someone think twice about picking a lock or unpinning a hinge. If your door enters onto a public hallway, make sure it is not just a common hollow-core variety door. One swift kick from a thief is all it takes to punch a hole next to the knob. If replacing the door with a solid one would prove to be too expensive, consider screwing a sheet of oak plywood to the inside of the door. All windows should have secure locks and those facing alleys or dark streets should have bars on them. As most dealers will agree, your money is better invested in a sound security system than a security sound system. Rather than announcing his arrival, consider not sending a potential thief an open invitation instead.

III

RELATED SERVICES

Introduction

Most people with only a casual interest in antiques are aware that numerous opportunities await those who are anxious to either buy or sell antiques and collectibles. Few realize, however, the vast number of related services that can be operated out of the home on a part-time basis. Seldom do any require expensive equipment and most can be started with only minimal financial investment. The idea, naturally, is to take an existing interest and skill and find an antiques-related service wherein the two can be directed toward intrinsic and monetary rewards.

One danger, however, is the temptation to solicit work before being both properly trained for the technical element of the service and properly prepared for its business aspects. Failure to recognize a lack of training may cause permanent damage to an antique; refusal to admit to a lack of preparedness in financial matters may lead to business failure on the part of the individual. Neither is a desirable goal.

Before you embark on even a part-time service-related career it is imperative that you follow these six basic steps:

(1) Research the subject.
(2) Observe specialists at their work.
(3) Practice on undistinguished pieces.
(4) Practice on personal pieces.

269

(5) Service on standard customer pieces.

(6) Service on challenging customer pieces.

Rates for various services vary from state to state and often from year to year, so you must research and establish guidelines on an individual basis. Generally all that is required are a few phone calls and conversations with persons currently offering the particular service that interests you.

The future, it has often been noted, will find us becoming more and more a service-oriented society rather than a production-oriented one. Nowhere else can you find a better example than in the field of antiques, where antiques dealers, collectors, auctioneers, and hobbyists are crying out for reliable, competent craftspersons to care for, repair, and restore their antiques.

Are you ready to help fill that need?

Whether it is called a dome-top, a curved-top, or a camel-back trunk (c. 1900), the combination of firmly riveted oak slats over tin-covered wood has accounted for the large number of surviving examples. Their availability, low cost, and practicality inspire collectors not only to purchase these trunks, but to invest in their repair and restoration as well. Wood rot and rust, however, are two enemies of trunks that can require extensive, expensive, and sometimes impractical restoration. Never buy a trunk without first turning it over to inspect the bottom.

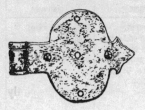

Hand-forged hinges such as the one pictured here will be found on early nineteenth-century case pieces. They will often need repair or, on some occasions, a matched mate. If an original piece of hardware or even a section of hardware is replaced, the original must be tagged, identified, and kept with the antique for future verification.

Many late nineteenth-century ceiling lamps such as the one illustrated here originally burned kerosene, and were either switched to electricity or may be brought to you by someone wanting them converted. Parts, including shades, are now readily available through specialty companies.

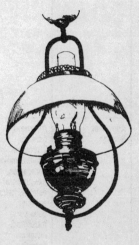

Like the furniture of the parallel Golden Oak era, wicker must be carefully inspected to distinguish between the lower and higher quality pieces. This rolled arm and curved back model (c. 1885) featured a caned seat and reinforced base structure. Heavy strands, tight weaves, intricate patterns, a natural finish, and a strong, durable framework are the ingredients of a valuable piece of furniture.

Service	Clientele	Training	Equipment
Advertising Agent	Antiques dealers, refinishing shops, auctioneers, related service occupations.	Background in advertising and sales; knowledge of antiques; experience in ad layout, design, and typography essential.	Desk, file cabinet, telephone; extra bedroom or corner of large room.
Appraisal Service	Attorneys, bankers, insurance agents, moving companies, executors of estates, heirs, antiques collectors, museums, historical societies.	Classes in various aspects of antiques; extensive reading and research; experience buying and selling, attendance at shows and auctions; interviews, observations, and experience with veteran appraisers.	Desk, typewriter, file cabinet, bookcases, reference books, and price guides; spare bedroom or corner of large family room.

Advertising	Organizations	Publications	Comments
Business cards, references, samples of previous work and potential ads for new client; ad in antiques publications.	American Advertising Federation 1400 K Street NW, Suite 1000 Washington, DC 20005	*Advertising Age* Crain Communications 740 North Rush Street Chicago, IL 60611 *Sales and Marketing Management* 633 3rd Avenue New York, NY 10017	Best suited for urban areas where businesses are accustomed to working with advertising agencies. Combination of previous experience in advertising and knowledge of antiques will distinguish you from other ad agents. Consider publishing a giveaway brochure of antiques shops, a restaurant placemat with listings of antiques shops, or a free directory of area antiques shops and related services—each with various sizes of paid ads and a map. Start-up costs: under $500.
Telephone book, area antiques brochures and directories, local antiques publications, direct mail to persons on clientele listing.	American Society of Appraisers PO Box 17625 Washington, DC 20041 Antique Appraisal Association of America 11361 Garden Grove Boulevard Garden Grove, CA 92643 Appraisers Association of America 60 East 42nd Street New York, NY 10017 Mid-American Antique Appraisers Association PO Box 981 C.S.S. Springfield, MO 65803	Materials and periodicals distributed by organizations listed.	Every appraiser is dependent on his/her reputation for the amount of work received. Be prompt, fair, and honest. Avoid conflict of interest charges; do not use an appraisal service as a means of buying antiques. Meticulous research and careful observation are basic tools of the trade. The reward for excellent work: valuable references, flexible hours, and a steady income. Start-up costs: under $500.

Service	Clientele	Training	Equipment
Chair Caning and Seat Weaving	Antiques dealers, refinishing shops, auctioneers, general public.	Classes, private instruction from experienced caner; can be self-taught from books and pamphlets. Buy inexpensive chairs at auctions to practice on.	Common household tools (knife, plastic bucket, pliers, awl); pegs and wedges from supply companies; small room or area for storage of tools, materials, and chairs.
China, Glass, and Porcelain Repair	Antiques dealers, advanced collectors, area museums and historical societies, general public.	Lengthy apprenticeship program and/or degree from accredited institution; background in art and/or ceramics beneficial.	Unique combination of common, speciality, and improvised tools; separate room with color-balanced lighting, heat and humidity control, two or three workbenches and storage space. Highly technical materials and tools available from companies such as Talas, Division of Technical Library Services, Inc., 130 Fifth Avenue, New York, NY 10003.

Advertising	Organizations	Publications	Comments
Telephone book, call on and send letters to antiques dealers, refinishing shops, and auctioneers. Provide example of work. Yellow Pages ad for increased number of customers. Distribute business cards at shops and shows.	American Antiques and Crafts Society Fame Avenue Hanover, PA 17331	Many produced and distributed by national firms that supply caning tools and materials: Cane and Basket Supply Co. 1238 South Cochran Avenue Los Angeles, CA 90019 The H. H. Perkins Co. 10 South Bradley Road Woodbridge, CT 06525 Connecticut Cane and Reed Company PO Box 1276 Manchester, CT 06040	Rates will be competitive among area caners and seat weavers. Antiques dealers and refinishing shops can be wooed with discounts and speedy completion times. Less profit per chair, but more chairs with less advertising. Extra income: simple re-gluing and repairs on chairs brought in, teaching classes for community education programs, or selling caning supplies to do-it-yourselfers. Start-up costs: under $500.
Antiques dealers and advanced collectors rely on personal references; general public turns to Yellow Pages advertising and antiques publications. Distribute cards and display work at rented booth in area antiques shows.	American Institute for Conservation 1522 K Street NW, #804 Washington, DC 20005 Art and Historical Glass Foundation PO Box 7413 Toledo, OH 43615	Many produced and distributed by: American Institute for Conservation of Historical and Artistic Works 3545 Williamsburg Lane NW Washington, DC 20008	Before enrolling in a lengthy degree or apprenticeship program, it would be advisable to spend a few days observing an established china, glass, and porcelain restoration expert. The commitment necessary to prepare oneself for such a career dictates a clear understanding of the training required before your services can be offered to the public. The eventual rewards, both financially and personally, are excellent incentives, but the field is not one which can be entered half-heartedly. Start-up costs: $500–$1,500.

Service	Clientele	Training	Equipment
Clock and Watch Repair	General public, jewelry stores, antiques dealers, restoration shops.	Lengthy apprenticeship or classroom program; limited number of books available for self-teaching; knowledge and experience of an experienced repairperson and teacher needed.	Small space, but large number of technical tools (watchmaker's bench, lathe, light, punches, pliers) for both repairing and fabricating wood and metal parts.
Doll Restoration	Antiques dealers, doll collectors, general public.	Apprenticeship program; classes, if available; numerous illustrated books and pamphlets obtainable; self-taught method too slow and too risky.	Well-lit workbenches; ordinary tools, but wide variety of specialized materials required (molds, glues, glazes); small room.
Furniture Repair and Restoration	Antiques dealers, general public, restaurants, businesses, fraternities, historical	Classes, apprenticeship program, personal experience; numerous books, magazine articles, and booklets available. Learn and	Wide variety of woodworking and specialty tools and materials (clamps, drills, fillers, finishes); several workbenches; well-ventilated areas

Advertising	Organizations	Publications	Comments
Yellow Pages advertising, plus ads in area antiques publications; business cards left at antiques and restoration shops and jewelry stores.	National Association of Watch and Clock Collectors, Inc. 514 Poplar Street PO Box 33 Columbia, PA 17512 International Wristwatch and Cigarette Lighter Club 832 Lexington Ave. New York, NY 10021	*Clockwise* magazine 1236 East Main Street Ventura, CA 93001 (Most organizations also have regular publications.)	If you have either a background or an interest in clocks and watches, steady work awaits you in this field. Few dealers or refinishers attempt even a simple cleaning of antique clocks and watches. Additional income can be generated through the refinishing and restoration of wooden clock cases. Potentially valuable timepieces needing only to be cleaned sell far below their actual value at auctions and in shops simply because buyers are frightened away by clocks that do not work. Start-up costs: $500–$1,500.
Reach area customers through ads in antiques publications, business cards distributed through antiques shops; reach regional or national clientele through trade publications.	United Federation of Doll Clubs Main Street Parkville, MO 64152 International Doll Makers' Association 3364 Pine Creek Drive San Jose, CA 95132	*Bambini* magazine PO Box 33 Highland, IL 62249 *Yesteryears Museum News* Main and River Streets Sandwich, MA 02563 *The Dollmaker* magazine PO Box 247 Washington, NJ 07882	Just as important as learning the technical aspects of doll restoration is the need to know the history behind each doll. Proper restoration is based on knowledge of original materials and techniques. Study the history of doll making along with the technical aspects. As with all service fields, success is directly related to reputation. Start-up costs: under $500.
Yellow Pages, area newspapers, flyers, business cards, playbills, antiques directories.	Association for Preservation Techniques Box 2487 Station D Ottawa, Ontario, Canada	*Fine Woodworking* magazine Taunton Press, Inc. PO Box 355 Newtown, CT 06470	Many amateur refinishers have seen their hobby grow into a full-time business. With fewer do-it-yourselfers and a dramatic increase in the value of antiques,

Service	Clientele	Training	Equipment
Furniture Repair and Restoration (continued)	societies, museums.	experiment on inexpensive furniture.	for stripping and finishing furniture; van or truck for deliveries.
Hardware Repair and Replacement	Antiques dealers, professional and amateur refinishers, auctioneers.	Knowledge of furniture styles and appropriate hardware. Background in casting or metalwork for matching or repair service.	Sales of reproduction hardware require display boards; casting and repair equipment too costly to purchase for these services only; should be offered only if equipment already available.
Lampshade Reproduction	antiques dealers, lamp collectors.	Classes or instruction, if available; self-taught through study of original lampshades; experience in hand and machine sewing.	Sewing machine, hand sewing supplies, worktables in small room.

Advertising	Organizations	Publications	Comments
	(offers numerous publications).		demand for competent restoration services is greater than ever before. Thorough estimates and dependable deadlines, along with quality work, will assure you of continued success. Start-up costs: $1,500–$4,500.
Antiques publications; direct contact with area antiques dealers and refinishing shops; sample display boards at antiques shows and shops.	Association for Preservation Techniques Box 2487 Station D Ottawa, Ontario, Canada Art and Antique Dealers League of America 353 East 53rd Street #2G New York, NY 10022	Send for catalogues of hardware companies advertising in antiques publications: Horton Brasses PO Box 95 Nooks Hill Road Cromwell, CT 06416 18th Century Hardware Co., Inc. 131 East 3rd Street Derry, PA 15627	Unless you purchase large quantities of reproduction hardware from other companies, assemble your own catalogue, and do a regional or national mailing and advertising campaign, this will not become a large volume business. Work in conjunction with established antiques shop or restoration business with steady traffic flow. Casting duplicates should be restricted to persons with necessary equipment and experience. Start-up costs: $500–$1,500.
Services section of newspaper; antiques publications; direct contact with dealers and show exhibitors.	The Questers 217 South Quince Street Philadelphia, PA 19107	Send for catalogues of companies selling materials, patterns, forms (*Kovels' Collectors' Source Book*, Crown Publishers, NY): Shades of the Past PO Box 502 Corte Madera, CA 94925 Burdoch Silk Lampshade Co. 3283 Loma Riviera Drive San Diego, CA 92110	Though probably not destined to become a large volume business, a reliable lampshade reproduction service will develop a loyal clientele. Ease in mailing expands clientele area if you wish to advertise in larger antiques publications. Start-up costs: under $500.

Service	Clientele	Training	Equipment
Lighting Repair and Conversion	General public, antiques dealers, restoration shops.	Basic knowledge of electricity, either through classes or private instruction; knowledge of styles of lighting fixtures.	Standard electrician's tools; workbench with multiple outlets; conversion parts from electrical supply companies; small space in corner of garage or basement.
Lock and Key Service	Antiques dealers, restoration shops, collectors.	Self-taught through study and experimentation with locks on old furniture; instruction from veteran locksmith; study information available in books and catalogues.	Few simple tools, workbench large enough to support dresser drawers, armoire doors; toolbox for house calls.
Mall Proprietor	Antiques dealers, general public.	Experience as an antiques dealer; ability to organize, lead, supervise, negotiate; bookkeeping and business experience;	Building in good location with adequate parking; desk, file cabinet, good lighting; policy handbook.

BARNES & NOBLE: 1983
PALM BEACH, FL. (407) 627-2828

REG#04   BOOKSELLER#004
RECEIPT#   19893 10/12/97   6:01 PM

S 0345346246   HT MAKE 20000 A YEAR ANT
                  1 @   6.99   6.99

SUBTOTAL   6.99
SALES TAX - 6%   .42
TOTAL   7.41
CASH PAYMENT   20.45
CHANGE   13.04

BOOKSELLERS SINCE 1873

Advertising	Organizations	Publications	Comments
Services section of newspapers; direct contact with potential clientele through flyers ad business cards; display at antiques show.	Aladdin Knight (club and newsletter re: Aladdin lamps) Route 1 Simpson, IL 62985	*Font & Flue* (newsletter about kerosene lamps) PO Box 68 Pattonsburg, MO 64670	Dozens of companies offer replacement parts ranging from conversion kits to chimneys to shades, plus instructions for both rewiring and converting old lamps without affecting their antique value. Consult the *Kovels' Collectors' Source Book* (Crown Publishers, NY) for names and addresses. Additional income available through polishing brass lamps or refinishing those with wooden bases. Start-up costs: under $500.
Services section of newspaper; area antiques publications; direct contact with dealers and restoration shops; business cards at antiques shows.	American Lock Collectors Association 37076 Grennada Livonia, MI 48154 Key Collectors International PO Box 9397 Phoenix, AZ 85068	Newsletters, bulletins, and other printed materials are available through the organizations listed here.	You will want a steady supply of keys to fit old locks. A few of the companies whose catalogues you are going to want to have are: 18th Century Hardware Co. 131 East 3rd Street Derry, PA 15627 Noel Wise Company 6503 St. Claude Avenue Arabi, LA 70032 This service might not grow to large proportions, but will gain the continued loyalty of dealers and refinishers who encounter stubborn and damaged locks weekly. Start-up costs: under $500.
For dealers: area antiques publications; for customers: Yellow Pages, newspapers, brochure ads,	Art and Antique Dealers League of America 353 East 53rd Street #2G New York, NY 10022	*Antiques Dealers* magazine 1115 Clifton Avenue Clifton, NJ 07015	The single most important thing an antiques dealer can do to prepare to become a mall proprietor is to talk with other mall proprietors. Call malls advertising in an-

Service	Clientele	Training	Equipment
Mall Proprietor (continued)		study policies of other malls, talk with proprietors.	
Matching Service	Advanced collectors, antiques dealers.	Thorough knowledge of field; sources for inventory; experience buying and selling.	Telephone, desk, storage for inventory, workbench for cleaning and tagging new inventory; workbench for packaging sold inventory; mailing materials, 35mm camera.
Metal Polishing	Antiques dealers, restoration shops, general public.	Can be self-taught using available books and tips from experienced polishers.	Small chemical bath tank, buffing wheel and buffing compounds, materials; small room with good lighting, ventilation and storage.
Mirror Resilvering	General public, furniture restoration	Apprenticeship or private instruction. Self-taught method	Special acid resistant trays, burners, running water,

Advertising	Organizations	Publications	Comments
radio, flyers, antiques publications, billboards.			tiques publications; most proprietors and managers will be helpful and honest. Analyze potential sites carefully; exposure and traffic essential to success. Start-up costs: $3,000–$6,000.
Large circulation trade papers; specialty publications.	Many exist for specific collections: Tea Leaf Club International PO Box 904 Mt. Prospect, IL 60056 China, Glass and Giftware Association 1115 Clifton Avenue Clifton, NJ 07015	Many newsletters are published by and for specific organizations (e.g., *Depression Glass Daze*, PO Box 57, Otisville, MI 48463). Check with organizations listed in *Kovels' Collectors' Source book* (Crown Publishers, NY). *American Glass Review* 1115 Clifton Avenue Clifton, NJ 07015	Traditionally matching services have focused on china, glass, and silver—all easy to identify and ship. What also might work in an urban area would be a search and find service for furniture, aimed at people who have neither time nor sources to find a piece they want (e.g. a hutch to match their table, antique end tables to go with their couch). Small ad in local paper could test demand for such a service. Start-up costs: under $500 (excluding inventory).
Area newspapers and antiques trade publications; flyers and business cards at antiques shows and shops; direct contact with restoration shops and dealers.	Metal Polishers, Buffers, Platers Union 5578 Montgomery Road Cincinnati, OH 45212	*Antiques and Art: Care and Restoration* by Edward J. Stanek, published by Wallace-Homestead Book Co. 580 Waters Edge Road Lombard, IL 60148	Metal polishing is a service for which will grow as people discover that it is available. Brass lamps, copper boilers, hinges, latches, pulls—all need attention at some time. Careful estimates, proper tagging and storage, and dependable completion dates are essential to a successful business. Start-up costs: $500–$1,000.
Area newspapers and antiques	American Institute for Conservation of Historic and	Write to the American Institute for Conservation	The expense and danger of mirror resilvering has kept most people from

Service	Clientele	Training	Equipment
Mirror Resilvering (continued)	shops, antiques dealers.	too dangerous and costly.	workbenches, excellent lighting, and good ventilation to prevent exposure to toxic fumes; small, securable room with locked cabinets for toxic materials.
Oil Painting Restoration	Antiques dealers, general public, collectors.	Apprenticeship program, classes and/or private instruction in art history, preservation, and restoration.	Color-balanced lighting, two or three workbenches in heat and humidity controlled room; simple artists' tools and a wide variety of special materials; safe storage area.
Photographing Antiques	Auctioneers, antiques publications, antiques dealers, restoration shops.	Experience and classes in 35mm photography.	35mm camera and attachments; portable lighting. Optional: darkroom and developing equipment.

Advertising	Organizations	Publications	Comments
publications; ad in Yellow Pages, antiques brochures; business cards in antiques shops and at shows.	Artistic Works 3545 Williamsburg Lane NW Washington, DC 20008	for printed materials.	attempting it themselves or doing it for others; thus those who offer the service find a steady demand. If you plan to operate out of your home in a residential or rural location, arrange with an established antiques or restoration shop to permit customers to drop off and pick up mirrors there. A standard price sheet and profit percentage for the shop will pave the way for smooth relations. Start-up costs: $1,500–$4,500.
Yellow Pages ad, business cards, ads in playbills and antiques brochures; direct contact with interior designers, art galleries, and collectors; displays at antiques shows with before and after photographs and examples.	The International Foundation for Art Research 46 East 70th Street New York, NY 10021 American Institute for Conservation of Historic and Artistic Works 3545 Williamsburg Lane NW Washington, DC 20008	*The ARTnewsletter* 5 West 37th Street New York, NY 10018	While interest in oil paintings and their restoration has been established in urban areas for decades, many rural areas and smaller cities are not served by reliable restorers. Though it is not a field to be entered lightly, those with the proper training and background who find themselves in an area without adequate art restoration service can find a steady source of income by cleaning and restoring artwork. Start-up costs: $500–$1,500.
Direct contact with potential clients; business cards and samples of work; ad in antiques brochure.	National Freelance Photographers Association Box 629 Doylestown, PA 18901	*Modern Photography* 825 7th Avenue New York, NY 10019 *Popular Photography* 1 Park Avenue New York, NY 10016	In addition to providing quality photographs for use by auctioneers and antiques show dealers, a photographer with solid journalism skills can freelance for various antiques publications. More than fifty regional and national publications use freelance photogra-

Service	Clientele	Training	Equipment
Photographing Antiques (continued)			
Picture Frame Restoration	Antiques and art collectors, antiques dealers, furniture restoration shops, art galleries.	Classes in art history, framing, and picture frame restoration; private instruction in plaster repairs and gold leaf; experience in regluing loose joints; practice on inexpensive frames from antiques shops and auctions.	Workbenches and lighting; clamps and glues for mitre joint repairs; basic woodworking hand tools; artists' brushes and materials; storage for projects.
Public Speaking about Antiques	Area civic groups and organizations.	Thorough knowledge of topic; experience in speaking before groups; classes in public speaking.	Slide projector, slides, and screen optional; handouts of information and/or illustrations pertaining to topic.
Quilt Repair and Restoration	General public, antiques dealers, quilt collectors.	Background, experience, and study in history of quilts, appraisals of quilts, fabrics, and hand stitching.	Room for quilting frame, sewing machine, and storage of quilts.

Advertising	Organizations	Publications	Comments
			phers to supplement the work of their full-time staff. Once impressed with the quality of your work, editors will continue to approach you with assignments. Start-up costs: $500–$1,500.
Yellow Pages ad; business cards and flyers for direct contact with frame shops, art galleries, furniture restoration, and antiques shops.	American Institute for Conservation of Historic and Artistic Works 3545 Williamsburg Lane NW Washington, DC 20008	Available through American Institute for Conservation. A valuable book is *Antiques and Art: Care and Restoration* by Edward Stanek, Wallace-Homestead Book Co. (Lombard, IL).	While physically related to oil painting restoration, does not require as lengthy a training. Few frame shops restore antique frames, thus welcome the opportunity to refer customers to someone who does. Start-up costs: under $500.
Resumés sent to organization presidents and Chambers of Commerce.	Toastmasters International PO Box 10400 2200 North Grand Avenue Santa Ana, CA 92711 International Toastmasters Clubs 2519 Woodland Drive Anaheim, CA 92801	Some of the best material on the subject is published by the many national and regional organizations whose members share an interest in public speaking. The organizations listed here will be able to supply you with helpful materials and information.	While a career as a public speaker is unlikely to produce a sizable income, talks before civic groups are guaranteed to create excellent publicity for an existing antiques or antiques-related business. Any small honorarium or lunch aside, the goodwill, contacts, and publicity generated will more than reward you for the time invested. Start-up costs: under $100.
Small ads in area papers and antiques publications; direct contact with antiques dealers (from whom you can get the names of quilt buyers and collectors); displays at antiques shows;	National Quilting Association PO Box 62 Greenbelt, MD 20770 American Quilt Study Group 105 Molino Avenue Mill Valley, CA 94941	*Quilter's Newsletter* 6700 West 44th Avenue Wheat Ridge, CO 80033 *Quilt World* House of White Birches, Inc. PO Box 337 Seabrook, NH 03874	The steady increase in interest in and the value of quilts guarantees a growing need for the services of quilt restoration experts. Careful study, experience, and research must come first, however, to insure the continued support of dealers and collectors. Start-up costs: $250–$750.

Service	Clientele	Training	Equipment
Quilt Repair and Restoration (continued)			
Show Promoter	Antiques dealers, general public.	Experience as antiques dealer; experience with advertising; ability to plan, organize, and promote.	Reliable reputation; building with easy accessibility and convenient parking; desk and file cabinet at home for information, contracts, and dealer files.
Stained Glass Repair	General public, antiques dealers, restoration shops, churches.	Classes in stained glass, private instruction from experienced craftsmen, self-taught using illustrated books and information.	Well-lit workbench, hand tools, soldering iron, glass cutter, supply of old colored glass.
Teaching Crafts and Antiques	Community colleges, city recreation departments, senior citizen centers, public schools, antiques shops and shows.	Thorough knowledge of subject; experience teaching; ability to organize and present a subject in an informative and interesting manner.	Materials related to subject (e.g., quilts, caning chairs); slides and projector helpful; handouts of illustrative material; classroom for private instruction.

Advertising	Organizations	Publications	Comments
business cards available at shops.			
Exhibitors: in antiques trade publications. General public: area newspapers, radio, flyers, television.	National Association of Dealers in Antiques 5859 North Main Road Rockford, IL 61103 Association of Antique Dealers of America Box 88454 Indianapolis, IN 46208	*Antiques Dealer* magazine 1115 Clifton Avenue Clifton, NJ 07015	Building a reputation as a show promoter is a slow task, but you can speed up the process by carefully choosing your show dates, exhibitors, and location. Avoid competing with other shows or major social events; pay the higher rent necessary for a better location; go after important exhibitors whose presence will give the show—and you—respect. Start-up costs: $3,000–$8,000.
Yellow Pages ads, antiques brochures, business cards, direct contact with area antiques dealers and furniture restoration shops.	Stained Glass Association of America 1125 Wilmington Avenue St. Louis, MO 63111	Literature available from Stained Glass Association of America	Supplementary restoration income available by purchasing damaged windows, cleaning and repairing glass, reframing them, and selling the windows complete with eyelets and chain through shops, shows, and craft fairs. Check with dealers who may have old glass suitable for repairs. Start-up costs: under $500.
Area and antiques newspapers, flyers in shops and at shows.	National Education Association 1201 16th Street NW Washington, DC 20036	Numerous publications containing tips and techniques for teaching available through the National Education Association and your public library.	Good teachers in this area are always in demand. While most work through a community college that provides the advertising, registration, and classroom and, in turn, takes most of the registration fee, a few are teaching out of their homes or shops, paying for their own advertising and dividing the fees by one instead of two. This

Service	Clientele	Training	Equipment
Teaching Crafts and Antiques (continued)			
Trunk Restoration	General public.	Self-taught using booklets available from parts supply companies.	Small basement or garage area with workbenches and storage space; common woodworking tools; special parts.
Upholstery	Antiques, collectors, dealers, refinishers.	Apprenticeship, classes and/or private instruction in upholstery techniques; basic furniture repair and refinishing experience; knowledge of furniture styles and corresponding fabrics; business experience.	Heat and humidity controlled room large enough for a commercial sewing machine, two workbenches, padded sawhorses, assortment of woodworking and upholstery hand tools, and storage for furniture, foam, and fabrics; vehicle for transporting customer pieces.
Wicker Repair and Restoration	General public, furniture restoration shops, antiques dealers.	Classes and/or private instruction; self-taught using furniture restoration books and other illustrative material.	Simple hand tools; electric drill; small padded sawhorses; small room for workbenches and storage.

Advertising	Organizations	Publications	Comments
			involves more work but offers more potential reward. Start-up costs: under $500.
Small ads in area newspapers and antiques publications; business cards at shops selling old trunks; sample of work (possibly being sold on consignment) with business cards in antiques shops.	Association for Preservation Techniques PO Box 2487 Station D Ottawa, Ontario, Canada	Several of the companies that stock trunk parts and hardware offer instructional booklets on both the history and the restoration of antique trunks. Two of them are: Charlotte Ford Trunks Ltd. PO Box 536 Spearman, TX 79081 Antique Trunk Company 3706 West 169th Street Cleveland, OH 44111	Most furniture restoration shops prefer not to restore trunks primarily because of the special stock of hardware required. Alert them to your service, offering to send furniture work to them in exchange for trunk restoration references. Additional income available by buying inexpensive trunks, restoring them, and reselling through antiques, crafts, and "country" gift shops. Start-up costs: $250–$750.
Yellow Pages advertising, newspapers, antiques publications; direct contact with furniture restoration shops, restaurants, and interior designers.	National Association for Professional Upholsterers PO Box 1424 Riverton, NJ 08077	*The Professional Upholsterer* Communications Today Ltd. PO Box 1424 Riverton, NJ 08077	As the price of new furniture escalates, so does the demand for competent upholsterers. Work is steady; profits from labor and markup on fabric rewarding. Additional help often required to move and transport couches and large chairs. Start-up costs: $1,500–$4,500.
Small ad in area newspapers and antiques publications; direct contact with antiques	Association for Preservation Techniques PO Box 2487 Station D Ottawa, Ontario,	*American Indian Basketry* magazine PO Box 66124 Portland, OR 97266	Increased interest in wicker furniture insures a steady demand for wicker restoration specialists. Opportunity awaits craftspersons

Service	Clientele	Training	Equipment
Wicker Repair and Restoration (continued)			
Wood Carving	Restoration shops, amateur refinishers, antiques dealers.	Basic wood carving classes; experimentation and self-teaching through illustrated materials; knowledge of furniture styles and woods.	Set of wood carving tools; power and hand saws for rough shaping; standard woodworking hand tools; workbenches and vises; small area with good lighting.
Wood Turning	Antiques dealers, amateur refinishers.	Woodworking class or private instruction on basic lathe operation; experience, practice, and experimentation on lathe; knowledge of furniture woods.	Wood lathe and turning tools; simple hand woodworking tools, including saws for cutting stock; small area that is not inconvenienced by dust and chips.
Writing about Antiques	Editors and publishers of newsletters, tabloids, newspapers, and magazines dealing regularly with antiques (complete listing available through *Writers Market*, Writers Digest Books,	Thorough knowledge of subject through research and experience; ability to organize a topic, develop an idea logically, and present it clearly; writing classes, if necessary; ability to combine interviews and research.	Good quality typewriter, desk, file cabinet, reference books; corner of bedroom.

Advertising	Organizations	Publications	Comments
dealers buying and selling wicker; direct contact with furniture restoration shops and interior designers.	Canada		who are not afraid to buy inexpensive damaged wicker furniture, restore it, and then re-sell it either privately or through an antiques shop. Start-up costs: under $500.
Direct contact with antiques dealers and restoration shops; business card at shops and shows; display samples at same. Antiques brochures and publications.	National Wood Carvers Association 7424 Miami Avenue Cincinnati, OH 45243	*Chip Chats* National Wood Carvers Association 7424 Miami Avenue Cincinnati, OH 45243	For all but a few, wood carving is destined to remain a hobby, but that does not mean a hobby cannot produce financial rewards, regardless of how infrequent. Exposure is crucial; ask permission to display boards of work samples in area antiques shops. Start-up costs: $250–$750.
Business cards posted and distributed in lumber yards, hardware stores, antiques shops, craft shops; turning demonstrations at outdoor crafts and antiques shows.	Wood Products Manufacturing Association (formerly Wood Turners & Shapers Association) 52 Racette Avenue Gardner, MA 01440	*Fine Woodworking* magazine Taunton Press, Inc. PO Box 355 Newtown, CT 06470	A dependable woodturner can quickly develop a steady clientele of amateur furniture refinishers. Additional income can come from simple chair regluing, since many clients will not have the means or the time to install the pieces you turn for them. Start-up costs: $500–$1,500.
Letters to editors of antiques publications (see Query Letters section in *Writers Market*).	American Society of Journalists & Authors 1501 Broadway, Suite 1907 New York, NY 10036 National Writers' Club 1450 South Havana, Suite 620 Aurora, CO 80012	*Writer* magazine PO Box 892 Boston, MA 02117 *Writer's Digest* 9933 Alliance Road Cincinnati, OH 45242	By volunteering to cover area antiques shows and auctions for regional publications in return for a byline, you can gain experience and tearsheets to show larger publications, including national magazines, when you query them about potential articles. Ability to provide quality 35mm photographs will

Service	Clientele	Training	Equipment
Writing about Antiques (continued)	Cincinnati, OH).		

Advertising	Organizations	Publications	Comments
			help sway editors. Follow submission formats suggested in writing guides. Start-up costs: under $500.

Index

NOTE: Page references in italics refer to illustrations.